THE COLLECTED WRITINGS OF SHERMAN AND GRACE COOLIDGE

THE COLLECTED WRITINGS OF SHERMAN *and* GRACE COOLIDGE

Sherman Coolidge and
Grace Coolidge

EDITED BY
Tadeusz Lewandowski

UNIVERSITY OF NEBRASKA PRESS LINCOLN

The University of Nebraska Press is part of a land-grant institution with campuses and programs on the past, present, and future homelands of the Pawnee, Ponca, Otoe-Missouria, Omaha, Dakota, Lakota, Kaw, Cheyenne, and Arapaho Peoples, as well as those of the relocated Ho-Chunk, Sac and Fox, and Iowa Peoples.

Library of Congress Cataloging-in-Publication Data
Names: Coolidge, Sherman, author. | Coolidge, Grace, author. | Coolidge, Sherman. Works. Selections. | Coolidge, Grace. Works. Selections. | Lewandowski, Tadeusz, 1973– editor.
Title: The collected writings of Sherman and Grace Coolidge / Sherman Coolidge and Grace Coolidge ; edited by Tadeusz Lewandowski.
Description: Lincoln : University of Nebraska, [2023] | Includes bibliographical references and index.
Identifiers: LCCN 2022031518
ISBN 9781496234056 (hardback)
ISBN 9781496234872 (epub)
ISBN 9781496234889 (pdf)
Subjects: LCSH: Coolidge, Sherman. | Coolidge, Grace. | United States—History—1865– | United States—Race relations—History—19th century. | Indians of North America—Missions—History. | Episcopal Church—Clergy—United States—Biography. | Arapaho Indians—Biography. | Heiresses—Biography. | Interracial marriage—United States—History.
Classification: LCC E663 .L49 2023 | DDC 973.04/97354—dc23/eng/20220720
LC record available at https://lccn.loc.gov/2022031518

Set in Ehrhardt by Mikala R. Kolander.
Designed by N. Putens.

Cover image: Grace and Sherman Coolidge at home on the ranch shortly after their wedding in 1902. Courtesy of the American Heritage Center, University of Wyoming.

For my parents

CONTENTS

PART 2. GRACE COOLIDGE:
WRITINGS, LETTERS, AND POEMS

ILLUSTRATIONS

ACKNOWLEDGMENTS

I would like to thank the Pioneers Museum in Colorado Springs, Colorado, for allowing me to publish some of the materials held in the Coolidge-Heinicke Collection, and archivist Hillary C. Mannion for all her patient help over the past years.

EDITORIAL POLICY

The writings collected in this volume have required very little editing. More than half of the contents are from proofread published articles devoid of typographical errors. In the rare case an error in spelling or punctuation does appear, the emendation is silent. Archaic spellings, such as "centre" or variants such as "saviour," are however retained, as are idiosyncratic capitalizations and emphases in italics. Annotations are offered in endnotes when obscure figures or references can be identified.

Fortunately, Grace Coolidge's letters have been copied from generally error-free, typewritten transcriptions made approximately twenty years ago and held in the Coolidge-Heinicke Collection in the Pioneers Museum, Colorado Springs, Colorado. The originals are no longer available. Grace often used abbreviations such as "*yr.*" for "your," "*shd*" for "should," "*wd*" for "would," and "*wh.*" for "which." These abbreviations have been retained. Underlined words have been rendered in italics. Though occasional errors in spelling or punctuation found in the transcripts are emended silently, the only significant change made is in their standardized formatting, with dates and locations presented in a uniform manner preceding the body of the text and with closings and signatures following the closing paragraph. As with the articles, annotations with biographical or background information (when available) are provided in endnotes when obscure personages or events appear. When the transcriber was unable to decipher Grace's handwriting, [illegible] appears in brackets. When a part of the letter is missing, [fragment missing] appears in brackets.

THE COLLECTED WRITINGS OF SHERMAN AND GRACE COOLIDGE

Sherman and Grace Coolidge

A BIOGRAPHICAL SKETCH

When the Arapaho priest and missionary Sherman Coolidge and New York hotel heiress Grace Darling Wetherbee wed in a small ceremony at Fort Washakie mission, Wind River Reservation, Wyoming, on October 8, 1902, neither suspected the national attention they would attract.[1] In the days that followed, the *New York Times* announced that Grace's father had, shockingly, given his "full consent" to the union, while an extensive article in the *Denver Post* informed readers that Sherman, hoping to please his new bride, had reluctantly forsaken his tepee for a modern home. Over the ensuing weeks, more papers picked up the sensational story of the mixed-race marriage between the "society belle" and the "red-skinned missionary" born among the "savage and warlike" Arapahos; they produced a stream of reports that amused Sherman and Grace tremendously.[2] Friends even sent them clippings that Sherman recited aloud at the dinner table with "great unction." Their favorite quote read, "If the details could be known, the story of their courtship would read like a chapter from a Romance."[3] That was hardly true, but one daily correctly stated an unquestionable fact: Sherman Coolidge's dramatic life story would make "an excellent subject for a novel."[4]

Sherman Coolidge was born into a band of Northern Arapahos in the early 1860s somewhere along the Goose Creek, a tributary of the Tongue River that flows into the Wind River Basin in present-day Wyoming.[5] His parents, Banasda (Big Heart) and Ba-ahnoce (Turtle Woman), gave him the name Des-che-wa-wah, translated as "Runs On Top," or "Runs Mysteriously Over Ice," after an ancestor who had escaped an enemy war party by leading his people over a frozen lake.[6] Coolidge's recollections of his first years on the Great Plains were sometimes nostalgic. The Arapahos' migratory lifeways of hunting and gathering had not yet been erased, allowing Runs On Top, his little brother, and half-siblings (born to his father's second wife, Ba-ahnoce's sister) a life of stable abundance.[7] Yet there was another side to Runs On Top's Indian boyhood that directly stemmed from conflicts with white settlers and their protectors, the U.S. military.

In July 1865, the Arapahos' allies, the Lakotas, killed over two dozen soldiers at Platte Bridge Station, which guarded a river crossing along the Oregon Trail.[8] Retaliation was swift. A month later, Gen. Patrick E. Connor's punitive expedition came upon a large Arapaho encampment situated along the Tongue River. The village, led by Chiefs Black Bear and Medicine Man, included Runs On Top's family. Believing the inhabitants to be Lakotas, Connor attacked under a hail of howitzer fire, slaughtering indiscriminately. Ba-ahnoce grabbed her older son and fled while a cousin scooped up her youngest, but not all the family escaped. Runs On Top's grandmother, aunt, and uncle were shot down, as were many of the band's elderly and children. Sherman Coolidge later wrote that his father, Banasda, contemplated revenge and that Connor's soldiers had departed, "rejoicing over their victory, the lives they had blighted, and the families they had broken up."[9] This was only one part of a larger tragedy. Smallpox epidemics and cholera had already depleted the Northern Arapahos, leaving them dependent on the Lakotas and vulnerable to adversaries such as the Eastern Shoshones and Bannocks, who competed for the region's diminishing resources. Horses, necessary for bison hunting, became a cherished object of theft.[10]

Two years later, in 1867, an event occurred that Sherman Coolidge would recall vividly for the rest of his life. In the early spring, his family and two others broke off from Black Bear's band to take an alternate route to new camping grounds. On the first evening, the families' three tepees came under attack by Bannock warriors hoping to scare them into abandoning their horses. In the initial chaos of the assault, Ba-ahnoce slipped under her tepee's bottom with her younger child in her arms. Runs On Top was left behind with his father, who, unlike the other men in his party, remained to fend off the assailants in defense of his loved ones. Banasda lifted the tepee flap and ordered his son to run. Runs On Top obeyed, scrambling over a frozen stream and sprinting at full speed through the dark night, only to bump into his mother moments later. Not knowing what had occurred back at camp, he, his mother, and his baby brother walked for days to find safety among the remainder of their tribe. An Arapaho war party subsequently investigated the scene. Sadly, they found Banasda shot through the chest and riddled with spear and arrow wounds. His body, however, had been placed neatly in a buffalo robe as a sign of respect for his bravery.[11] Ba-ahnoce, her sister, and their children were left to mourn a man Sherman Coolidge later called "the bravest, the wisest, and the best of chiefs."[12]

The death of Banasda occurred at a time of escalating violence on the Great Plains.[13] The newly established Bozeman Trail, leading through Wyoming Territory's Powder River Basin to gold fields in present-day Montana, became a magnet for Indian anger at white intrusion. Unable to prevent raids on wagon trains and attacks on military forts by the Lakotas, Cheyennes, and Arapahos, Washington sought peace. While the ensuing 1868 Treaty of Fort Laramie created the Great Sioux Reservation—including the Black Hills of the Dakotas—for the powerful Lakotas, the less populous Northern Arapahos were left without a reserve of their own. Wanting to inhabit their traditional lands, the leadership began lobbying U.S. commissioners for permission to relocate to Wind River Reservation, which was established in the 1860s for the Eastern Shoshones under Chief Washakie. Washington brokered a tentative agreement, but the Arapahos were unwelcome guests. When Black Bear's band approached the reservation's center, Camp Brown, to do some trading in the spring of 1870, they were assaulted by Shoshones, Bannocks, and white mobs alike.[14] Thus came the third major upheaval for Runs On Top. Within the space of a day, his life would change more dramatically than he could ever conceive.

On the morning of April 8, 1870, Ba-ahnoce, the children under her care, and several neighbors sat camped along the Popo Agie River. Upon hearing war cries, the band of one elderly man, three women, and eight or nine children raced down the middle of the Popo Agie to obscure any tracks. The gambit failed. Pursued on horseback by Shoshone warriors, the exhausted group was quickly captured after taking cover under some brush. Runs On Top cowered next to his mother while the warriors surrounding them calmly assessed his potential to take revenge. "Look at his scalp," one observed. "He is old enough to shoot us with an arrow." As the men debated, a Shoshone scout named Ezac suddenly intervened, insisting that the terrified captives be surrendered at Camp Brown. The warriors assented, but first they shot and scalped the elderly man in front of his shrieking wife and children.

When the Shoshones handed over their prisoners to U.S. troops later that day, officers rode out to collect Ba-ahnoce's tepee and her few worldly possessions.[15] There was now little for her to do but wait for a military escort back to the main body of the Arapahos. Then Lt. Charles Frederick Larrabee approached her. Seeing the mother's state, Larrabee offered to take her younger child, Runs On Top's little brother, thus guaranteeing his survival. Ba-ahnoce hesitated, explaining that she had been widowed and that she feared for the future. Larrabee could have her child on one condition: he would also have to find a guardian for Runs On Top to lessen the blow of their separation. The camp surgeon, Dr. Shapleigh, begrudgingly accepted care of the boy, giving him the name William Tecumseh Sherman after the famous Union army general and the Shawnee chief who had resisted American expansion in the early 1800s. Sherman's little brother was meanwhile named Philip Larrabee.[16] A detachment of soldiers later returned Ba-ahnoce to her people under cover of night, leaving a traumatized Runs On Top to grieve the loss of his mother.[17] Then matters somehow got worse. Shapleigh treated Runs On Top abusively and in a short time began trying to get rid of him.[18] Fortuitously, new guardians unexpectedly presented themselves a month later.

In May 1870, the Seventh U.S. Infantry began marching north from Utah to Montana Territory, joining troops from Camp Brown en route. Among the Seventh were Lt. Charles Austin Coolidge, a mustached man of Pilgrim ancestry, and his young wife, Sophie, who took an immediate interest in Runs On Top. Seeing that he was dressed only in a "bread cloth," she asked Dr. Shapleigh if she could take the child.[19] Shapleigh answered that she could, provided she promised never to bring him back.[20] Sophie's act, however, was not one strictly of compassion. She surmised that the Arapaho boy might make a decent servant; good help was hard to find in the West.[21] Soon after, Charles was called east for recruiting work, and he and Sophie took their new ward, renamed Sherman Coolidge, into a world he had never known. His brother, Philip, was left behind. The boys would never see each other again.

For the next three years, Sherman attended a school for African American children in New York City, where he imbibed all the fervent patriotism, unquestioning ethnocentrism, and deep Episcopal devotion of his adoptive guardians.[22] At the mere age of eleven years old, he decided to become a missionary to other Indians. With the aid of a local priest, Sherman even received an offer to study at Shattuck Military Academy in Minnesota under the state's Episcopal bishop, Henry Benjamin Whipple. Sophie, however, insisted that her boy was still too immature for boarding school.[23] The Coolidges' stay in Manhattan ended in 1873 when Charles was ordered back west.[24]

In the interim, Runs On Top's Northern Arapahos had fared badly. Bison were scarce due to an army policy of mass culling, and rations promised under treaties were so meager that the bands had taken to eating their horses. In desperation, the Arapahos intermittently raided the Shoshones and white settlers in the Wind River Basin. U.S. troops joined the Shoshones in counterattacks.[25] Still, these outbursts of violence paled in comparison to the coming explosion. In 1874 Lt. Col. George Armstrong Custer led an incursion into the Black Hills and verified the existence of rich gold deposits. As the U.S. government aggressively (and unsuccessfully) maneuvered to purchase the area, the military ceased evicting white prospectors illegally searching for riches. President Ulysses S. Grant decided to abandon treaty obligations, and Indian agents received word in early 1876 that all Native signatories to the Laramie treaty outside reservation boundaries would be treated as hostile. In June, Custer made a foolish attack on a large village of Lakotas, Cheyennes, and Arapahos camped alongside the Little Bighorn River and speedily met his death.[26] Upon hearing the news, Charles Coolidge's unit immediately marched to the scene and began burying the dead.[27] Sherman, by now about sixteen years old, accompanied his adoptive father in subsequent expeditions against the Lakotas.[28] This proved a difficult time for the young man. After receiving news that his little brother, Philip, was living happily in Massachusetts, word abruptly came that he had succumbed to consumption.[29] Experiencing this loss in the midst of the Great Sioux War of 1876–77 convinced Sherman to eschew all violence and to push harder for a life in the ministry. Fortunately, Sophie respected his wishes. She wrote Bishop Whipple, attempting to revive the offer to have Sherman study at Shattuck. Whipple responded enthusiastically.

In mid-1877 Sherman Coolidge set off for Faribault, Minnesota, where he would study for the next seven years—first at Shattuck, then at Seabury

Divinity School. Coolidge was ordained into the deaconate by Whipple in 1884, and within months he headed back west, determined to convert his former tribe.[30] During his time away, the Northern Arapahos had failed in their quest to secure a reservation and had instead settled at Wind River alongside the Eastern Shoshones.[31] These once-warring nations now kept an uneasy peace while trying to preserve their cultures under the Office of Indian Affairs, or Indian Bureau, which enforced a strict assimilationist program of white education, Christianity, and farming.[32]

Coolidge arrived at Wind River by stagecoach in the fall of 1884, though rumors of his impending arrival preceded him. When he alighted the coach, his aged mother, Ba-ahnoce, who had somehow survived fifteen years of violence and privation, was waiting anxiously. To her long-lost son's deep surprise, she and a large group of relatives greeted him in a moment of utter poignancy, each lining up to embrace him. Tears flowed copiously.[33] Unfortunately, this promising start did not augur success. After being advanced to the priesthood in 1885, Coolidge, known on the reservation as the "Arapahoe Whiteman," commenced work educating, in his words, "the weaker race of the inferior language, life, and religion into the better language, life and religion of the stronger race."[34] As one can imagine, among a people proud of their own long-cherished traditions, this kind of attitude only heightened their resistance to his assimilationist efforts. Ignoring this dynamic, Coolidge deemed Native religious expressions such as the annual Sun Dance as "pagan" and aggressively did all he could to influence Indian children away from the customs of their parents. Coolidge's relations with whites also suffered. He did not get along with the Episcopal mission's head, Rev. John Roberts, at Fort Washakie (formerly Camp Brown), so he established his own home and mission among the Arapaho camps.

But then Coolidge came into serious conflict with a group of Catholic missionaries proselytizing nearby. The Wind River agent, Col. Thomas M. Jones, had allowed these Jesuits 160 acres on which to operate, a fact that enraged Coolidge deeply. Fearing the Catholics' influence among the Indians, he entered into a brazen conspiracy with the superintendent of the Wind River government school, A. M. Johnson. The men's plan, in essence, was to poison the Arapahos and Shoshones against the Catholic mission and simultaneously foment a rebellion among the Arapahos to have Agent

Jones removed. When Jones learned of the plot in May 1887, he threatened Coolidge and Johnson with legal action and effectively exiled them from the reservation. The local white community, meanwhile, became so incensed at Coolidge that he feared for his life.[35] In the end, his only recourse was to leave Wyoming—quickly. Chastened, he headed east to New York State, where he attended Hobart College for several years until Jones left his post, and matters calmed enough for Sherman to return.[36]

Regrettably, Coolidge's second tenure at Wind River, from 1890 to 1910, turned out to be no less controversial. Adamant that the Indian Bureau's "civilizing" regime was proper and just, he consistently sided with the new Wind River agent, Herman Nickerson, against the Northern Arapahos. Coolidge first threw his support behind the cession of the "Smoking Waters" hot springs. Then he attempted to play the younger "progressive" Arapahos against their elders in a bid to implement allotment under the 1887 Dawes Act, which sought to end collective land ownership by dividing parcels among individuals. In 1901 Coolidge falsely informed the Indian Bureau that the "progressive" half of the Arapahos had consented and that allotment could proceed. Wind River's Catholic missionaries, once the victim of his machinations, here managed to turn the tables. They informed Washington of the subterfuge and even managed to get Nickerson terminated.[37] Allotment eventually proceeded after the bureau made a host of concessions to the Arapahos, but the incident soured many against Coolidge for good.[38]

Indeed, Coolidge's only redeemable actions during this period, it appears, took place off the reservation. On regular trips to the East, he never failed to charm Episcopal congregations and secure generous donations for the Arapahos and Shoshones at Wind River.[39] A penchant for humor was the key to his success. At one meeting, he referred to himself and a fellow priest as the "wild Indian and the wild Irishman." The *Church Standard* recorded: "All who heard his address felt that if there were a few more just such 'wild Indians' in the Church, and speaking for their race, the Indian work would not languish."[40] Nonetheless, these efforts at consciousness raising did very little to correct the problems of penury, disease, and undernourishment that came with U.S. reservation policy. Such work had to be performed on the ground, and one young eastern woman in Sherman Coolidge's orbit was determined to see it done.

Grace Darling Wetherbee first visited Wind River in the summer of 1896 as the guest of her college friend, Anne Talbot, who was the daughter of Ethelbert Talbot, the first Episcopal bishop of Wyoming.[41] An urbanite, Grace had only recently become enamored of the West. Born on July 25, 1873, in Auburndale, Massachusetts, to Gardner and Hannah Nye Wetherbee, she descended from the original New England colonizers, including the illustrious Coolidges who were related to Sherman's adoptive father, Charles. Grace's father owned and operated the sixteen-story Hotel Manhattan, located on Madison Avenue and Forty-Second Street, and reputed to be the tallest hotel in the world. Thirty blocks north on Seventy-Second Street, the Wetherbee family owned a palatial townhouse, in which Grace was raised. Well-traveled and educated, she spent much of her leisure time at the Metropolitan Opera House.[42] But despite this decadent veneer, Grace craved an existence of greater meaning. Though her family was not religious, she underwent baptism and confirmation in the Episcopal Church in her twenties, stating that all the years prior had been "wasted."[43] Her sister, Alice, had married a Hungarian count in Paris, pleasing Hannah Wetherbee greatly. Grace, in contrast, refused a comfortable upper-class marriage in favor of St. Faith's Deaconess Training School, which she attended from 1900 to 1902. The unusual decision drove her mother to distraction, causing a rift that would only grow as time passed.

Anne Talbot, with whom Grace studied at Ogontz College, Pennsylvania, had been the inspiration for her friend's intense religious devotion.[44] And if all this were not unconventional enough, it appears that Grace struggled with intense romantic feelings for Anne, who evidently reciprocated.[45] Yet were it not for Anne, Grace would have never met Sherman Coolidge. On her first trip to Wind River, Grace encountered Sherman in the now-defunct town of Rongis.[46] He flirted wildly (as he did with most young women), and the two crossed paths whenever Sherman traveled east on church business. Grace initially took no interest in his fervent attentions, but in a friendly gesture, she bestowed upon him the nicknames Pokey, Poke, and Cousin.[47]

Grace Darling Wetherbee, for whatever inscrutable reason, always felt that she had a deep connection to Native peoples, whom she called "cousins."[48] Since childhood, she had even believed that she would one day marry one.[49] Through Anne Talbot, Grace became increasingly involved in Indian welfare, and in the summer of 1901—against her mother's passionate protestations—she worked as an assistant missionary on the Uintah and Ouray Reservation in Utah.[50] When she returned to New York, she found herself disgusted by the city's poverty, and she resolved to move west permanently after graduating from St. Faith's.[51] This chance came a year later when John Roberts, moved by her consistent donations, invited Grace to Fort Washakie in 1902 to take charge of the mission girls' school.[52] Grace arrived in the summer, full of enthusiasm, and took up residence in a crude cabin. Over the next few months, however, she faced insidious boredom as Roberts assigned her fewer and fewer duties. Her expanding free time was thankfully taken up by Sherman, then living at Fort Washakie's hotel.[53] Slowly, a relationship developed from hand-holding to what Grace called "twosing," contemporary slang for "petting."[54] Forty-year-old Sherman proposed, but Grace, then nearing thirty, was deeply uncertain. When she finally accepted, marrying in the manner she wished became an obstacle. Roberts, who had always disliked Coolidge, refused to wed the couple on the grounds that Grace's father had not explicitly approved the union.[55] This was true. Despite later *New York Times* reporting, Gardner Wetherbee never gave his "full consent." In fact, he answered his daughter's request to marry Sherman with a curt telegram, reading: "Under the circumstances I withdraw my decision and leave the responsibility with you."[56] Following much arguing and acrimony, Roberts finally relented and performed the ceremony, perhaps fearing that his superiors in the Episcopal Church might frown upon his denial of a fellow clergyman's request.[57]

Sherman and Grace's marriage in October 1902 inspired headlines across America such as "Society Girl's Heart and Hand Captured by an Indian." But if "the story of their courtship" did truly "read like a chapter from a Romance"—as their favorite quote suggested—more than a little tragedy soon ensued. The evening of their wedding, the Coolidges relocated to Sherman's old home among the Arapaho camps. Grace pronounced it "the worst looking place you ever saw," but over the next eight years the couple developed the property into a working ranch.[58] Though Grace was now free of her disapproving parents, criticism of her new husband emanating from family and friends angered her greatly and eventually led to a complete break with her mother.[59] Now reduced to living on Sherman's meager missionary salary, the couple struggled to support themselves.[60] Sadly, their first three children died in infancy between 1904 and 1905, leaving Grace devastated.[61] As a means of coping, she resolved to honor their memory through service to the reservation's Indians, working in camps, administering medicine to the ill, and providing meals to the hungry. A news report from the time even detailed her efforts under the title "Society Belle Turns Squaw."[62] These helpful acts, however, were combined with a brand of Christian evangelicalism and "progressive" ideology that alienated many Arapahos. Sherman enjoyed the support of a small group of relatives who had converted to Christianity and taken up farming, but most of the tribe resented his past interference in reservation politics.[63] Nonetheless, the Coolidges managed to adopt two girls from the local Indian communities: a six-year-old Arapaho named Virginia, whose mother had died, and an eight-year-old Shoshone orphan named Effie. Grace finally gave birth to a surviving child, Sallie, in 1907 in Salt Lake City, Utah.[64] While away, an incident occurred at Wind River that highlighted the Arapahos' simmering ire at the missionary presence, previous land losses, and the Indian Bureau's continuing curtailment of freedoms.

Back in 1904, Sherman Coolidge had supported the U.S. government in an agreement to cede a vast portion of the reservation. When promised compensation was repeatedly withheld by Washington, the Arapahos' aggravation intensified. Another source of frustration was a strict ban on the Sun Dance. One February evening in 1907 these tensions exploded when Coolidge's missionary colleague, John Roberts, crossed the border of the reservation on a trip home from the nearby town of Lander. A group of disaffected Arapahos gave chase, intending to murder him. Roberts hurriedly retreated and telephoned Fort Washakie. The commanding officer there quickly dispatched soldiers to collect Roberts's wife and children, also potential targets of assassination. Coolidge immediately returned from Utah to exercise any calming influence he could, but the incident had laid bare the Arapahos' resistance to reservation missionary work.[65] Displeased, the Episcopal hierarchy began considering changes, and in 1910 Coolidge was abruptly transferred to the Southern Cheyenne Reservation in Oklahoma.[66] In fact, he and Grace were happy to leave Wind River, each having grown weary of the hostile environment.[67]

Sherman's transfer came not long after Grace's mother, Hannah Wetherbee, died in New York at the age of sixty-nine. Hannah's passing, however, allowed Grace to reestablish relations with her more sympathetic father.[68] She headed east with the children while Sherman shuttered the ranch and boarded a train to Oklahoma. There, he settled in the small town of Enid and wrote Grace enthusiastically about his new work at St. Luke's mission in Whirlwind, ten miles away. Although Sherman was impressed by his warm welcome from the Cheyenne community and the mission's teacher, Harriet Bedell, he quickly found that the demands of the position were more than anticipated.[69] After months of enduring the constant travel to various parishes at his own cost, the regular guest lectures at the local Chilocco Indian School, the discomforts of a dilapidated old house, and the increasing criticism from Miss Bedell, Sherman asked Oklahoma's bishop for a transfer. The bishop summarily refused.[70] Meanwhile, Grace and the children arrived and took an instant dislike to the state.[71] Sherman, now more determined to escape, successfully put in for another transfer, requesting Faribault, Minnesota, where he had studied as a youth.[72] The family relocated in 1912, welcoming another daughter, Rosie, that same year.[73] Life in Faribault was pleasant but a bit too calm. Grace went so far as to dub the city the "land of the Lotus Eaters."[74] Sherman's duties consisted of ministering to a mixed congregation of Dakotas and whites, who kept a strict but tacit code of segregation on separate sides of the church.[75]

Though the time spent in Oklahoma and Minnesota failed to please, the early 1910s became crucial to Sherman Coolidge's development as a reformer and activist of national stature. In October 1911, he attended the first annual meeting of the Society of American Indians (SAI) in Columbus, Ohio. This group, which included the Yavapai physician Dr. Carlos Montezuma, Seneca museum director Arthur C. Parker, and Santee Dakota writer and physician Charles Eastman, encouraged assimilation into mainstream Euro-American society but insisted that Indians had "certain contributions of value to offer our government and our people."[76] In early 1912, Coolidge was chosen as the SAI president after the prominent Omaha attorney Thomas Sloan withdrew from consideration.[77] Luckily, the role played to Coolidge's strengths. He had always displayed a talent for communicating with white audiences and took seriously his mission to raise awareness of Indian issues. Working in the society also influenced his thinking. Surrounded by eminent Indian colleagues who venerated their Native heritage, he began to vigorously promote the integrity of Indigenous cultures. As president, Coolidge established himself as a moderate, pleading with SAI members to work together in "strength and harmony," and espousing cooperation with the government as essential to gaining influence over Indian policy.[78] As a public speaker, he became known for his quick wit and strong condemnations of white violence and greed, which had reduced an "independent, free, noble race" to "a caricature."[79]

Yet as time passed, Coolidge became increasingly discouraged by the society's lack of political progress. Matters worsened when, at the 1915 annual conference in Lawrence, Kansas, Carlos Montezuma advocated the immediate liquidation of the Indian Bureau to free the "prisoners" living within the reservation system.[80] The radical idea split the SAI into factions, and Coolidge, loathsome of battles and aware that his moderate approach was failing, looked for a way out.[81] At the 1916 conference in Cedar Rapids, Iowa, he abdicated his presidency, perhaps fearful he would not garner enough votes to continue in the role.[82] By then, however, his personal circumstances had changed tremendously.

In March 1916, Grace's father, Gardner Wetherbee, died in Manhattan at age eighty-two.[83] Grace embarked for New York, where she learned that she had inherited over $1 million, or nearly $25 million today.[84] During the previous five years she had remained home—"a martyr to babes and food," in her words—while Sherman had traveled from conference to conference across the United States.[85] Fighting domestic ennui with her pen, she had composed a series of stories inspired by her time at Wind River. Several appeared in periodicals such as *Collier's* and the *Outlook* in 1912 and 1913.[86] Grace nonetheless struggled to publish her main project, a book of twenty-nine vignettes detailing the near starvation, the high rates of infant mortality, and the profound demoralization many Wind River Arapahos suffered under the reservation system. Editors simply found the pieces too sad.[87] Fortunately, Grace eventually prevailed, and Four Seas Press in Boston published her *Teepee Neighbors* in 1917.

For the two years following their windfall inheritance, the Coolidges moved frequently, searching for a better place than Faribault to settle for good. Sherman first took the position of canon at St. Matthew's Cathedral in Laramie, Wyoming, in 1917, but he left soon after.[88] In 1918 the Coolidges gave Reno, Nevada, a trial run. Within a month, Grace decided that the city was as "nondescript and uninteresting" as Oklahoma—the ultimate insult.[89] Finally, the Coolidges settled in Colorado, where Sherman became the canon at the St. John's Cathedral in the Wilderness in Denver.[90]

Despite his new millionaire status, Sherman Coolidge did not relinquish his activist pursuits. Instead, he made a comeback run for the presidency of the Society of American Indians at the 1918 annual conference, only to be defeated by the anti–Indian Bureau Thomas Sloan, who had long wanted to take the society along a more radical course. In reaction, the Indian Bureau branded the SAI a pariah, and the organization effectively expired not long afterward. Coolidge was one of just eight stalwart members to attend the 1921 annual meeting.[91] Nevertheless, he was not quite finished. Coolidge took the opportunity to serve on the Committee of One Hundred, chosen by Secretary of the Interior Hubert W. Work to investigate reservation conditions and report on the challenges facing Native peoples across the United States. Following the issuance of the committee's report in December 1923, Sherman Coolidge, accompanied by the Cherokee poet, educator, and activist Ruth Muskrat Bronson, appeared with President Calvin Coolidge in a public ceremony.[92] The two men had met before, during the president's time as the governor of Massachusetts. Calvin Coolidge had exclaimed, "An Indian, named Coolidge! Why, all the Coolidges I have ever heard of were New Englanders whose ancestors came over on the Mayflower." The remark allowed Sherman to quip: "My ancestors were on the reception committee which met them."[93]

Back in Colorado, the Coolidges moved into a quieter neighborhood in Colorado Springs. Their sprawling, Spanish-style home still stands on Third Street and Mesa Avenue today.[94] Wanting to keep busy, Sherman took the position of canon at the city's Church of the Good Shepherd, establishing himself as a well-liked local figure.[95] Once a staunch assimilationist, he had grown to cherish Native cultures and values. In his sermons and public talks, he admonished Euro-American society for its materialism and lack of communitarian spirit while lauding Indian spirituality. In summers, he and Grace sometimes visited Wind River to observe the Arapahos perform the Sun Dance, which he no longer deemed a pagan ritual but instead saw as a "deeply religious observance."[96] Here, we see the great intellectual reversal of Sherman Coolidge's life: Having spent the first part of his career as a missionary trying to teach Indians to be like whites, he was now counseling whites to be more like Indians. Crucially, his revised philosophy of assimilation rejected the idea that Indians should fully adapt to new circumstances and instead insisted that the United States adapt to Indians. Humane assimilation meant building a communal, pluralistic America that accepted all humans as equals and embraced Natives with respect and tolerance.

Unfortunately, the 1920s brought tragedy to the Coolidge family. Adoptive daughters Effie and Virginia both had a mental illness and were committed to institutions.[97] Sherman's physical health also worsened. Spells of dizziness "tortured" him, and episodic heart palpitations made him "miserable."[98] Doctors suggested a warmer climate, so in late 1931 he joined his daughter Sallie in Los Angeles, where she had settled.[99] He was hospitalized soon after his arrival but appeared stable. Then one evening his condition abruptly deteriorated, and hours later on January 24, 1932, Sherman Runs On Top Coolidge died at approximately age seventy.[100] At his service in Colorado Springs, Bishop Irving Peake Johnson of Colorado characterized Coolidge as "a witness to the power of the gospel which could produce in one who was born in a teepee the grace to become the peer of any of us as a Christian gentleman and a godly priest."[101] Regrettably, the remark contained undercurrents of the racism and ethnocentrism that the deceased had fought against much of his life.

Following the funeral, Grace took up residence in Colorado Springs' Broadmoor Hotel, just three blocks from her old home. She traveled for some years, visiting Hawaii and California, and was happy to see her two biological daughters marry.[102] In November 1937, Grace sustained a broken hip and remained bedridden until her death on December 28 at age sixty-four.[103] She was buried next to Sherman in Evergreen Cemetery, Colorado Springs.[104] Three Episcopal bishops attended Grace's funeral to pay respects for her life-long charity work.[105]

The Coolidges' union lasted almost thirty years from the day the *New York Times* erroneously announced that Grace's father had given his "full consent" for them to marry. Nevertheless, in later years Sherman drew on his own life experience to devise a nonpolitical solution to the Indian problem. In one interview, he ruminated on the strong, initial prejudice against his marriage to Grace but noted that "those things pass when there is a true mating." He added, "On the great Happy Hunting Ground, we are all going to be surprised at the racial diversity of the chosen."[106] Reconciliation between Natives and whites, then, might best be achieved through intermarriage.[107] This belief reflected Sherman Coolidge's ultimate development into an expansive pluralist who ended his life defending the Native religious traditions that he once vowed to eliminate as a Wind River missionary so many decades earlier.

Sherman and Grace Coolidge's writings, collected here for the first time, provide us with remarkable portraits of epochs past and lives fully lived. Reading what they left for posterity, we not only gain valuable insights into such subjects as turn-of-the-century reservation life and the intertribal organizing of the Progressive era but we also uncover intimate details of Sherman's Arapaho childhood, Grace's struggles to define herself as a young woman, and the couple's courtship and early marriage. The Coolidges' enduring partnership has long languished in relative obscurity. This volume is a tribute to their once-great trials, triumphs, and aspirations.

1. A young Sherman Coolidge in clerical garb, ca. 1880s. The image is found in the *Colorado Magazine*, 1893.

Notes on the Writings of Sherman Coolidge

In November 1917, Grace Coolidge wrote her husband from a hotel in California, where she was vacationing with the children. Sherman had recently been appointed the canon of St. Matthew's Cathedral in Laramie, Wyoming, and had been traveling the state taking care of assorted business. Grace, who had recently published her collection of Wind River sketches, *Teepee Neighbors*, now encouraged Sherman to do some writing of his own. "Why not go down to the public stenographer in Sheridan and let her take down your 'recollections' and get that job really done this winter?" she asked. "Do, Sherman," the letter admonished. "You owe it to the children."[1] Grace was referencing an autobiography that her husband had planned to write for years but never did.[2] For this reason, Sherman Coolidge has been denied the recognition other Native men of his generation enjoy today. The works of his contemporaries Charles Eastman and Luther Standing Bear offer detailed accounts of their Native childhoods and entries into white "civilization," as well as penetrating critiques of Euro-American society.[3] Coolidge's own story and writings, though equally dramatic and incisive, have been confined to the margins. His is, without a doubt, a neglected voice.[4]

We can, however, forgive Coolidge for his lack of output—at least concerning his early life. Eastman was fifteen years old when his long-lost father suddenly located him in Canada and brought him south to embark on a life among whites.[5] Standing Bear was around eleven years old when his father sent him east to study at Richard Henry Pratt's Carlisle Indian Industrial School in Pennsylvania.[6] In their cases, the transition into "civilization," though difficult, was partially guided by family members. In Coolidge's case, the entrée into "civilization" was tragically abrupt, following several years—half his brief life, really—of intense violence and deep trauma. Within this backdrop, there existed few romantic recollections of his Indian boyhood, little memory of the ways of his people, and eventually no memory of his first language.[7] As a result, his foster parents, Charles and Sophie Coolidge, were apparently able to reform Sherman's thinking entirely. While young Eastman and Standing Bear could express their skepticism of the white ways and beliefs presented to them, Coolidge had an unstable standpoint from which to do so. He instead imbibed his new culture so ferociously that he became a model of Euro-American ethnocentrism, unable to detect any hint of hypocrisy in U.S. government policy toward Indians or anything wrong with white conceptions of Indians as heathens.

For instance, when sixteen-year-old Coolidge received word from Sophie that he would soon be studying for the ministry in Minnesota, his response read: "I would gladly do something toward having some of my race taught to believe in God. I know how ignorant they are of the Bible and of Good. . . . I will do my best, for my pity at their ignorance of God and of the Bible is so great that I will happily do all I can possibly, to learn to teach and preach the Gospel to them, and if I succeed in doing this I would not ask for any better work in this world."[8] Indeed, for a long time Coolidge saw his own people as "savage men" who needed the example of Christ as much to live in peace as to save their benighted souls.[9] His job, he felt, was to "conquer the barbarian" by assimilating Indians into a life of dignity in the United States, a "new order of a civilization" that existed in "union with God through the Prince of Peace."[10] This unquestioning attitude, however, eventually underwent significant evolution; and though Coolidge never wrote his autobiography—or very much at all for public consumption—this volume can at least trace the arc of his thinking and offer valuable details about his early life.

It bears mentioning that were it not for Grace Coolidge's prodding, we would probably have virtually no information on Sherman's Arapaho boyhood. He just did not care to write. In 1926 and 1927, the Wyoming historian Grace Hebard tried in vain to get him to record his recollections of Shoshone chief Washakie for a school textbook she was preparing. Sherman assured her that he was working on the article multiple times. In the end, she never got a word out of him.[11] Luckily, one afternoon during this period Grace

Coolidge managed to sit him down and forced him to speak of his childhood memories, which she typed up, likely for the children, and stored with the rest of the family papers until her death. These short pieces commence part 1 of this volume, and though they are in no way as extensive as the writings of Eastman or Standing Bear, they do give us snapshots of a once-happy life blighted by deadly violence.

Sherman Coolidge's first memory as a boy named Runs On Top appears to have been of his father or rather waiting for his father, Banasda, who had left camp to hunt eagles in the traditional Arapaho manner. When Banasda finally appears with two eagles slung across his back, Runs On Top, then perhaps three or four years old, shouts excitedly that his father has returned with two crows.[12] This unanticipated misidentification reinforces an underlying current of humor in Coolidge's recollections, whether when his mother, Ba-ahnoce, intentionally topples over his colt with a sack of berries just to get a rise out of him or when he foolishly loses his bow and arrows in a shooting contest with an older Arapaho. That particular night, Runs On Top breaks down in tears and cannot fall asleep until his mother promises that his newborn baby brother will go and win back the items in the night. The following morning a welcome surprise awaits.[13] Runs On Top finally turns the tables on at least one of his elders when an uncle challenges him to a horse race, which Runs On Top improbably wins in the home stretch thanks to the spontaneous intervention of some tree branches.[14] This carefree childhood ends abruptly in the early spring of 1867, after Runs On Top's father makes the fatal decision to break off from the main Arapaho band and take an alternate route to new camping grounds. The family is surrounded by enemies in the night, and only Banasda stays to fight off the attackers and allows the others to flee to safety. This act of sacrifice ends in his death. Yet the most poignant aspect of Coolidge's description of the incident is its postscript. He reveals that years later, he learned that the Bannocks who intruded on his camp that evening had no intention of murdering anyone. They had merely wanted to steal the small band's horses. Coolidge does not make explicit the conclusion that his father would have lived had he simply run away with the rest of his family. Perhaps stating that fact would have been too painful.

Little surprise, then, that Coolidge prefaces one of his childhood recollections by stressing how it is "almost impossible to convey to the ordinary civilized man's mind the cruel uncertainty of life as the Indians in the old days knew it."[15] Such tenuousness of existence emerges as a major theme in much of Coolidge's later writings and statements. Ultimately, he viewed his early life as one of trauma best forgotten. For instance, he barely recorded a word about the 1865 Battle of the Tongue River. Perhaps he did remember being picked up by his mother under a hail of howitzer fire. Perhaps he did remember images of his aunt, grandmother, and uncle sprawled out dead in the aftermath.[16] We do not know. Coolidge's last memory of life among the Arapahos, of course, was being taken prisoner by the Shoshones and almost murdered. It is thus understandable that he may have been reluctant to delve into the painful past or speak of his scattered impressions of death and separation from every loved one who defined his previous life.

As such, Sherman Coolidge did not leave a first-person account of the day, three years following the loss of his father, that he parted from his mother at Camp Brown and found himself the ward of an abusive army surgeon.[17] Nor do we have a detailed description of how he felt once forced into life as the servant of a military man's wife. Coolidge was an able but not avid writer, and details of these times can only be extracted and pieced together from speeches and interviews published later in his life. We have only a few of his thoughts on the period just after 1870, when he commenced an unimaginable transition into an entirely foreign world, but almost nothing on the period leading up to his 1884 return to Wind River as a newly minted Christian missionary determined to convert his former tribe. Even his remarkable reunion with his mother and relatives at Fort Washakie warranted only a single mention to his mentor, Henry Whipple, a full three years after its occurrence. The entire description read: "I arrived here about the 2nd of October 1884, and I found my mother and other relatives."[18] Thankfully, Coolidge was under some obligation to write reports for the *Spirit of Missions*, a monthly journal inaugurated in 1836 and published by the Board of Missions of the Episcopal Church. An annual subscription cost a dollar, certainly a fair price for the well-illustrated, informative record of Episcopal missionary activities worldwide.[19] Coolidge, however, cannot be counted as an active contributor. His reports number a mere six scattered dispatches dating from 1885 to 1899. Unsurprisingly, Ethelbert Talbot, the bishop overseeing his work, once scolded Coolidge for providing so little information on his doings.[20] From what Coolidge did intermittently report we can at least learn of how he first constructed his log home among the Arapaho camps south of Fort Washakie and, perhaps more importantly, get some idea of how he represented (or misrepresented) his work to readers in the East.

If there is a common refrain in these *Spirit of Missions* reports, amid their full displays of ethnocentrism, it is "progress." Coolidge is insistent that the Arapahos are almost wholly accepting of his "civilizing" imperatives and willing to adopt the superior life offered by Christianity and farming. The Wind River Industrial School, he claims, "is doing as much good as any other institution of its class in the United States," while the Episcopal Church is actively aiding a "heathen people" eagerly awaiting "the reception of the Gospel story of the love of God."[21] On this religious front, Coolidge lists the baptisms, confirmations, and Christian marriages he has performed to demonstrate that his "aggressive and progressive" labors are showing results. Coolidge also paints a rather quaint picture of his life on the reservation, preaching in his own mission's pine log chapel, built in 1898 with donations from the East. His dissemination of "pure religion" to both the Arapahos and the Shoshones not only casts off "ignorance and injurious superstition" but also allows these "hereditary foes" to "live side by side in peace and harmony." In one of the first instances of his penchant for humor in print, Coolidge does however admit that the only problem remaining is that "the Arapahoe thinks he is better than the Shoshone, and *vice versa*." In fairness, Coolidge as well remarks on the "clannish" nature of both tribes, perhaps a subtle admission that his toil is not appreciated to the extent he wishes.[22] The Arapahos were, after all, generally resistant to efforts at conversion.[23] Every baptism Coolidge performed prior to 1904 was received by boarding school students who had little idea of what the ceremony meant and who probably had no choice in the matter anyway. Sherman and Grace Coolidge were therefore mildly shocked when a small village of Arapahos under a friend named Mule agreed to let their children be baptized that same year. It was apparently the first time any such thing had happened at Wind River.[24]

Coolidge's rosy depictions for the *Spirit of Missions* present an interesting contrast to several of his articles from the same period. In 1887 he published "Education of Indians," a piece that openly admits the failures of the reservation system. At Wind River, "ill-paid and responsible employees" face the discouraging task of "overseeing starving human beings" in "a land bursting with plenty." The dire situation is compounded by the number of children who perish every year in assimilationist boarding schools. Still, Coolidge finds space to chastise Indian parents for their "limited range of thought" in refusing to send their offspring off the reservation. His solution is easily anticipated—on-reservation, religious education that will allow Native peoples to rise from a "barbarian" to "progressive" state.[25] This stress on education appears again in Coolidge's speech at the Seventh Annual Meeting of the Lake Mohonk Conference of the Friends of the Indian, which he attended in 1889 while studying at Hobart College in New York State. Interestingly, his remarks relate his personal struggle to read as an eleven-year-old boy. Just as tears once rolled down his cheeks in frustration, Indian children, born to a "helpless and perishing people," are now "crying for education" in a different sense. Only with this civilizing balm can the Indian "show his ability, his humanity, [and] his capability of mental culture" and be rapidly assimilated.[26]

Coolidge's preoccupation with assimilation produced probably the most offensive statement he ever made, "The Indian of To-Day," published in the *Colorado Magazine* four years later in 1893. The article appeared during the tenure of P. H. Ray as the Wind River agent and at a time when Coolidge had begun to align himself more closely with Indian Bureau policy. Ray, a former army officer, was especially adamant about assimilating the Shoshones and Arapahos to Euro-American ways. He imprisoned polygamists, banned giveaways, and undermined the Arapaho chiefs' authority by distributing rations directly to heads of households. Ray's apparent centerpiece, though, was the recruitment of the male population for military service.[27] Coolidge takes an equally hard line in "The Indian of To-Day," lauding Ray's program for "the wild camp savage," whose "undisciplined valor" can now finally be channeled into worthy ends. This is not a one-sided bargain. Coolidge makes his first full-throated call for the U.S. government to do the "fair thing" and grant Native peoples American citizenship—a goal that can only be achieved by educating "the weaker race of the inferior language, life, and religion into the better language, life and religion of the stronger race." With this process complete, Natives worshiping "the true God together at the Christian altar" will never take up arms against one another, or Americans, again.

Coolidge's goal of establishing peace was of course inspired by the intertribal violence of his childhood. However, his occasional suggestions that Indians are naturally warlike (he uses the term "aboriginal son of Mars" on one occasion) seem to have undergone some reevaluation toward the end of the 1890s.[28] In his private writings, Coolidge sometimes noted that there were similarities between the Arapahos' religion and Christianity.[29] He also began developing a theory that Adam and Eve were the first members of his tribe.[30] More evidence that Coolidge had begun to reject what he had learned of his people in white society appears in a wide-ranging 1894 government report on Native peoples published by the U.S. Department of the Interior. His contribution, "Indians in Wyoming," reveals a softening of his view that Arapaho culture is necessarily degraded, bellicose, and pagan. Quite the contrary, Coolidge writes of the Arapahos' monotheistic vision of God and realization that "the good and bad on earth will be rewarded and punished beyond the grave."[31]

By 1894 Coolidge had lived at Wind River for over a decade, witnessing enormous poverty on a daily basis. He had seen how in the winters, the Arapahos resorted to eating cattle and sheep herds dead of starvation and disease and that their infants frequently died of malnutrition.[32] When the Arapahos took ill, they mostly refused to consult the reservation physician, whom Coolidge himself secretly regarded as a "very poor excuse of a man."[33] At some point, these circumstances started to affect his thinking profoundly, and he began laying greater blame on the Indian Bureau, feeling that the Arapahos had a cultural basis for "progress" that was being thwarted by government policy. His "Indians in Wyoming" even evinces a strong nostalgia for the precontact past, when the Arapahos once thrived in the "bosom of mother earth," consumed "wild meat and fruit in abundance," and "had no fear or knowledge of syphilis, scrofula, or consumption." Now denied the best "medical science of the enlightened nineteenth century," the tribe has understandably fallen back on old beliefs.[34] If the Indian Bureau is to justify its power and fulfill its "civilizing" mission, Coolidge suggests that legitimate medical care is a good place to start.

Coolidge's growing respect for Arapaho customs and his disillusionment with the bureau quickly evolved into a more critical public stance soon after his entry into the Society of American Indians in 1911. Surrounded by

Natives who venerated their ancestry and insisted that they, as a group, had important contributions to make to the nation, Coolidge appeared emboldened. In his speeches, writings, and statements as the SAI president and later as a member of the rank and file, he began expressing open criticisms that shifted from the Indian Bureau to larger white society and developing a more sympathetic view of Indians as spiritual and unmaterialistic. Reading such statements, one detects strong traces of Charles Eastman's depiction of the Indian as "the highest type of pagan" and Arthur C. Parker's characterization of American capitalism as a "commercial sea filled with long fanged sharks."[35] Both men certainly influenced Coolidge, as did the Arapahos at Wind River, probably equally so.

At the first annual SAI conference, held in Columbus, Ohio, Coolidge spoke spontaneously of an incident that had occurred over twenty years earlier. When asked to deliver a sermon at "a very aristocratic church" in New York, he refused after realizing that the resident priest had allowed a "pew-rent system." Wealthier worshipers paid for the privilege of proximity to the altar, while the poor squeezed into two pews placed off in a rear corner. Offended, Coolidge announced to the stunned congregants that he preferred his ancestors' religion to one of "commerce," which was "auctioned off" in such a manner. As he explained to those in Columbus, whatever the Arapahos' faults, the democratic nature of their religion showed it was "not so very bad after all."[36] This declaration amounted to a significant reversal. In fact, from 1911 we almost see an entirely new Coolidge, praising ancient Indian ways and condemning modern white society in every breath and stroke of the pen. No longer is the Indian a "degraded savage." He is instead "a brave warrior and a noble patriot" who defended his rightful lands.[37] No longer is the United States the "new order of a civilization" in "union with God through the Prince of Peace."[38] It is instead a nation of "invaders" who have carried out a "policy of war and extermination."[39]

Coolidge delivered his first major statement as the SAI president (a post he held from 1912 to 1916) at the society's second annual conference in Columbus, Ohio. Later printed in the *Quarterly Journal* under the title "The Indian American: His Duty to His Race and to His Country, the United States of America," the speech encompasses themes that Coolidge would stress until his death: contradicting negative stereotypes of Indians, challenging whites to understand the Indian's perspective, advancing notions of mutual responsibility for reconciliation, and promoting Indian citizenship. That day, Coolidge cited the timeworn saying "The dead Indian is the only good Indian" and quickly reminded his audience, "But so is the live one!" In one of the most powerful passages from his entire body of work, he wondered aloud:

> Who is this Indian? What is he? Where does he live? Above all, why is he a problem? If these questions were asked of the average white man, the answers would be both inaccurate and confusing. In our early school-days, the Indian was defined as a savage who lived by hunting and fishing; who lived in a wigwam or teepee. He was a fierce, ferocious, cruel, crafty, treacherous, blood-thirsty red devil! Exterminate him! Exterminate him! Again, he has been described as a dirty, lazy, shiftless loafer, beggar and drunkard. No wonder "the only good Indian is the dead one!"

The reason this reputation prevails is found the history of Indian retaliation and the brutal acts sometimes committed against settlers. Yet Coolidge pointedly asks his white audience, "What would you have done?" The Indian, after all, was merely defending "his lands, his people and his teepee home." Now, with this fight lost, the Indian has become a "civic freak," forced to battle for his natural rights through political organization. But in this endeavor, Coolidge points out, the responsibility is mutual. Just as Indians must fight on, they deserve aid from the government and larger Euro-American society. With understanding, acceptance, and citizenship, each will someday proudly state, "Civis Americanus sum."[40]

It is difficult to imagine that anyone who heard Sherman Coolidge speak in the 1910s was left unmoved. After hearing the preceding speech in Columbus, Richard Henry Pratt called it "as near being a classic as anything yet written by an Indian on Indian matters."[41] Coolidge continued to impress in public forums over the next four years, declaring in addresses such as "American Indians for the Honor of Their Race" that "the Indian must be made free," while asking that whites help "redeem" historical wrongs by joining the Society of American Indians in serving "all humanity."[42] The basis for this union, he often pointed out, was not a shared history of relentless conflict but sometimes one of important cooperation. In his speech for the 1913 SAI conference in Denver, Colorado, Coolidge highlights Native contributions to America's creation. Despite their consistently poor treatment, Indigenous peoples have fought alongside whites since the Revolutionary War. While making this point, though, he inserts a subtle claim to primacy. He discusses meeting another man named Coolidge, descended from the Pilgrims. A bystander asks how they have ended up with the same last name, and the white man takes pains to distinguish himself from his Arapaho counterpart. "I'm a real Coolidge," he asserts. "My ancestors came over in the Mayflower." "Yes," Sherman Coolidge responds, "but mine were on the reception committee when they arrived."[43]

This blend of cajoling humor and underlying substance, disseminated from a clearly charismatic figure, had a revelatory effect on some listeners. One Colorado monthly, the *Trail*, ran a long article on the 1913 Denver meeting, extolling Sherman Coolidge's "overflowing geniality" and "superior culture" in rallying whites to the Indian cause.[44] The reporter's reaction shows how Coolidge was able to open the minds of those who perceived Native peoples through negative stereotypes, thus becoming an effective mediator who could use language such as "white invaders" but somehow avoid giving offense. Coolidge's 1914 "The Function of the Society of American Indians" asks readers to reflect on the "war and extermination policy" of the U.S. government and to reject the idea of the Indian as a "degraded savage." Addressing an issue he would later speak on publicly, Coolidge designates the "deep-seated disease germ of the whole Indian problem" within overweening Euro-American ethnocentrism and false notions of white supremacy. Mainstream society needs to respect the Indian's values and "blame him not if he refuses to become an imitation white man; if he bows not the knee to commercialism, or fails to admit that the white man is the ultimate model of the best citizenship or of noblest manhood."[45]

Coolidge, of course, lectured not only before white audiences during his tenure as the SAI president. Much of his work consisted of trips to speak at Indian schools throughout the nation. He related one such trip to California before the student body at the Haskell Institute in Lawrence, Kansas, during the 1915 SAI conference. Condemning the deep prejudice against California's Indians, derogatorily called "Diggers," Coolidge mentions a Paiute boy reacting to the statement that the Indian should be given "the white man's chance": "Yes; give us half the white man's chance," he answers, "and we will take the other half." Coolidge then muses, "That is the spirit of those Digger Indians: We must take a stand." This stand, he makes clear, is distinguished from the racist basis of white society yet one still anchored in racial pride. Soliciting help from the young for the "great work of uplift for our race," he stresses how the Society of American Indians bars none—"no sex, sect, or section"—from its ranks.[46]

The racial pride in this equation of "uplift" is reflected in Coolidge's declaration, at Haskell, of an "American Indian Day" to be celebrated on the second Saturday of every May as "a memorial to the Red Race of America and to a wise consideration of its future."[47] American Indian Day received some national attention and was observed in public schools the following year. Nonetheless, some SAI members saw it as an offensively ineffectual gimmick. Carlos Montezuma in particular called the idea a "farce."[48] His controversial speech at Haskell, "Let My People Go," reflected his frustration with the SAI and became a turning point in the young history of the organization. Denouncing the Indian Bureau's "slimy clutches of horrid greed," Montezuma called for freeing the Indian "prisoners" of the reservation system. The society, he charged, had renounced its mission of liberation in favor of taking a soft line on the bureau, when members should be pushing for abolition.[49] Arthur C. Parker later called the collective response to the radical proposal "a riot," and Coolidge, who saw cooperation as the only route to attaining influence in Washington, roundly humiliated Montezuma before those in attendance.[50] Only Philip Gordon, a young Ojibwe Catholic priest and newcomer to the SAI, came away deeply impressed by Montezuma's principled and fearless stand.[51] Gordon responded with action, nominating the anti-bureau Omaha attorney Thomas Sloan for SAI president.[52] In the voting, Coolidge barely retained his position.[53] A "radical" faction had emerged, and the old leadership was under threat.[54]

Carlos Montezuma was hardly the only SAI activist exasperated at the lack of political progress made in the mid-1910s. Coolidge, too, was angered at the indifference of Washington to Indian matters, especially at Wind River. His 1916 written statement to the U.S. Senate Committee on Indian Affairs paints a stark portrait of his old home and amounts to another sharp reversal. In the 1890s and early 1900s, Coolidge had strongly supported reservation land cessions to the U.S. government against the interests of the Arapahos, who largely rejected the loss of territory and fumed over the interminable delay in their promised payments.[55] With these monies still pending, Coolidge requests that the 1904 cession be canceled, the lands be returned, and the water rights, soon to expire without action from tribal members, be secured. Coolidge's letter also exposes what he calls "an old story" on the reservation. Many Arapahos and Shoshones, "driven by hunger," regularly consume "sheep and stock that had died from disease." Before the Senate committee, Assistant Commissioner of Indian Affairs E. B. Merritt responded to Coolidge's allegations, maintaining that water rights were indeed secure. Coolidge's claims of chronic hunger and calls to restore lands were ignored.[56]

The situation at Wind River was not the only source of Coolidge's frustration. From its inception, the society had agitated for the U.S. government to pass two legislative measures: the Carter Code Bill, meant to define the legal status of Native Americans, and the Stephens Bill, which sought to open an Indian court of claims as a route to compensation for broken treaties.[57] To achieve any progress on either front, the SAI would have to work in concentrated fashion to influence those in power. It is in this context we must read Coolidge's opening speech at the 1916 annual conference in Cedar Rapids, Iowa. His plea to work in a "union of strength and harmony" in tackling the "problem into which the race has been thrust by the white race" is coupled with the grim admission that without a long-sought resolution to issues of legal status, Indians writ large will remain in "a state of chaos."[58] Montezuma and Gordon, predictably, ignored Coolidge's entreaty, and the gathering quickly devolved into a fractious debate later published in the renamed *Quarterly Journal*, the *American Indian Magazine*. Montezuma unabashedly declares that "Indian employees in the service of the Indian bureau could not be loyal to the Indian race," prompting Coolidge to defend bureau employees. Though Montezuma is momentarily silenced, Philip Gordon intervenes, repeating it is impossible for a bureau employee to be "loyal to this Society." Gordon's comments then invite vociferous objections from others. Ojibwe Indian Bureau accountant Marie Baldwin insists she maintains her own freedom of thought and speech. Yankton Dakota writer Gertrude Bonnin agrees, noting it is absurd to believe that "just out of consideration of holding a job and getting a very small salary," a Native bureau employee would forgo criticism on an important issue.[59]

Before Coolidge terminated the debate, an incident occurred that several press outlets picked up and that later became part of SAI lore. At one point, Montezuma jumped out of his chair and waved his arms, shouting at Coolidge, "I am an Apache . . . and you are an Arapahoe. I can lick you. My tribe has licked your tribe before!" Coolidge, who stood at least a head taller than Montezuma and probably outweighed him by fifty pounds, coolly replied, "Well, I am from Missouri."[60] The humorous rejoinder referenced the slogan of the "Show-Me" state, as if to say to Montezuma, "Let's see you try." The remark also caused a ripple of laughter that immediately broke the tension, but headlines reading "Tribal War Averted at Indian Meeting" ran the next morning in local papers.[61] Such coverage, needless to say, hardly reflected the "harmony" that Coolidge had envisioned. Before leaving Cedar Rapids, however, he at least got some of his substantive message printed in the local press with the headline "Escaped Massacre to Be Taken by White Folk and Educated for Ministry—Story of an Indian Boy." In this public interview held at the Hotel Montrose, Coolidge explains how "the European looked on the Indian's civilization as different from his, therefore inferior." This perspective, along with expecting an ancient people to become "an imitation white man," is an example of sheer folly. Humane assimilation can only be expedited through cooperation with the government that will allow the SAI to "write a new history of the Indian with honor to himself and the nation."[62]

If this were ever to occur, it would be without Coolidge at the helm. Knowing that his moderate reign as SAI president was coming to an end, he declined to seek another term at the 1916 conference's close.[63] Relations with Montezuma had seriously deteriorated. The Yavapai doctor later excoriated Coolidge in his Indian rights journal, *Wassaja*. "Ex-President Coolidge of the Society of American Indians says that he can be loyal to the Indian race and at the same time serve the Indian Bureau," the attack reads. "*Wassaja* wonders if he serves God and the Devil in the same way."[64]

Remarkably, the fissures in the society were about to get worse. In 1914 World War I commenced in Europe. U.S. intervention, accompanied by a massive propaganda offensive declaring the imminent triumph of global democracy, came in the spring of 1917.[65] Commissioner of Indian Affairs Cato Sells began aggressively recruiting on reservations, enlisting Indian men for service in segregated units.[66] Montezuma and Gordon supported the policy of separation.[67] The new SAI president Arthur C. Parker and secretary Gertrude Bonnin meanwhile expressed horror at the notion of a "walking reservation."[68] Yet once the War Department rejected these plans, the SAI—Coolidge included—fully endorsed the Indians' joining the service.[69] Only Montezuma dared ask whether Indians, languishing under "Indian Bureauism"—also termed the "Kaiserism of America"—should fight at all.[70] The society, however, had a goal in mind: The leadership hoped that Indian service abroad could spur the granting of citizenship at home when the war had ended. Even though Coolidge had often rebuked the white "invaders" of Indian lands, he now publicly agitated for an all-Indian regiment, which would, as he told a reporter from the Nevada *Sunset* magazine, "add glory to our history."[71]

Coolidge may have later regretted this statement. In the ensuing years, he watched as the wounded returned, Native and white, and slowly realized that patriotic Indian participation had brought no political change but only loss. Native American soldiers suffered a 5 percent mortality rate, which was 400 percent greater than that of their white counterparts.[72] This tragic backdrop certainly informed Coolidge's only surviving sermon, "Ye Cannot Serve God and Mammon," dating from the 1920s. In it, he takes the stance that the "proudest militaristic nations in the world took a pacifist Jewish peasant for their guide and easily reconciled His teachings with bombs, poison gas, secret treaties, and all the lies of official propaganda." His point, though, is much broader. Elaborating on the dictum that "there is no compromise between the love for God and love for riches," the sermon criticizes how "Europeanized" civilization demands a "cut throat principle" that begets "cruel strife among men with its intendant greed." Whites, encouraged by the economic system, willingly kill for material gain. Indians may have killed for revenge but never for riches. In this way, "the Indian lived his religion," believing it "vital" to every part of life and evincing a spirituality sorely lacking in mainstream America.[73] Having once deemed Indians "the weaker race of the inferior language, life, and religion," Coolidge had made quite an intellectual turnaround.[74] Native peoples, with their communal values, had essential lessons to teach white society—lessons more akin to Christianity than the vast white citizenry could comfortably admit. He asked, in essence, that the United States shed its rank materialism, greed, and ethnocentrism, and finally embody the democratic ideals that were present in the national narrative but absent in everyday life. These steps were necessary toward creating a new, pluralistic America defined by tolerance for racial, ethnic, and cultural differences, and by respect for the continent's rich and distinguished past.

Indians finally gained U.S. citizenship in 1924.[75] Still, Coolidge saw this ostensible extension of rights as inadequate for those who remained on reservations, subject to the oversight of the bureau. With the Society of American Indians having disintegrated in the early 1920s under the anti-bureau faction, he acted as a lone voice when he could, holding open lectures near his home in Colorado Springs. In 1926 the *Colorado Springs Gazette* recorded his last political remarks. Before a group of whites gathered in the town's courthouse, Coolidge criticizes an American public "so engrossed" in "material things," lauds Indian religiosity, and speaks of the over seventeen thousand Indians who fought in the Great War, only to come home to second-class citizenship.[76] These strong sentiments probably elicited only a passing interest from Colorado Springs' wealthy residents.

When Sherman Coolidge passed from this life in 1932, Grace Coolidge's first instinct was to bury him at Wind River. It was January, though, and the earth was frozen over, and Wyoming was very far away. Given these circumstances, Colorado Springs would have to do.[77] Perhaps one might conjecture that Sherman would have preferred burial in the lands of his birth, for intellectually, he had already returned home. Even if his long-promised autobiography remained forever unwritten, he died having developed a critique of Euro-America as powerful as those of his more prolific contemporaries, Charles Eastman and Luther Standing Bear. And most notably, after a full sixty years of assimilation and acculturation to white ways, Sherman Coolidge ended his life a critic. He was no longer interested in recasting Indians in the mold of modernity; instead, he was determined to alert whites to the errors of their society and teach them that the remedies lay in implementing the values of Indians. It is curious how so many prominent Natives of the Progressive era, having made the transition into "civilization," in the end came down on the side of their supposedly "savage" ancestors.

2. A young Grace Darling Wetherbee Coolidge in an undated studio portrait. Courtesy of the Colorado Springs Pioneers Museum.

Notes on the Writings of Grace Coolidge

Grace Darling Wetherbee Coolidge first tried her hand at writing as a young woman. In the 1890s, she occasionally submitted to the Episcopal journal the *Spirit of Missions*, and in one letter from that time she even mentions having composed a "clergyman story," perhaps based on her future husband, Sherman, whom she had met less than a year prior.[1] It was not until Grace was in her forties, however, that she began to acquire some distinct success. *Collier's* and the *Outlook* featured several of her stories in the 1910s, while Rand McNally & Co. published her children's book, *Paddy-Paws: Four Adventures of the Prairie Dog with a Red Coat*, in 1914.[2] But when Grace is remembered today, it is inevitably for her 1917 collection of Wind River sketches, *Teepee Neighbors*, which H. L. Mencken admiringly deemed "a book that leaves something behind it."[3] Unfortunately, nothing else followed. One reason may have been that publishing *Teepee Neighbors* proved more of a struggle than Grace had anticipated. Finding a commercial press interested in producing a book of sad vignettes detailing the daily life on a reservation had proven difficult, and no writer enjoys rejection.[4] Composing the pieces had also left her feeling like a "squeezed lemon." Each, in her words, had been "all true."[5] Thus, *Teepee Neighbors* turned out to be the culmination of Grace Coolidge's published work. Why she wrote nothing further is simple to discern: The vast majority of her creative writing sprang from her time at Wind River, and once her stories were told, there were no more.

Grace Coolidge's other writings are scant indeed. Only six of her efforts, dating from 1903, 1905, 1917, and 1918, appear elsewhere in print. The first two, written for the *Spirit of Missions*, detail Grace and Sherman's efforts at converting their Arapaho neighbors. Grace believed deeply in this mission; so in late December 1902, after she and Sherman had been married less than three months, they struck on a plan. Having gathered candy, peanuts, toys, and a tree left over from a benefit at the agency church, the couple loaded the goods on their wagon and set off from their ranch to Big Wind River, aiming to hold the first Christmas celebration for the Arapaho band living there. The Coolidges received a warm welcome from Sherman's relatives and friends, among them his half-white cousin Herbert Welsh, and a headman named Mule.[6] The following day in the village's large council house, everyone gathered to hear Sherman give a short talk on "the wonderful birth of the Saviour."[7] Grace deemed the event such a success that after returning home, she announced to her friend Anne Talbot, "I'm going to try to write that Xmas tree up for the Spirit of Missions."[8] And that she did. "An Arapahoe Christmas Tree" appeared in the January 1903 issue of the journal.

"An Arapahoe Christmas Tree" has a propagandistic feel. Like Sherman's missionary reports from the 1880s and '90s, the article assures the largely engaged white Episcopal readership that "progress" is occurring unabated at Wind River. Grace places a focus on the accoutrements of "civilization" adopted by the Arapaho, such as the pride they take in farming yields and their successful exploitation of resources. Her descriptions, however, unwittingly betray how greatly Wind River's natural environment has deteriorated. The "beaver is gone," Grace writes, "but his friendship for the Indian" remains in the irrigation ditches that now crisscross the reservation. Cultural changes are also occurring. As the Arapaho men work together, they speak English—more supposed proof that they are "progressive." In the past, the tribe's warriors had been "a terror to the people of this region." Now, through education and example, they have abandoned "scalp dances" in favor of the "improvement of themselves and of their land."[9]

Two years later, in 1905, Grace reported on this "improvement" in another article for the *Missions*, "A Christmas Tree that Bore Souls." Following the 1902 gathering, headman Mule had asked to be baptized along with all of the children in his village. In February 1903, Sherman baptized him with several members of his family in a grand ceremony. Grace admits that this was an unprecedented event. Previously, Sherman had only baptized schoolchildren "under Christian influence from six years of age." Spurred on by such "progress," in 1905 the Coolidges held another Christmas event, aided by boxes of toys from the Woman's Auxiliary of Ohio. By the time it concluded, Sherman had baptized fifty-nine children with their parents' consent. Grace thanks the Woman's Auxiliary of Ohio for their generosity in this mission; it was key to showing the Indian children the good that comes with worshiping Christ. At Sunday school, her students had recently been discussing a section of the Catechism: "That we may worship Him, serve Him, obey Him as we ought to do." The girls understood the meanings of "worship" and "obey," but they were "perplexed" about the concept of "serve." "And how about the fifty-two dolls that came with your Christmas things?" Grace asks them. "Who dressed them for you? And the hoods for the little children? And the candy? And the money to build your churches? What were the people doing who sent you all these things?" "Serving God," the students answer in one voice. "Now," Grace concludes, "if only we can teach these Indians to serve God, too, in the same way!"[10]

Here, we encounter more than a little irony. Grace undoubtedly boasted pure intentions, but the vision of a Euro-American heiress instructing a tribal people on generosity and community—not to mention worship—does not fail to raise an eyebrow. On display, unfortunately, is the ethnocentric disconnect that alienated the Arapahos from the Coolidges the longer they remained at Wind River. Grace's work with the Sunday schoolchildren, in fact, was the kind of interference that Northern Arapaho elders had been trying to counter since their arrival on the reservation. As she and Sherman were promoting the Indians' conversion to Christianity and "progressive" lifestyles, the Arapahos were doing everything possible to preserve their long-held traditions. This meant discouraging children from listening to schoolteachers and missionaries, and clandestinely continuing religious rituals, lodges, and ceremonies, changing them, if necessary, to assuage the Indian Bureau. When Arapaho children or even adults did accept baptism, as the Coolidges advertised, the act often meant very little to those on the receiving end.[11] Men such as Mule and Herbert Welsh, meanwhile, were exceptions; the other Arapahos may have disliked them intensely. In 1901 Welsh had been involved in a conspiracy (along with Coolidge) to keep a deeply unpopular agent, Herman G. Nickerson, in his post after the Arapahos had rejected his policy on allotment. Nickerson, hoping a petition might improve his chances of staying on, had paid Welsh two dollars to lobby for him in the Arapaho camps.[12] The scheme, predictably, was a complete failure. Even when the Dawes Act allotment was later pushed through in the mid-1900s, its individualistic basis was nullified by tribal collectivism. As suggested in Grace's "An Arapahoe Christmas Tree," even "progressive" Arapaho villages managed lands communally, distributing surpluses to tribal members in need.[13]

Eventually, the Coolidges began to comprehend the enmity many felt against them and to realize the lack of "progress" they were making in their missionary efforts. After moving off the reservation, one of the things that Grace enjoyed most was finally having neighbors who liked her.[14] Nonetheless, she believed in Christianization until the end of her life. One of her last acts was donating seven thousand dollars to one of Wind River's missions, St. Michael's.[15] Yet whatever blame one might lay at Grace's feet for fostering forced assimilation has to be seen in the larger context of her deep concern for the Arapaho and Shoshone children.

In 1917 Grace Coolidge penned her only overtly political article, "Wanted: To Save the Babies," for the *American Indian Magazine*. Her opening paragraph conjures up the image of a serene winter evening in a snug log cabin suddenly "assailed by a wild weird cry"—the "Indian wail for the newly dead."[16] This was something Grace had experienced personally.[17] She goes on to explain how Indian deaths per thousand at Wind River are double that of the surrounding white settler population, with the main reason being infant mortality. Then-commissioner of Indian affairs Cato Sells had recently issued a pamphlet titled "Save the Babies," which promoted a four-pronged solution: "Teach, Urge, Improve, Extend." Grace treats the prescription as a morbid joke. Most Indian women have been "taught" in government schools, most have been "urged" by missionaries, and most live in "improved" white-style homes. What, then, is there to "extend"? The fact remains that the babies die, in most cases, for lack of milk in their second year—something easily preventable through government intervention.

Interestingly, Grace does not solely blame the Indian Bureau for this situation. She also condemns the "unchecked demands of custom and precedent" that some Indian mothers must endure, such as the birthing of babies in "hastily erected" lodges that leave young mothers and their offspring vulnerable to exposure. Also noted is that not all babies are wanted—proof, she writes ironically, that "the Indians are advancing in civilization." White influence, it turns out, does have its negative side. Grace then lists a series of incidents of which she apparently has personal knowledge. At Wind River, sick babies die when elders refuse the help of agency physicians, newborn infants are buried with mothers who have died in childbirth, and babies are left on hillsides to be eaten by coyotes. Meanwhile, diseases such as diphtheria ravage Indian children because school officials willfully ignore quarantine protocols. In all these cases, no one is held responsible because the Indian Bureau does not bother to investigate Indian deaths.[18] Grace's painstaking account of infant mortality at Wind River is certainly difficult to read, but it is unfortunate that she did not do more of such writing. Without question, her talent for description and argument could have moved many a reader to join national reform movements.

That same talent is in evidence in three stories Grace contributed to the *American Indian Magazine* later in 1917 grouped under the title "The White Plague." Here, she sparsely depicts the effect of tuberculosis on the population of Wind River. The images she conjures up, one must note, are unusually depressing. One even wonders whether the publisher of *Teepee Neighbors* rejected these three vignettes because of their stark quality. In one, a young woman from an eastern tribe, an "alien wife," arrives on the reservation with her returned husband, a baker. The young couple struggles financially while the woman finds it impossible to integrate into the local community. Eventually, she travels east to die. In the second story, subtitled "A Tale of the Boy Who Coughed," a skeletal orphaned child perishes slowly of consumption while reservation authorities look on, unable or unwilling to render him care. The decline of this "little shrunken bundle" is presented as simply inevitable. The last, "A Family Reaping," follows the fate of a young Indian mother lucky enough to have two living children and thus to be envied by all. In time, however, they both succumb to consumption, and the young mother expires a year later, to be laid out next to her dead offspring "upon the warm, all-embracing bosom of the earth."[19] Each of these stories—undoubtedly true—are enormously affecting. With just a few hundred words, Grace Coolidge creates memorable images and evokes strong emotions. The terse, spare writing is reminiscent of Ernest Hemingway's, though it predates his literary influence by decades.

Grace contributed two other sketches to the *American Indian Magazine* during her association with the Society of American Indians: "The Carpenter Who Had No One to Set Him Straight" and "Justice on a Reservation." Both were based—as one would expect—on events she witnessed at Wind River. The first is a short, almost humorous depiction of an Indian man, Daniel Blind Bull, attempting to build his own house. As a carpenter, his "imagination ran but a little beyond his skill," yet this is no fault of his own. In trying to construct a cozy cabin for his wife and new baby, he receives no aid from the agency carpenter, who ignores his requests for advice and spends his time making repairs to the reservation agent's home. In the end, Daniel's failed efforts become a source of ridicule to his neighbors. His wife admits to Grace that the home is really just "a shed," even while defending her husband's ambition. "But Dan he work hard, only he don't know how, and there's nobody around here to tell him nothin'," she explains with a sigh, positing that eventually they'll use the cabin's logs for firewood.[20] The message, of course, is clear: the desire and ability to work go to waste on the reservation without proper training; and the Indian Bureau consequently fails its wards once again.

"Justice on a Reservation"—the title meant ironically—is apparently Grace's final published effort, dating from 1918. It is a more ambitious work and reveals the rank unfairness of the bureau's power structure and the U.S. court system toward Native peoples. A "good-looking" Indian policeman named Harry Little Dog comes into conflict with a government school superintendent over his relations with a student, Pauline, "the prettiest and most troublesome girl in the school." When the superintendent finds the pair harmlessly giggling together in the building's basement, he insults Pauline's honor and slaps Harry, prompting him to instinctively reach for his sidearm—though not draw it. After the agent's inquiry, in which the superintendent disingenuously exaggerates the incident into a threat of death, Harry is put on trial in the county seat. A jury of whites issues a predictable verdict and harsh sentence. Grace contrasts this miscarriage of justice with another. After a Shoshone man is shot dead around the same time, his Arapaho killer claims self-defense. Though witnesses, two Indian women, contradict the story and describe nothing less than a cold-blooded murder, the Wind River agent ignores the entire issue—not deeming the death of an Indian worthy of investigation. Thus a guilty man remains free, while an innocent man is sent to prison. The story's last lines comment on the nature of lady justice, who on the reservation must wear blinders like a pack mule lest she "kick every blame thing to smithereens."[21]

Even if Grace Coolidge produced no other published writings, her pen rarely rested. "Isn't it nice we are scribbling so often," she wrote to Anne Talbot in 1897. "I only hope it will continue for the next 50 years or so."[22] Instead, it would continue for forty, ending with Grace's death in 1937. Thanks to this diligent correspondence and Talbot's foresight, we have an unusually intimate view of Grace's life. Talbot saved almost every letter sent to her, and she later handed them over to Grace's children before her own passing.[23] This valuable cache of documents records Grace's struggles to become a missionary, Sherman's courtship and their early marriage at Wind River, and the couple's later life. While many of the missives deal with mundane family matters, the ones offered in part 2 of this volume provide extraordinary details and, put simply, make for good reading. Here, Grace gives us what Sherman never did—a detailed record of the couple's life together that boasts tremendous biographical value for the researcher.

Grace's correspondence is divided into three sections. "Dearest Reddy, 1896–1901," commences with the first extant letter Grace wrote to the red-haired, green-eyed Anne Talbot. "I'm nearly bursting with delight for I don't see any reason why I shouldn't start for Wyo. a week from next Monday or Tuesday!!!!!!!!" it opens.[24] She is speaking of her impending trip to Wind River as a guest of Anne and her parents. Grace's stay in Wyoming begins a love affair not only with the West but perhaps with her old friend as well. Initially, the infatuation does not seem serious. When Anne takes ill and the women are unable to meet again in California, Grace admits that she is "just aching to pet somebody," and there are "moments, even, when the aching gets so pronounced (usually at night) that this foolish child pretends with the maddest glee that Annie is just on the other side of the bed." Another line reads, "Oh, Annie, *how* I longed for you—it almost hurt—way down in my tummy. You know that place. What an Annie you are to me."[25] Is this just joking? For a while it seems so.

The feelings in Grace's "tummy" subside when she travels to Europe and Russia, then to Wyoming and Colorado as Anne herself embarks for

Britain. In letters from these far-flung places, we view Grace's privilege and personality. In the spa town of Karlsbad, her judgmental side deems Germans a "degenerate little people."[26] At Grand Lake, Colorado, her carefree side almost gets her killed when she ascends a high peak with only her Kodak camera and some bread, then gets lost and spends a night in the woods as search parties futilely comb the surrounding area. She never feels fear, though, and in the end the "little adventure" merely provides "a fine feeling of independence."[27] By 1899, however, Grace seems to have become dependent on Anne. Interpreting this series of letters as a whole, one gets the vague impression that Grace divulged romantic feelings for her friend, who reciprocated but could not bring herself to break free of social convention. Concerned about such desires, Anne seems to have fallen back on her religious teachings, asking Grace to stop pressing the matter of their mutual attraction and instead devote herself to God and charity work. Grace, meanwhile, holds Anne up as a moral paragon, begging for love "in spite of everything" and for forgiveness for having "fallen short" in good deeds and perhaps the suppression of her emotions.[28]

Was this a romantic relationship? Was it a "romantic friendship" devoid of physical expression? How is one to take passages such as "When a time comes when I really love you better than I do myself I want to go to you, to fly to you, Annie—only tonight what I most want to do is to kiss you and kiss you"?[29] And what of comments such as "Of course the thing I wanted to say in this letter is what I have left unsaid, but you know what I have been thinking every time I have thought of you. Oh dear! There are such things I want to say but I mustn't"?[30] Lesbian relationships were no rarer at the turn of the twentieth century than now—and in Episcopal circles no less. Evangeline Marrs Whipple, the wife of Bishop Henry Whipple (Sherman Coolidge's mentor), famously carried on a love affair with acting first lady Rose Cleveland, the sister of the president. After Henry Whipple's death in 1901, the women resumed their relationship and eventually left for Italy to live out the remainder of their lives as partners.[31] "Reddy, I've always had a deadly feeling that to find a man as fine as a woman was impossible," Grace states while discussing one of Anne's suitors and eventual husband, Francis Donaldson.[32]

Whatever the nature of the relationship, Anne had a tremendous influence on the direction of Grace's life. She mentions reading Thomas à Kempis "every night," seemingly inspired by his quote from *The Imitation of Christ*, book 1, chapter 3: "At the Day of Judgement we shall not be asked what we have read, but what we have done." This yearning to act brings conflict into the palatial Wetherbee home.[33] Grace resolves to enter St. Faith's and become a deaconess, confounding her mother, who comes down on her "like a wolf on the fold"—an allusion to Lord Byron's "The Destruction of Sennacherib."[34] Refusing to conform to Hannah Wetherbee's mold, Grace travels west again in the summer of 1901, having secured a position as an assistant missionary on the Ouray and Uintah Reservation in Utah, home to the Ute Indians. She is so eager to get there that during a few days' stopover in Evanston, Wyoming, she convinces her hosts, a couple named the Huntings, to drive her to Utah in their buggy over a snow-covered mountain road used primarily to haul iron ore.[35] Once in the agency center of Whiterocks, Grace works teaching schoolchildren and, in one instance, helps amputate a Ute man's mangled finger. One also gets the impression this is the first time in her life she ever cooked for herself.[36] Being out West on her own and serving others teach her that she can "get along" without Anne and that Anne has been correct to suggest they "break off." Grace even seems to view her life as a choice between her feelings for "Reddy" and her Christian duty to do good. Realizing that one "can't serve two masters," she misses Anne, fearing "the same two things that used to be all the trouble to me in you."[37] What precisely this "trouble" was, and if it ever became physical, we can only guess—though later missives provide scattered clues.

This volume's second selection of letters, "Love, Marriage, and Death at Wind River, 1902–5," begins when Grace travels to Fort Washakie at the invitation of John Roberts. Then nearing thirty years of age, she has gone there against her parents' wishes to oversee the reservation's Shoshone girls' school. Though she has no inkling whatsoever, Grace will marry in less than four months' time. The letters that flow out of this period give us a detailed account of her relationship with Sherman Coolidge. What stands out is Grace's initial uncertainty about what precisely she is doing. After two months or so, Roberts stops assigning her work and she is left idle.[38] Sherman, who does nothing all day but sit in an old Fort Washakie warehouse listlessly peeking out the window for potential converts, makes for good company.[39] Both are bored, educated, and lonely. Soon, they began talking and joking late into the evening and even smoking gold-tipped cigarettes in secret behind lowered shades.[40] Grace worries that her behavior might be "unwomanly." Sherman does not, and he eventually opens up to her about his difficult life and the constant bigotry he has suffered. Grace feels moved to touch him but controls her impulse.[41]

This budding relationship, however, is not devoid of tensions. Despite her general love for Indians, Grace held deeply racist views all too typical of her white Anglo-Saxon Protestant milieu (and also typical of many "Red Progressives" such as Gertrude Bonnin, Marie Baldwin, and Arthur C. Parker).[42] Her correspondence is littered with racial slurs against African Americans—whom she feels bring bad luck—and hateful comments about Jewish Americans.[43] Grace felt some license as well to poke fun at Indians by using broken English, words like "heap" and the salutation "How." "Injun" and "Injuny" were among her other favorites. One evening, Sherman apparently had enough. He accuses Grace of saying "something awfully mean and heartless," putting her "right down with all those people who say mean things to him because he is Injun." This reaction sends Grace reeling, and three days pass before they speak again. Grace concedes that it all "hurt like fire" but privately deems Sherman "absurdly sensitive."[44] Yet the fight brings the two closer together. Some initial hand-holding advances to "twosing," the nineteenth-century slang for sexual "petting." How heavy Grace does not specify, but she does admit to not feeling "fit for church."

Still, there is no intention of marriage. Instead, Grace's thoughts return to Anne. These letters provide the strongest suggestions that the women's relationship had indeed been physical. "Don't you believe you better come out and take care of me?" Grace asks. ". . . My but I wanted you that first night, I'm awfully green for my years. But I always thought men were just about like women. Indians don't seem to be, anyhow. Well, if I hadn't you, I never would dare go as far as I have. If you tell me to stop, I will."[45] It is because Sherman is an Indian that Grace feels the twosing is "natural." His is "so much realer than any (man) body" she has ever encountered.[46] We can assume, possibly, that she is more familiar with the bodies of women. Regardless, being with Sherman feels so "comfortable" that, as Grace puts it to Anne, "I might as well buck at kissing you."[47] Within less than two weeks, Sherman asks Grace for her hand. "Reddy," she reveals, "I almost died right there and then." In truth, Grace has not the "vaguest idea" of what to do, but she appreciates how she feels "dead comfortable and happy when he is here," inevitably because "he is Injun."[48] Anne expresses envy at this new attraction. "You needn't be jealous," Grace assures her. "I tell Sherman every time the subject comes up that you are the only man I ever loved."[49]

Grace agrees to marry Sherman in late September. His reaction is jubilant, but serious troubles follow. John Roberts refuses to perform the ceremony, offering a series of poor, bumbling excuses. First, he says he needs time, then the consent of Grace's father. The real issue, of course, is Sherman's race. One evening, Sherman breaks down in tears, crying "like a baby" because their marriage might be thwarted indefinitely.[50] He was then around forty years old and had endured the breakup of several previous serious relationships.[51] In 1887, for instance, he had been about to marry an assistant matron at the Wind River school until his conspiracy against the Jesuits resulted in his temporary exile.[52] Sherman and Grace thus are left trying to figure out some way to wed in dignity, without the black mark of Roberts's refusal. Grace never manages to obtain explicit parental consent, but eventually Roberts yields under pressure and marries them in early October. Grace provides a step-by-step description of the entire day, starting with a hurried expedition to the town of Lander for a marriage license and ending with the Coolidges' ride down to their new home at Sherman's ranch, having been accompanied by an impromptu children's chorus of "John Brown's Body"—a hilarious moment the Coolidges remembered and referenced on anniversaries.[53]

Why Roberts relented remains the real question. If he feared those in the Episcopal Church would negatively construe his denial, his instincts were wise. Coolidge's superiors, it turned out, approved of the union. Ethelbert Talbot even took credit for bringing Grace and Sherman together, but he admitted that his daughter Anne's warnings had mitigated the "shock" and enabled him to "survive" the news.[54] As her correspondence indicates, Grace's family and friends in the East were not as supportive. She is constantly forced to defend her choice and even dispel rumors that she has married a "blanket Indian."[55] Not recorded in these letters is that Grace's aunt Sarah cut her off completely for several years following the marriage.[56] When Sarah did allow Grace to visit her home again in 1910, she treated the Coolidge children with simmering contempt.[57]

Despite her family's disapproval, Grace is initially thrilled with her new life on the ranch. Sherman's relatives often camp nearby and treat her with complete acceptance.[58] By 1904 Grace has given birth to two "young squallers." Her first is an "awfully sweet" boy named Louis, whom she keeps in a traditional Arapaho baby carrier.[59] The second is a girl, born prematurely, named Grace Ann, after Anne Talbot.[60] Then suddenly in November 1904, Louis dies of typhoid fever, a common illness at Wind River. Grace's only wish is "to go to him." Five months later, Grace Ann dies of pneumonia.[61] What keeps Grace going in her grief is Sherman's unwavering faith in an afterlife and that she will soon give birth again.[62] A son named Philip arrives in October 1905 but dies twelve days later due to a congenital heart defect, resting in Grace's arms as she tries to revive him in a warm bath. "What will you say when I tell you that my little son is dead too?" she asks Anne. "You ought to see those three little graves in a row, Grace in the middle and the boys on the outside."[63]

These devastating deaths developed in Grace the deep empathy that marks the rest of her life. Once ensconced in wealth and privilege, she had found herself in the same position as many an Indian mother at Wind River, and she never forgot it. She vowed, after her first child's death, to "make the best come out of it" and to "see that his death and his life too for that matter of that, were not in vain."[64] This meant helping those around her. Grace kept her promise by doing whatever she could for Wind River's young ones until her departure from the reservation in 1910. The *Spirit of Missions* even dubbed Grace "God's own blessing sent to the Indian babies of the reservation," explaining that the children "she does not adopt she cares for in one way or another, and the Indian mothers bring their babies to her whenever they are ill."[65] Grace often traversed the reservation, sometimes alone, sometimes with an interpreter, offering to take in orphaned or needy children. Whether some mothers saw this as interference is of course possible. Grace found, in most cases, that the Arapahos and Shoshones were reluctant to give orphaned children to a white woman.[66] In 1906 the Coolidges finally managed to adopt an eight-year-old Shoshone girl named Effie, who had been orphaned.[67] While Grace was pregnant a fourth time, they took in six-year-old Virginia, the daughter of one of Sherman's relatives.[68] In the 1920s, the Coolidges also hosted ill Indian children in their home during summers.[69] Perhaps these acts of compassion and generosity helped—at least marginally—to heal the wounds caused by their own children's deaths. Regardless, there is no question that the Coolidges' marriage endured events that would have broken many others.

The brief final section of letters, "Later Missives, 1911–32," gives us five snapshots from the last third of Grace Coolidge's life. It opens with her confession to having done "something horribly audacious." For the past few months in Enid, Oklahoma, Grace has been composing what she herself calls "snapshots" of her eight years at Wind River. This "audacity" would become her book *Teepee Neighbors* six years later.[70] Audacity, perhaps, but one could also argue that the book grew out of the empathy Grace had acquired on the reservation. Mencken, incidentally, read this empathy as "the great quality of pity."[71] Well, even the greatest of critics can err. Why Grace felt compelled to return to the past was a mystery to her. She tells Talbot: "It's funny I'm writing again after all those stuffed up years in Wyoming. It's not worth it, I'm convinced but I tell you solemnly *I can't help it*. The things are in you and they stir to get out and what's more they have to come out just as absolutely as the babies do." Whether the pieces were published was almost secondary. "Well, I've *loved* doing them," she writes, "and they can at least be buried with me."[72]

Grace's references to babies and death were appropriate in light of ensuing events. As the next letter details, Grace gives birth to her last daughter, Rosie, in September 1912 while living in Faribault, Minnesota.[73] Six months later, the Coolidge family almost returns to dust when their buggy is hit by an express train while out for a Sunday ride. Rosie is catapulted through the air and miraculously lands unscathed; the rest of the family suffers serious injuries. Even though Grace's "respected nose" is broken and she almost loses an eye, her thoughts on the accident typify her lifelong carefree attitude. "Wasn't that funny!?" she asks Anne.[74] On the first anniversary of the buggy accident, another brush with death occurs. Grace and Sherman are woken in the night by the cries of baby Rosie, and they quickly realize their home is on fire. Sherman barrels downstairs trying to find the source, then runs back up to collect the children, exit the house, and call for help. The incident is not without humor. As he bursts into a neighbor's home, Sherman finds "the young girl of the family" on the couch entangled with her "beau." "Love's Young Dream," as Grace calls it, is brusquely interrupted. In the end, the fire department ascertains that the Coolidges have been the victim of a defective flue. Rosie's cries, it bears noting, saved the family from certain death by asphyxiation.[75]

The final letter in this section dates from February 1932, a month following Sherman's death in Los Angeles. Four years earlier, he and Grace had placed daughters Sallie, then twenty-one years old, and Rosie, sixteen, in schools in California.[76] With the children out of the house, a new, more relaxed period began. "Sherman and I are really quite enjoying arranging our own lives and eating what we please after long years of slavery to the young," Grace wrote Anne in October 1928.[77] During this time of long-awaited freedom, the couple traveled, sometimes with friends, in their Franklin touring car. While negotiating steep mountain roads, Grace's habit was to assist the driver by standing on the auto's running board and shouting out instructions.[78] She and Sherman sailed to Alaska in 1931 and more than once visited Wyoming to observe the Sun Dance.[79] At Wind River, Grace sometimes felt a wistfulness that provoked "spells of talking about building up the ranch and going back for a while every year." This was mere nostalgia. "You can't go back and recapture vanished phases of life," Grace admitted to Anne in October 1931. "The thing has to flow on, and if you hold it back you only make backwaters."[80] Grace did not know that in three months the major phase of her life, her marriage, would vanish with Sherman's death. Nor did she know that she would be absent when his death came. Sherman's health had been deteriorating for years, so when doctors suggested a warmer climate, he left for Los Angeles, where Sallie had settled. Grace saw him off at the train station on New Year's Day 1932.[81] Her February letter describes what occurred over the next several weeks, the funeral, her grief, and her ultimate contentment at making Sherman's life "richer and happier." "Isn't it funny," she remarks to Anne, "to think that you were the one who first brought us together?"[82]

This volume closes with two of Grace's unpublished poems, which she shared with Anne Talbot in May 1911. The first, "The Offering of the Goddess," reflects her apparently unshakable conviction that Native peoples required the enlightenment of the Gospel. Her poem traces the transformation of a "heathen maid," bathed by pagan priests in the blood of beasts and men, into an acolyte of Christ. Having once lived "alone and very blind" in "lands remote," she gives up her name before the cross when reborn, having nothing else to offer in penitence.

Grace's second poem, the arguably more successful "On Finishing a Book," well captures the experience of being immersed in literature before the advent of commercial radio. Having finished a novel, the poem's narrator searches her home "from room to room" for the emotions inspired by the pages she has turned. These feelings, such as "love" and "anguish," have brought tears never to be replicated by a story now lying in a "grave." Even the book's author has lost his own creation. One's only recourse, the poem suggests, is to embark on a fresh search for stimulation and meaning, for a book, when finished, is forever "gone."[83] True enough, though reading Grace Coolidge's writing always "leaves something behind it."

PART 1

Sherman Coolidge *Stories, Articles, Speeches, and Statements*

Scenes from an Arapaho Boyhood

CROW AND EAGLE

To get eagle feathers, tail feathers for war bonnets, the wing feathers for fans, or for arrow tips, etc., the Arapahoe men were often obliged to go several days from the camp to the locality where eagles were more likely to be found than in the creek bottoms where we made camp when possible. I remember on one occasion my father moved with his family to such a place among the rocks in a mountainous region. It was in the winter time. Early in the morning he would get up and go off on foot and stay all day, watching his chance hidden in a little retreat made of whatever material was at hand . . . cedar or pine branches covered with a little earth and rocks. He would put bait of raw meat close by his hiding place, near enough to make his shooting with a bow and arrow sure, and wait there in the cold of the mountains wrapped in his buffalo robe.

One day, on this trip of which I speak he came home toward evening bringing two eagles on his back. I kept poking my head out of the tepee door to see if he was coming until he appeared . . . when I, standing halfway out of the tepee cried out the news to those inside. But being still only a little boy, I knew only the name of crow and that would do for any kind of bird. So I called out proudly, "Here comes father with crows on his back!"

THE COLT

When I was a little boy, I should think about three or four years old, my mother gave me a colt. I remember on a beautiful day my grandmother, aunt and mother, Turtle Woman, were picking berries on some big river . . .

I think the Platte. They were picking buffalo berries to dry for our use during the winter. Also to make a kind of drink from these berries by crushing the juice out of them while fresh and putting water to it, making as near as I can describe, a sort of pink lemonade which was greatly enjoyed by us all . . . especially the youngsters. Berry picking time was always a picnic time with us and we enjoyed the outing as much as the older people. They had gathered all they could put in their sacks of buckskin and rawhide "trunks" and had packed them on our horses all except one good-sized sack.

My mother said "Where shall we put this one?"

Noticing my colt standing by its mother . . . it must have been three or four months old at that time . . . laughing, she said, "I know what I will do with this one. I will put it on Runs-on-the-Top's horse!" And with that she threw it on the colt's back and the little fellow keeled over under its weight.

"You've killed my horse," I screamed as loud as I could. The women all had a good laugh over it till my mother had pity and took the sack off him. I must have been a very little boy at this time for I cannot remember my half-sister, Sings First, who was only two years younger than I was, being with us.

A LITTLE GAMBLER

It was perhaps the next summer that my little brother came. Later he was named Left Hand because he turned out to be left-handed, but the first name, or rather birth name, which he had and the name by which he always went with the Indians, was Nee-netch-a or One-Who-Dies-and-Comes-To-Life-Again. It is the same word, we now use in the Arapahoe translation of the Apostles' Creed. "He Died." This somewhat singular name was given to my baby brother from the habit he had of crying and holding his breath till he would almost lose consciousness.

My father was in the habit of taking me to the council of chiefs and leading men which met in the center of the village. I had a little bow and arrows; next to my brother my chiefest possession. An uncle of mine had made it for me. One of the young chiefs asked me, in all seriousness, to have a game with him in which our respective bows and arrows should be the stake. Our game which we played with our arrows rebounding from the bow to a certain mark stuck in the ground was a familiar Indian one. Naturally my opponent being much more expert than I won, one by one, my precious arrows and finally my bow. I bore up like a man as I thought! . . . while with the men, but when bedtime came a great sense of my loss came over me and I cried and cried while my mother tried in vain to comfort me. Finally she told me to go to sleep and that while I slept my brother, the little bundle of buffalo robe tied up and tucked into my mother's bed, would go in the night and win the arrows back for me. I had not had much experience with little brothers, not, indeed enough to make me doubt my mother's words. So I shut my eyes and fell asleep, and in the morning when I poked my head out from under the robes, there on the floor of my bed lay my bow and arrows. I think no boy was ever prouder of his little brother than I was from that day on, of mine!

A HORSE RACE

I was old enough to have and ride a real horse of my own . . . perhaps it was the colt of the berry-picking days now grown up, or perhaps it was a horse my oldest brother, really half-brother, Beaver Sing (Singing Beaver) had given me. I know I was the proud owner of two horses. At first, I used to be tied on one of my horses with a rope going around the animal's body and over my knees . . . my father leading the horse with a buffalo hide lariat. On one occasion as we were going from one camping place to another, following a trail, my father walking as usual leading my horse, one of my uncles riding up beside me challenged me to a race with him. He proposed if I won the race he should give me the next antelope he killed and if he won it my father should do likewise for me. I agreed and we made ready to start. We agreed on the distance and the course, which we picked out among the scrub cedar and pine that dotted that part of the country. My little pony was no match for his even with my light weight, but in good faith we wheeled our horses side by side, he laughing at my approaching defeat and I in dead earnest self to prove the merit of both myself and my horse. We started and ran side by side for a little way till suddenly and without warning my uncle's horse bolted, came in contact with one of the scrub cedars, got all tangled up in the branches, and left me alone to pursue my way at my own gait to the end of the course.

So I won my first race and my uncle, true to our bet, gave me the next antelope he killed.

THE DEATH OF BIG HEART (BRAVE HEART)

It is almost impossible to convey to the ordinary civilized man's mind the cruel uncertainty of life as the Indians in the old days knew it. My own realization of it came in a sudden and tragic way and in a scene which, little boy though I was, is fixed as clearly in my mind as though it happened yesterday. I speak of the death of my dear and much-loved father, Big Heart.

At a meeting of the Council of which my father was a member there had been a division of opinion as to which route through what I now judge must have been the Big Horn Country to affect a juncture with the friendly Crows. The majority of the Council was in favor of following the main stream of the river on which we were encamped while my father and a few others favored following a smaller branch and then making a cut-off through the hills taking, in fact, the course that the Crows themselves had taken when they left us a short time before. The division of opinion occasioned the tribes dividing into two bands, the main portion followed the council of the majority . . . while my father with his family (consisting of my mother, her younger sister—also my father's wife, for it was a custom of the Arapahoes often to marry the sisters of their older wife), their children and the children of their sister killed in the fight with the Whites not long before. With my father were two friends of his and their families. Their names or who they were I do not know. In all there were three tepees in our little band.

The first night after leaving the main body of the tribe we camped on the little stream in the old camping place of the Crows. There was a circular clear space surrounded by a thick growth of quaking aspens through which a trail led into the clear space and out again. It was, I should judge, a favorite camping place for moving bands of Indians from its sheltered position and its nearness to wood and water. We reached this place and made camp about sunset.

Just as we reached our camping place we saw across a wide valley on the other side of the stream, on bluffs, a small group of Indians apparently cutting up a buffalo they had just killed. My father and his two friends riding side by side in the lead of our little band noticed and talked over these Indians. There was nothing at that distance by which they could identify the tribe of these Indians, but feeling sure there were no hostile Indians in that part of the country they came to the unanimous decision that they were a band of Crows and went into camp in what they believed the greatest security from harm.

Supper eaten and the horses staked out in the enclosure, everybody went to bed early, I remember, only my older brother, Singing Beaver, and I were sitting up by the little fire in the center of my father's tepee while he was telling me ghost stories. At the end of the story we crawled in under our buffalo robes and went to bed. But I, excited by the story, still sat staring into the dying fire. Finally, I too got up and crossed over to where my brother was already asleep and lifted the blanket to crawl under, when suddenly out of the night, seemingly on all sides of us, rose the shriek of the war cry. We were surrounded. In one instant, the tepee inmates had leapt into life and terror, and in one instant more someone raised the back a little and all had crawled outside. The tepee stood close to the brush and backing up to the trail which led out of the clearing. The enemy had neglected to guard this outlet and the position of the lodge was such that it cast a black shadow, the night being a bright moonlight one, so that all who got outside were hid for the instant it took to get from the tepee into the thick growth of brush.

I tried to follow the others but could not lift the heavy hide of the tepee enough to let me crawl under. I turned and saw my father standing alone in the lodge loading by the little light of the embers his old muzzle loading rifle from a powder horn. He never made any effort to escape. He stayed behind with the simple object of holding the enemy off until we could make our escape. He was the only one of our little band who was killed.

When he had finished loading his gun he started for the door, I following him. When he saw me he told me to come with him out of the tepee and then to run into the trail, by which the others had gone and he would stay and fight. We emerged and I did as he bade me. I saw nothing of any of the enemy. They must have been hiding in the thick trees for their war cry had been very near. They were quiet as we came forth.

I ran into the trail which led me soon to the little stream. It was about the time that winter was breaking up. The stream was still frozen but the ice was thin. I saw a man and a woman, one of the other families. The woman had broken through the ice and was struggling in the shallow water. Her husband was trying to help her. As I came up on the bank on the other side a heavy cloud darkened the moon. I could see nobody. I began calling, calling for my mother and running as I called, till suddenly I ran right into her. She had not dared answer me for fear of drawing the attention of the enemy.

It always seemed strange to me that none of the enemy followed us. We all, except my father, escaped. Many years after my return to my people in the Wind River Reservation, a scout, a white man, connected with Fort Washakie, told me that he had heard from the Shoshones (who are friends and of the same race as the Bannocks), the Indians who killed my father, that the expedition was for horse stealing. The band of Indians which we had seen across the valley at sundown must have numbered twenty-five. Our horses all stayed in the enclosure and I suppose they considered themselves lucky to get the animals so easily and did not care to risk a night attack on the rest of us.

My mother and I did not know where the others were. My little brother was on her back. We walked on and on over the frozen ground until our moccasins were worn through. When it got light so that we could see a little by daylight we saw a boy about as big as my brother, Singing Beaver, coming down from a little hill where a little clump of pines grew. We recognized him as he came nearer as the son of the woman whom I had seen struggling in the water. He kept calling to my mother "Turtle Woman, Turtle Woman." We waited till he caught up with us when he told us that his father had sent him to tell my mother that his wife was up under those pine trees and had just given birth to a baby. Because his wife was in such a condition that he could not leave her was why he had not stayed to help my father fight. I might say in this connection that I never knew why the other man ran away. The boy went back and my mother and I kept on following the Crow trail.

Just a little after this, we were able to make out in the twilight a big band of Indians coming toward us on the trail . . . and soon we could see that it was an Arapahoe and Crow war party. As soon as they saw us they surrounded my mother and asked particulars about the location of our camp and what, according to her knowledge, had occurred. Singing Beaver, it seemed, had made great time through the night and had reached the main Arapahoe camp which had already joined the Crows, and had given the alarm. The war party directed us to follow along the trail we were on and we would soon make the main camp. We left them and a little farther on met a Crow man out hunting horses. We asked him about the camp and he gave us the same directions the others had done. Then we came to the main stream and met still another Crow man. He showed us how to cross the stream where the ice was firm and went with us to his tepee, the first of the main camp of the Crows beyond which was the Arapahoe camp. It was then about sun-up. They gave us food and a pair of moccasins to my mother and two to me. Then they showed us the way to the Arapahoe camp and we went to my uncle Bald Head's tepee. The old man still lives on the reservation.

One singular thing I must mention here: after I had been taken by the whites and was living with General (then first lieutenant) Charles Austin Coolidge, in the winter of 1870 (it must have been about five years after my father's death), Lt. Coolidge was stationed at the Crow agency near Livingstone, Montana. There was a great gathering of the Crows who came to the agency to receive their annuities. Several men came into the Coolidges' house and Mrs. Coolidge sent them into the kitchen to get warm. I stood by the door watching them. One man noticed me and turned to the two or three others talking to them in Crow at the same time using with his hands the sign language, a way in which the older Indians have of emphasizing what they are telling. I could understand the signs but not the Crow language. The man said, as near as I could understand, that I reminded him of an Arapahoe boy whom he had seen escaping with his mother from an attack by the Bannocks. He then went on to describe my mother and myself and the fight in which my father lost his life. He was the man we had met hunting horses and who had directed us to the Crow camp. I was too shy, however, to make myself known to him.

Eventually, all the members of the three families of our camp reached the Arapahoe camp in safety.

The returning war party brought the first definite word of my father. They had found him lying dead within the enclosure of the camp, bearing the marks of bullet, spear and arrow wounds. His body was lying on a buffalo robe and covered by another. He was neither scalped nor mutilated, as was the usual Indian way of treating a fallen foe. He was treated thus as a mark of respect for his bravery, as high an honor as his foes could have paid him.

The tepees and horses were gone and the Bannocks had got such a good start that the Arapahoes considered it useless to pursue them. They buried my father and returned to us with the news.

My father's memory is still revered amongst the Arapahoes. To this day if one of the older men, my father's contemporaries, wishes to speak to me with special honor or to compliment me he will call me, instead of by my own name Runs-on-the-Surface (Runs-on-Top) by my father's instead, Brave Heart or Great Heart, the significance of the name in Arapahoe having not only the meaning of a heart big with kindness but with courage and manliness as well.

Dispatches from a Wind River Missionary

REPORT TO THE *SPIRIT OF MISSIONS*
August 1885

The following letter from the Indian Deacon, the Rev. Sherman Coolidge, who is at work at the Shoshone Agency, will interest his many friends and supporters in the East:

> My chief work during the past quarter has been in aiding the school work at this Agency, teaching in the Arapahoe department of the Government school. I find the Arapahoe and Shoshone children are docile and intelligent, as I have found Indian children to be among the Ojibways, the Santee, Sisseton, Yankton, Sioux, and other tribes; and they learn very willingly and very readily. Notwithstanding the fact that this Wind River School is only two years old, I believe it is doing as much good as any other institution of its class in the United States; and that the superintendent and his co-workers deserve any and every aid the Church, as well as the Government, can give them. And I doubt whether those who are doing its work and who bear its burdens can fully realize what they are doing for these poor uncivilized heathens, for their country, and the Christian religion. I have held Services and preached at Fort Washakie and Lander every other Sunday, and delivered one sermon at the Agency; I also have buried one Indian and visited about twenty-five tepees. I have succeeded to obtain the promise of three Arapahoes to commence farming and to continue until they have secured a home for themselves and their families. I am now very desirous to raise a fund to the amount of about seven hundred dollars with which to build a dwelling to be situated at my uncle "Sharp Nose's"[1] camp, about ten or twelve miles from here, and where, I understand, Bishop Spalding[2]

intends to locate a chapel; and if we establish a permanent Mission there I believe many of the Arapahoes will settle around and near it. I know of no State or Territory where the Church has a more glorious field as man's educator, "intellectual as well as spiritual," than she has in this, her new Missionary Jurisdiction of Wyoming Territory; and, more especially, on this reservation, where the need of civilization by savage men is so imperious and where heathen people are waiting so favorably for the reception of the Gospel story of the love of God.

REPORT TO THE *SPIRIT OF MISSIONS*
August 1886

Mr. Coolidge is laboring in the associated mission of the Shoshone Agency, Fort Washakie, North Fork, and Lander. He writes:

> I have been holding services at these different points alternately with the Rev. Mr. Roberts, the head of the Arapahoe and Shoshone school, at the Agency. I have been connected with the mission since October 2nd, 1884; and the Church has been making progress ever since especially in the way of buildings. The church building in Lander has been completed; the church at the Agency was completed last fall, with the adjoining rectory of the Rev. Mr. Roberts. I am grateful to add that I have been enabled to build and finish a house for myself through the generous and prompt aid of members of the mission and other kind friends. The Rev. Mr. Jones, missionary to the Shoshones, I regret to say, has been compelled to leave his field of labor on account of ill health, but I hope his place may soon be filled by some other missionary, as the tribe needs one very much.
>
> The Arapahoes are in favor of civilization and Christianity. They show it by the disposition and in beginning to farm and desiring to live in houses instead of tepees, as well as by their children outnumbering the Shoshone children in school attendance. In order to obtain good fence-poles, which are durable, they have to go from five to fifteen miles; some, however, use cotton wood poles, which they get from the river banks.

I have made some progress in my language; but until I have mastered the language my chief work will be to advance the civilization of the tribe. There were quite a number of Indians on the Reserve who commenced farming and fencing in considerable tracts of land last summer after my council with them on the subject.

Besides attending to my Church duties at Fort Washakie, Shoshone Agency, North Fork, and Lander, I have visited thirty tepees during the last quarter.

REPORT TO THE *SPIRIT OF MISSIONS*
March 1896

The Rev. Sherman Coolidge, native Indian missionary at the Shoshone Indian agency, Wyoming, reports for the quarter ending December 1st last as follows:

Since my last report we have had our Bishop[3] with us, which always gives a new impetus and assurance to our isolated work. An episcopal visitation always brightens us up and gives a new life. The Bishop confirmed five Arapahoes, young men, in the Indian mission church at the agency. He visited the Arapahoe settlement, where we sometimes hold services, and made a short address. The Indians there are building a new "council house" in which they intend to allow us to hold services and to give them religious instructions. In the early days of frontier life the Arapahoes had the reputation of being warlike, and ferocious, but they are naturally a good-hearted and peace-loving people.

I have administered the Holy Communion, preached, and held services at the Shoshone agency, Fort Washakie, and the government Indian school. I have married an Arapahoe couple, baptized seven Arapahoes (one young man and six young girls), from the government school. The St. Andrew's Brotherhood members have held their regular meetings, which were very well attended. We missed the inspiring presence of our faithful director, Fremont Arthur,[4] at our last meeting.

REPORT TO THE *SPIRIT OF MISSIONS*

July 1897

The Rev. Sherman Coolidge writes in his last quarterly report, dated September 1st, as follows:

> Our work among the Arapahoes is quite encouraging. We hope soon to build a log chapel in one of our settlements, near where our catechist lives. The ladies' guild has raised $100, with which we hope to have the chapel built. We may not have enough funds for a board floor, and may have to content ourselves with a dirt floor for awhile, but we expect to have boards for the chancel. We hold service and preach regularly in the Indian agency church, at the government Indian school, and among the Colored soldiers at Fort Washakie.

REPORT TO THE *SPIRIT OF MISSIONS*

December 1898

The Rev. Sherman Coolidge, himself an Arapahoe, writes:

> The bell which rings out every Sunday afternoon in the valley of the Little Wind river, six or seven miles east of the Shoshone agency and Fort Washakie, has on it the inscription: "To the Prince of Peace." It is the gift of friends of the east to the little mission church near the Arapahoe council house. The church is built of pine logs, and we were allowed by the Indian agent to saw them into squares by the agency mill in consideration of the use of the mowing machine belonging to the Shoshone Mission school.
>
> We had the encouraging presence of Chief Plenty Bear at one of the services recently, and he stopped after service long enough to say, "Some don't believe in religion. We (the Arapahoes) have all believed in God from our youth, and when we hear the Word of God preached to us we are glad; and while there are people who don't believe in God, yet we want to continue in our belief in God the Father and worship Him. We are also

especially glad to hear the good news of the rising again from the dead. We have heard what you have been teaching our children in the schools, they in turn tell us older people. I believe in your teachings." During the conversation the missionary remarked to the chief that "bad men fear neither God nor man, but a good man is not afraid of any man although he is afraid of God." The school-house and the church are the hope of our Indians. The introduction of both education and pure religion among these two native tribes on Wind River reservation will greatly diminish ignorance and injurious superstition.

REPORT TO THE *SPIRIT OF MISSIONS*
January 1899

The Rev. Sherman Coolidge, Indian missionary to the Indians on the Wind River reservation, Wyoming, reports as follows upon the work at different points:

During the past quarter one marriage has been solemnized, the Holy Communion celebrated on the first of each month, and a service, with sermon, has been conducted every Sunday morning at the Church of the Redeemer, Shoshone Agency. Every other Sunday there is an evening service at Fort Washakie for the benefit of the officers, soldiers, and civilian employees connected with the garrison. Every Sunday afternoon at three o'clock there is a service held in the Arapahoe language by our lay evangelist, Fremont Arthur, seven miles from here in our little new mission chapel. The attendance has been quite good.

The work among the Indians on the Wind River reservation is both aggressive and progressive; especially among the Arapahoes. Really, the Church work here embraces not only the Indians, but also white people, an element of Mexicans, and mixed bloods not a few. And while these may be grouped in a general way as human beings, yet they are a heterogeneous lot, and must be treated as such. The lines are not so sharply drawn as to be impassable, still they form quite distinct classes; the Mexicans make a party, the mixed-bloods have different cliques, and the Shoshones are as clannish as the Arapahoes. These two tribes were hereditary foes before they were brought together here by the government. Now they live side by side in peace and harmony, only the Arapahoe thinks he is better than the Shoshone, and *vice versa.* The brotherhood of Jesus Christ is a universal need.

Early Articles and Statements

EDUCATION OF INDIANS

Churchman, May 1887

Several years ago quite a number of Arapahoe and Shoshone children were sent to Carlisle, and while there, and after their return to the reservation, a large majority of them died. This, according to the Indians' limited range of thought, is a posteriori evidence that the Atlantic coast climate is unhealthy for their young people. There is probably some truth in this statement, but, without doubt, their deaths to a great extent were caused by disease. On this account parents and guardians are apprehensive about the effect of the eastern atmosphere upon the constitution of their youth; they are therefore unwilling to send their children and wards there, while at the same time Carlisle refuses to receive any pupils from these tribes, because of the usual delicate condition of their physical organism. It is manifest, then, that the work of education and civilization of the young of these two tribes must be performed in a Government industrial school or church institution on the reservation, or else in some training-school located west of the Mississippi river. The bulk of educational operations among the Indians must of necessity be carried out on the reservations and in the West; but the training-schools, such as Carlisle in Pennsylvania, Hampton in Virginia, Genoa in Nebraska, and Salem in Oregon, are to the reservation schools what colleges and universities are to high schools and academies. After a study of the subject, both pro and con, it is certainly a fair conclusion that there are as many good reasons for having the schools at, or near, the agencies, or among the tribes, as there are for putting them away from such surroundings.

It is a great misfortune, however, for these schools that the wisdom of the nation's legislators should have deemed it best to place them under the control of a department so inextricably mixed up with politics, partisan changes, and a pernicious system of patronage. As a consequence of the laxity of such a system, wide room is given to irregularity and injustice in the administration of Indian affairs.

Would you test the truth of what is here affirmed, go to the United States Indian Agent, or to the Agency School Superintendent and examine the piles and bundles of imperious orders which they have received from Washington, and many of whose contents are of the essence of nonsense in their relation to the real nature and state of affairs of their destination; when you have completed your investigation you will not wonder why these two ill-paid and responsible employees of the nation look so careworn and tormented; but stay awhile with them and in a short time you will be further convinced that they have enough things to give them sleepless nights without receiving additional ones from their headquarters, because they have not only a thousand and one things which demand their care and attention in the trying positions they endeavor to fill, but they have also the duty of overseeing starving human beings who are the wards of one of the foremost nations of the earth in a land bursting with plenty and whose coffers are more than full. "Starving the wards of the nation ought to cease to be the scandal of the American Government." This is only an instance of a multitude of similar cases in the service which could be furnished did time and space permit; there are many employees in the service with genuine interest in the welfare of this neglected and perishing race, who are hindered and hampered from doing what they would to ameliorate their destitution.

But this is the result of such a system of government. Instead of being accelerated and pushed on, the advancing tide of the much-needed and desired Indian progress is thus impeded. It is often asked, "Can Indians be civilized or Christianized?" You might as well ask, are they human beings? Such questions are absurd to the last degree. They can only emanate from viewing this unhappy race as entirely different from the white race. As to whether this savage race can be civilized, you are requested to take a brief glance at the present condition of the natives of the American Continent, and you will be surprised and astonished beyond measure, by the overwhelming number of answers coming from every side; for you will hear loud, distinct, unequivocal and intelligent voices of the educated, civilized and Christianized sons and daughters of red men from the direction of the cabin and the cottage, the government and mission schools, academies and high schools, schools of art and schools of theology, colleges and universities.

Now as to their capacity to receive the Christian religion. In reply to this you are pointed to native heathens, by the thousand, who have accepted Christian baptism, Sunday-school scholars, catechists and lay-readers, deacons and priests of the Episcopal Church. Nor need you by any means be confined to this Church; but you are invited to go farther for your information among other Christian bodies throughout the breadth and length of this land, who are giving "the first glimmerings of light" to those who are sitting in darkness and in the shadow of death.

This improved situation of the wards of the United States is the outcome of the revulsion of feeling which the philanthropic and Christian people have evinced toward the once powerful aborigines of the Western continent during the past comparatively few years. The rapidity of their "onward and upward" career as a barbarian people to their present progressive state is, on reflection, at once hopeful and phenomenal.

The drawbacks of the Indians are the concomitants of their previous manner of living, and the injury inflicted on them for over two hundred years, which will take time to outgrow. Not only the mere developing, strengthening, and cultivation of the industrial habits, the growth of the physical and the enlargement of the mental powers are necessary to this end, but also the spiritual nature which is the *conditio sine qua non* to education in its broadest and truest sense. Christian education is the hope of the Indians—in fact, it is the only hope of any race in any land in any clime. In the first place, its aim is the development of true manhood. It realizes that man is a trinity of being, composed of the *Soma*, *Psyche*, and the *Pneuma*, and it seeks to expand these in full. It recognizes in its system that it can improve by "proper food and exercise the physical man, the study of the arts and sciences for the intellectual man, God's law, grace, and salvation to care for the spiritual man;" and, furthermore, it strives to write the "law of God in the heart, and the law of science in the head." Dr. A. M. Johnson,[1] an able writer and an eminent Baptist theologian, in speaking of the consequence of the evil tendency of separating Christianity from education, says: "There is an immense field of labor for the members of the entire Church among these Indians, and they have every claim by every principle of patriotism, policy, of Christian justice and mercy on the Church people and citizens of this country. The Church should plant both a chapel and a church school in the midst of every tribe on all the reservations, and the conscience of the nation should not be satisfied until this portion of its population has every privilege of civilized citizenship. It is hard to see clearly how a Christian people can behold with cold indifference these needy wards of the nation, or repress the feelings of the deepest compassion for these poor, weak, despised, and dusk-browed sufferers when they are conscious of their presence at their very doors. There are obligations and requirements which apply in common to every disciple of the Saviour, and which derive special meaning and force when we are reminded that 'We bear the name of Christians, His name and sign we bear.'"

SPEECH AT THE SEVENTH ANNUAL MEETING OF THE LAKE MOHONK CONFERENCE OF THE FRIENDS OF THE INDIAN 1889

I appreciate the kindness to me, personally as well as for my race, of the friends who are here, and what they have been doing and are doing for this helpless and perishing people. When I was about eleven years old, I was just beginning my alphabet. I have sat by Mrs. Coolidge's knee; and, in the effort to learn my alphabet, the tears have rolled down my cheeks. But she made me learn that alphabet. Now the Indian children to-day are crying for education. As far as the Indian can show his ability, his humanity, his capability of mental culture, it will help to solve the Indian problem. It will help to solve the legal problem, but on the social side you must aid him in his advancement. The questions which have been brought up to-day show the intelligence as well as the civilization of the Mohonk tribe around the council-fire. It is the best pow-wow that I have ever attended. I am glad of this opportunity to express the gratitude that I feel, for myself and my race, in your friendship. I might express it in the way that an Indian expressed it once. A kindness had been shown to a chief of the reservation where I had been staying; and he said to the person that conveyed that kindness: "Tell that person who sent me this gift that, when a Frenchman receives a kindness, he is thankful in his head.

The head has a tongue: it can talk. But, when an Indian receives a kindness, he is thankful in his heart. His heart has no tongue: it cannot talk." So it is with me to-night. But I have learned by education that there is a communication between the heart and the brain, and what the heart feels the brain can express through the tongue.

THE INDIAN OF TO-DAY

Colorado Magazine, May 1893

I am requested to write of my work among the Indians, and my views of the policy of the Government in enlisting Indians as soldiers. Such a request is not only an evidence that the Indian still excites curiosity and attracts attention, but also that the patriotic chord of fairness has been struck, its reverberation reaching the ear and the great heart of the American people. It is true that the Government of the sovereign people of these United States has made mistakes in its dealings with the nation's wards; but it is substantially a princely Government, and it means to do the fair thing by the Indians of this continent. Most of the blunders have been made through ignorance; and such blunders may be educative. To help us in the sincere endeavor to understand one another and unite us more harmoniously is the office of an honest literature.

There are Indians in most of the states and in every territory in the Union, and the young commonwealth of Wyoming, a new star in the American constellation, has eighteen hundred natives. Near the center of the western half of the State, and on the east side of the Wind River Mountains, is the reservation of these Indians, one-half of whom are Arapahoes and the balance Shoshones. The Indian Agency and Fort Washakie are situated in one of our favored valleys and on the banks of the crystal streams at the foot of the mountains. The Wind River Reservation embraces a territory of about eighty miles square. The locality and its principal range of mountains, doubtless, derived their names from the Wind River, a large stream which flows through the reservation.

Now and again we see in our midst the improvements and discoveries made in the blazing light of the Nineteenth century. Through the telephone we receive messages in the twinkling of an eye; by a chain of electricity we have telegraphic communications; we have listened to the phonograph; and we hear the whistle of the modern flourmill, but not the whistle of the locomotive, blow it never so loud. The railroad has not as yet reached our neighborhood, and the steel track is still one hundred and fifty miles away. We say we are one hundred and fifty miles from Rawlins, our nearest railway station, but some contend that it is one hundred and forty-eight; to avoid uncertainty let us take a philosophical solution by accepting the fact that it is exactly as far from Rawlins to Shoshone Agency as from Shoshone Agency to Rawlins. At all events, it must be apparent that we dwell far in the interior and are quite isolated. Of a verity, this part of Wyoming is in the stage-coach and pack-mule age. So was it in other states now gridironed with car-tracks. If our Indians seem backward it may be on account of their isolation and want of more training. A few of them have become struggling farmers in embryo. "Intercourse is the soul of progress," and these people need more time and chance. Consider the primitive but fair English in the fields of their ancient isle; consider the Germanic tribes on their vast prairies and in their primeval forests; consider that it has taken them twenty centuries to reach the wonders of this magic age, and then ask whether or not it is reasonable to expect Indians to attain even a measure of it in a few short years. These Arabs of the western plains have lived a barbaric life for ages and require time to change their nature and mode of life. Nature works slowly, and will not alter her types and her tendencies suddenly.

The Arapahoes and Shoshones have always dwelt side by side in friendship. They were hereditary foes, and time was when a contact between them meant death to the one or the other. Both the reason of their truce-less war and the date when their forefathers first met in battle are lost in the obscurity of the past; but the writer has a distinct recollection of some of the fierce battles fought. The impressions could not but be vivid when one's dearest and nearest relatives were slain in all the horrors of savage hostilities; when one's grand-mother and an aunt were killed by United States soldiers; when an uncle fell at the hands of white and Mexican civilians; and a heroic father was lost while keeping back, single handed, thirty or more fierce Shoshones in order to save family, friends, and kindred. By the death of his father the writer was left the poorest of the very poor among his people and with a broken home; but he was also left with the memory of a loving parent, the bravest, the wisest, and the best of chiefs.

Aboriginal existence was uncertain at its best. On a moon-lit night an Indian camp might be calm and quiet, the ponies tethered close by their owner's tepee, all resting peacefully—till the war-whoop and the sharp report of a rifle are heard, and the frightened people rush out for their lives, some to escape, some to be shot down and scalped, and others to fall under the cruel blow of the flashing tomahawk. "Man's inhumanity to man makes countless thousands mourn." Thank God that His image has never been wholly obliterated from man; marred it has been, but never effaced. The new order of a civilization linked with the eternal has come, the new order of Divine Grace calling men to the supernatural adoption of sonship and union with God through the Prince of Peace; and this transforms both individuals and nations with a miracle as great as the creation of the world.

The Wind River country and parts adjacent, were favorite camp, hunting and battle grounds of different bands and tribes of Indians; and here in the winter of 1869, a treaty of peace was concluded between the Arapahoes and Shoshones—a treaty which has never been broken. The Arapahoes, however, were subsequently sent to live at Pine Ridge Reservation, South Dakota, with the Cheyennes and Sioux, which tribes had been associated with them from remote times.

But the Arapahoes had resided only a few years at the Pine Ridge Reservation when they began to long for the scenes of former days, for Wyoming with her game and streams, her mountains and climate. Such a longing is a sign of a human being and a patriot. Does an Indian become attached to his country? Love of country burns eternal in the native breast, and the dusky American is patriotic because he is human. Is it not a most grand reason? The bodies of their kindred who had succumbed to age, disease, or had died in all the glory of war, were resting in the soil of Wyoming. Small wonder, then, that the clannish Arapahoes became discontented even among their old friends and confederates, and were willing to make their permanent home with their once traditional enemies, the Shoshones, in order to be in their own land and among the spirits of their ancestors.

In 1876, having obtained permission of the Government and consent of the Shoshones, they moved to the Wind River Reservation; and from the day of their arrival a feeling of friendship has steadily grown between the two tribes. Nevertheless, someone published recently a libel to this friendship in Wyoming and Colorado papers, obviously with the mischief-making intention to poison the political wells against the Arapahoes. In these periodicals it was alleged that the Arapahoes had no right or title to any portion of the reservation, and that the Shoshone Chief Washakie threatened to lead his tribe in battle against the Arapahoes. This and other assertions of similar import have been circulated in the journalistic world. Major Fosher, the Indian Agent, read the article in the Wyoming paper to Chief Washakie in presence of the interpreter. The article was read slowly and a sentence at a time was interpreted to him. When the article was completed, Washakie was asked what he thought of it. He said it was a lie from beginning to end. He also said that the Government had acknowledged the rights of the Arapahoes; that there was land and room for all, and that they were in friendly relations and expected to so remain. Black Coal,[2] the Arapahoe Chief, expressed the same sentiments when interviewed, and said he was entirely satisfied with his treatment by the Government and the Shoshones.

Those who are interested in the advancement and welfare of these American Ishmaelites, these warriors of the American Desert, look forward to the time when they will be American citizens, when they will worship the true God together at the Christian altar, and when their hands will be with every man and every man's hand with them.

Our church work in this country was first started in 1871, when Bishop Randall,[3] of Colorado, sent Mr. Patten,[4] now of Lander, to organize a day school at the Agency. At that time there were about a thousand Shoshones on the reservation. Mr. Patten carried on the school in 1872, and again in 1873. The journey between Rawlins and Shoshone Agency is a hard one at all times, and the last trip cost the life of our aged bishop.

Joseph Cook may well say: "The churches in the East do not know, the churches in the West do not know, the self-sacrifices, the privations, the toils, the prayers, the tears, of the frontier missionaries. They are precious in the sight of God; and it is because I believe that Almighty Providence will second efforts as holy as these that I do not abate one jot of heart or hope concerning the solution of the Indian problem."[5]

In 1877, the Hon. J. I. Patten returned as the United States Indian Agent. He commenced school work again and started two institutions—one for each tribe; but these were discontinued in 1879.

In 1883 the Rev. John Roberts was sent to Wyoming by Bishop Spalding, of Colorado, and was stationed on the reservation as missionary to the Indians. With the cooperation of Dr. Irwin, the then Indian agent, Mr. Roberts established the present Wind River Industrial School for the Government. We carried on the school with an annual attendance of between eighty and ninety boarders until 1886. Eighty or ninety boarders were really more than the school building could comfortably accommodate, but so desirous were the parents for the education of their children that we were induced to take as many as possible.

The task of being at once a priest and a secular teacher is therefore not unknown to us.

But now the Government has completed the erection of three commodious brick buildings in a new location, and work has commenced in the new quarters. The object of this school is education and an industrial training. Part of the day is devoted to studies and the balance to various branches of civilized labor—labor hitherto unknown.

In May, 1890, the Rt. Rev. Ethelbert Talbot, Bishop of Wyoming and Idaho, laid the corner-stone of our Church School, which has since been finished and occupied. It has accommodations for thirteen girls, and is under the charge of the Rev. Mr. Roberts. It is called "The Bishop Talbot School," and is situated about a mile and a half west of the Agency, on the center of a fertile valley, through which flows a clear mountain stream. This institution, please God, will supply the wants of the physical, the intellectual and spiritual man. It is the function of the Christian Church and home, school and college, society and civilization, to teach what the Gospel of Reconciliation does for man, woman and child. It is, however, a sad fact that its worst representatives have been the van of civilization in our country, since they have condescended to the Indian in nothing but the gratification of his inordinate appetites and desires; but with these new institutions for learning and elevating, the character of the "crimesodden reservation" may be wholly changed.

The call to the Church to give better support to the work among the Indians is imperative. While part of our spiritual work must be weighed in the scales of Heaven, part must be measured by money. It is the habit to measure so many things by money in this our age, that religion has not escaped the rule, and our field in Wyoming is no exception to "the eternal want of pence" that constantly vexes missionary operations.

The servant of the King requires straw wherewith to make brick. Our base of operations is in the West but, to a considerable extent, we look to the East for our base of supplies. Most of our people reside there and a great deal of the money made here goes to enrich the capitalists in our large cities.

The Church of the Redeemer was built in 1885, by Miss Shields of Philadelphia, Pa., at a cost of two thousand dollars. Sunday School and divine worship have been conducted, the Gospel has been preached, the solemnization of matrimony has been performed, the apostolic rite of confirmation has been held, and the Holy Sacraments have been administered in this house consecrated to the service of Almighty God.

Aside from the use of the Church edifice we have preached in the schoolhouse, in the Post Hall at Fort Washakie, in the log-cabin and the native wigwam on the reservation.

The Rev. Mr. Roberts meets some of the Shoshones at Chief Washakie's house for religion instruction. This Chief has ever been a loyal friend of the white people and has stood many times like a wall between them and turbulent warriors.

The native missionary has likewise held such meetings with the Arapahoes at Little Wolf's Camp.[6] Little Wolf is his uncle and has most willingly allowed him the use of his log-cabin. Little Wolf is not only one of the principal chiefs, but he is also the "Grand Medicine Man" of the Arapahoes; and unlike the medicine men of Sioux and the Chippeway nations, he has not opposed the missionary, but on the contrary listens with interest and reverence to the story of the Great Physician of our souls.

Our work is not that of building up an Arapahoe or Shoshone church with an Indian liturgy in the Indian tongue. It is rather that of preparing these people for their duties in church and state. The missionary may learn the Indian language for the sake of preaching the gospel; but the main effort is to educate the weaker race of the inferior language, life, and religion into the better language, life and religion of the stronger race. Education promotes civilization and a common language promotes affiliation.

The question is frequently asked: Can the wild camp savage be trained as an American soldier? There is not the shade of a shadow of doubt of it. But he wants a friendly, sympathetic as well as an intelligent management. He wants a man of experience and judgment, in charge of him. He wants a superior officer whom he can trust and respect. The Indian is a man and knows his rights. Unlike the dreamy Asiatic Indian the American native, jealous of his freedom, would not surrender his sacred rights without a struggle; hence the past Indian hostilities. High-spirited, independent, and brave, he has fought with obstinate, if undisciplined valor against the white people, on the one hand, and traditional enemies, on the other. His occupation was war, and one of the cardinal virtues of his religion was bravery. To be a brave warrior was the height of his ambition.

The government has found it expedient to summon Indians to its aid in times of emergency. The auxiliaries have come hastily; and although poorly equipped they have been used successfully against their own tribes and species. While the Indian is independent and not servile, his nature is not incompatible with discipline. During the Civil War Indians soldiers were not wanting in the ranks of the United States service, and Indians there are who served meritoriously in that fierce conflict for the Union and against negro slavery. A Seneca sachem was an aide on the staff of General Grant.[7] Willingly they served the Government; willingly would they give their lives on the altar of the constitution.

It seems now that the make-shift has been organized into a permanency. We have the Indian contingent in the regular army, and on this subject many opinions wage war and many pens have been employed. It is a new venture, and like all innovations it is met with an agreeable surprise by its friends, and disgust and zealous opposition by its foes. We rejoice in the present peace policy; we deplore any reduction in appropriations for educating people whom we would civilize, and, verily, we endorse the enlistment in our army of men of a martial race.

"On March 7, 1891, an order was issued from the War Department, directing the enlistment of eight troops of cavalry and nineteen companies of infantry, each of fifty-five men, the recruiting to be carried on in the locality in which the regiments, to which these troops and companies belong, were stationed."

It goes without saying that more difficulty was experienced in obtaining men for the infantry than for the cavalry. Reckoned in the large, the Indians are naturally partial to horses, not altogether because of their so-called, par excellence, laziness; but because, like the sons of Arabian Desert, they have made the animals a part of their lives.

The new scheme is both an honorable and a good stroke of policy. The aboriginal son of Mars, in his neat army uniform and no longer in plumes and feathers, is a symbol of a step forward in the Indian problem. It opens a way to a profitable and a congenial occupation. If not the only way, certainly it is the quickest and best in which a considerable number of Indians can be brought under civilized influences. They were young men, just too old to be sent to school, and just old enough to be too proud, independent and indifferent for exertion toward civilization. Some were leaders in native fashion, some belonged to the soldier class, a few were sub-chiefs. They gambled and they danced and all were devotees at the race course. After a bath, a hair-cut and attired in their new clothes, it is hard to imagine them the same dusky warriors. The clothes do not make the man, but we venture to think that, at the end of five years, the clothes, the discipline and occupation will make a marked improvement. Discipline, habit, encouragement and intelligent management conspire to make a great change.

Then, too, the enlistment of natives lessens the chance of war among themselves and against the white people. The flower of the fighting element has been taken from the tribal forces. We opine, moreover, that it is better for the army and the Indians to fight, to subjugate, nay, to conquer the barbarian in peace than in all the horrors of savage warfare. "Peace has its victories as well as war."

There is plenty of labor in the Indian field for the members of the Church; and by every principle of patriotism, policy, Christian justice and mercy, the Indian has a strong claim on the people of the United States. The conscience of the nation should not be satisfied until the aborigine can stand before the world and say in the broadest sense: "Civis Americanus sum."

INDIANS IN WYOMING

Report on Indians Taxed and Indians Not Taxed in the United States (except Alaska) at the Eleventh Census: 1890, 1894

Tradition.—In regard to the creation the Arapahos say that long ago, before there were any animals, the earth was covered with water, with the exception of 1 mountain, and seated on this mountain was an Arapaho, crying and poor in distress. The gods looked at him and pitied him, and they created 3 ducks and sent them to him. The Arapaho told the ducks to dive down in the waters and find some dirt. One went down in the deep waters and was gone a long time, but failed. The second one went down and was gone a still longer time, and he also came up, having failed. The third then tried it; he was gone a long time. The waters where he went down had become still and quiet, and the Arapaho believed him to be dead, when he arose to the surface and had a little dirt in his mouth. Suddenly the waters subsided and disappeared, and left the Arapaho the sole possessor of the land. The water had gone so far it could not be seen from the highest mountains, but it still surrounded the earth, and does so to this day. Then the Arapaho made the rivers and the woods, placing a great deal near the streams. The whites were made beyond the ocean. There were then all different people, the same as at the present day. Then the Arapaho created buffaloes, elks, deer, antelopes, wolves, foxes, all the animals that are on the earth, all the birds of the air, all the fishes in the streams, the grasses, fruit, trees, bushes, all that is grown by planting seeds in the ground. This Arapaho was a god. He had a pipe and he gave it to the people. He showed them how to make bows and arrows, how to make fire by rubbing 2 sticks, how to talk with their hands, in fact, how to live. His head and his heart were good, and he told all the other people, all the surrounding tribes, to live at peace with the Arapahos, and the several tribes came to this central one (Arapaho). They came there poor and on foot, and Arapahos gave them of their goods, gave them ponies. The Sioux, the Cheyennes, the Snakes, all came. The Cheyennes came first and were given ponies; these ponies were "prairie gifts." The Snakes had no lodges, and with the ponies they gave them skin tepees. The Arapahos never let their hearts get tired with giving; then all the tribes loved the Arapaho.

Dances of the Arapahos.—Their customs, manners, and some of their laws were and are very much like those of the Sioux and Cheyenne. The "sun dance" was not compulsory; it had no religious character, and lasted 4 days and 4 nights, during which time the dancer neither ate nor drank. The "sun dance" was rather an occasion of national jubilee. The dancers were looked upon as heroes and gained a certain notoriety which is so dear to some natures. They had and have many dances: the buffalo, wolf, hungry, and the war dance.

History.—Very reliable tradition located this tribe in western Minnesota, several hundred years ago. The tribe scattered so that it is now divided into 3 separate bands, inhabiting sections of the country far apart. The 3 divisions consist of the Gros Ventres of the prairie and the Northern and Southern Arapahos. The Gros Ventres left the main body of the Arapahos during their western migration and then they reached the Missouri river, about the year 1820. They then went north and joined the Blackfeet, seldom afterward visiting the Northern Arapaho. They are now at Fort Belknap, Montana. The Northern and Southern Arapaho separated in 1868, on account of the refusal of the former tribe to join the latter in the war against the white people. During the same year the Northern Arapaho made a treaty in conjunction with the Sioux and Cheyennes. What the name "Arapaho" means, from what language it is derived, when they were first known by it, are matters of uncertainty. The Northern Arapahos call themselves by a name which means "the parent of nations" (anonai). The Southern Arapaho claim the word only means "the men, or the people." According to some historians the Arapahos are classified among the different branches of the Sioux family, but they are a tribe of Algonquin stock. The men of the tribe are intelligent and brave, and the people as a whole are not unlike the Sioux or Cheyennes in their physical and mental constitutions. The histories of these 2 tribes have been intermixed since they were together in Minnesota, especially these of the Cheyennes and Arapahos; indeed, they have been so to such an extent that they have been for all practical purposes one people. For many years they moved and camped with or near one another.

Language.—The vocal language of the Arapahos is different than any other; it is very guttural, somewhat similar in this respect to the Hebrew language, and it has a rich vocabulary; hence the statement that the sign language is a necessary aid to the vocal is a mistake. They have, however, the perfect use of the sign language.

Religion.—The religion of the Arapahos is monotheistic. They believe in a supreme being; he is the good and omnipotent spirit and is called E-jeb-bah-a-neatha, or "the White Man on High." They also believe in an evil spirit, who is a worker of evil, and is called A ja. They have a standard of right and wrong, though it is far inferior to that of civilized people. The good and the bad on earth will be rewarded and punished beyond the grave. The belief in ghosts is firmly implanted from their childhood. The belief in fairy stories is as prevalent as that of ghosts. The white buffalo has always been held sacred.

Civilization.—The civilization and Christianization of the Northern Arapaho is not so advanced as some other tribes, but the signs are by no means discouraging. Owing to the as yet undeveloped condition of the country, and being located far in the interior 250 miles from the railroad, their advantages for learning have necessarily been limited. But they have made a commendable start and with time and proper management they can become intelligent and self-supporting Christian citizens. Failures there are, failures there may be, failures there will be, but judging from their progress in the past they have shown a willing disposition to lay hold of facilities when they have been placed within their reach with gratifying results. They are beginning to build log cabins, to fence in land, and to cultivate the soil, besides sending all the children to school that can be accommodated at the different institutions; all this, too, in the face of insufficient food, lack of funds, and the want of that knowledge which is the inheritance of every American youth from free education and home training. There is now no doubt but that the Indian has capacity of education and civilization.

Sanitation Condition.—When the Arapaho were in Minnesota they had wild meat and fruit in abundance, and they had no fear or knowledge of syphilis, scrofula, or consumption; neither these diseases or insanity were inherited in families. Those were the days when they could lie in the bosom of mother earth almost with impunity, with only a blanket or skin between them and the ground. But the hygiene provisions of both the tepee and cabin are defective. Skins and furs are gone, and the quantity and quality of food and clothing obtained by these reservation Indians are at once insufficient and deficient, and the Indians are oftentimes compelled to eat such dead horses, cows, and calves as they may find, whether lean or fat, and not knowing whether they died of disease or were killed by accident. Now, under these circumstances, on the principle of self-preservation, they have relied on their own superstitious and ignorant medicine men. The Indians are quick to perceive and discriminate, and when they see the cures from the application of medical science of the enlightened nineteenth century they will come to it for help. They have been supplied with it to a very limited extent. The government has placed a physician at all, or nearly all, of the reservations, yet the physician does not always have the proper supervision of his patient, nor can he be at all sure that his instructions will be carried out by them or his medicine taken. What, then, will meet the demand for the alleviation of the dying and neglected sufferer and lessen the duration of curable diseases? The answer is plain: the skillful physician, and most of all, a properly constructed hospital at the reservation.

Sherman and the Society

THE INDIAN AMERICAN: HIS DUTY TO HIS RACE AND TO HIS COUNTRY, THE UNITED STATES OF AMERICA

Quarterly Journal of the Society of American Indians, January–April 1913

"Use Your Citizenship Worthily of the Gospel of Christ." These words were written by a citizen of Imperial Rome, and on the strength of that citizenship he appealed to Caesar. He was proud of being a citizen of "one of the most remarkable nations that ever rose and flourished and fell."

Christian citizenship is the highest type known; it is linked with the eternal. May it ever be the American ideal! Citizenship for the native ward is the aim of the United States and he must ultimately assume the duties and responsibilities involved in a Christian nation. To that end the existence of the Indian bureau must be terminated and the elimination of the Indian as a national ward must be effected as soon as may be possible. The great heart of the American people is in the right place and it is not their intention that the native of the soil shall remain a political nondescript forever. The Indian himself feels dissatisfied with the present scheme in vogue at Washington for his uplift. Every fibre of his manhood protests against being treated as a federal or civic freak. His friends have faith in him and he has faith in himself. He will not admit that he is a misfit on his own soil; on the contrary he believes that he has a niche to fill among the united races of America.

Is his own race worthwhile? Is the United States as a country worthwhile to him? Is it all worth living for? Is it worth dying for?

Prescott has well said, "Every step that the white man has taken in the new world has been over the corpse of an Indian."[1] Another man said, "The dead Indian is the only good Indian," but so is the *live* one! For three hundred years he has been defending his land, his people and his tepee home, and he is still on the sacred soil of his forefathers.

But the fight has shifted; he is on the same battlefield and his leaders are armed with new weapons,—the plow, the ballot and the pen. The struggle is even more terrific in the face of greed, self-interest, deceit, scandal, cruelty, ambition and lust. The Indian American is engaged in a real battle. True hearts and loyal souls must volunteer; must enlist to carry the banner of modern patriotism above the din and smoke of the conflict.

"Is any war, or peace, or traffic, or trade, or alliance, or acquisition, or measure of any kind, morally wrong? If so, it cannot be politically right. Moor the anchor of your politics to the Rock of Righteousness, not to the shifting sands of supposed interests, and it will hold amid the tide of popular opinion." In other words, make right might! So strives the Indian of to-day.

Christian citizenship means right between man and man, right between the home and the nation, right relationship between man and God. The greatest nation is the one that does not leave God out of its life. A God-fearing nation will take care of the homelife where God's children should be trained for the serious affairs and obligations of life. A Christian nation will have churches, schools, asylums and hospitals; it will have clean communities, clean cities, and clean industries. It will set its face against slavery and war and despotism.

The other day a distinguished Christian citizen said, "A Christian does not recognize such a thing as a necessary evil. If a thing is necessary, it is not evil; and if it is evil, it isn't necessary." This is a hot-shot against gambling, intemperance, divorce, child-labor, the red-light district, and all forms of vice.

The patriotic Indian American will consider these subjects; will face these problems for the good of the nation. Is he too cowardly, too lazy, or too dull to meet this crisis in his career? Hitherto his mode of life has been along different lines. The time to change his condition and habit has come. He is now asked *to adjust himself to the new order* of things. He must modify his customs, language and religion. The Indian has been a nomad, a mighty hunter, a brave warrior and a noble patriot. But the transformation takes time! When he saw his country overrun by another race, he made a determined resistance and fought his pale-face brother for three centuries, and still there are unwhipped Indians in the mountains of the West! The all but omnipotent white brother with his wealth, luxury, power and civilization demands that he yield submission to the law of human movement, to the logic of migration. The Indian did not see that all the required changes were meant for his good. His brain seethed with mutinous misunderstanding. And why not? The irony of alien control by alien methods, morals, and religion has eaten deeply into his high-spirited soul,—lo, these many centuries. The white man has a way of putting his European morals, religion and mental machinery inside of the Indian body and then mapping out the probable process of development accordingly. The inevitable result is that the Indian must spend much of his time and ingenuity in disentangling himself from mistaken policies and abuses. Here is a national problem concerning the 250,000 of the original land owners, and the problem also affects 10,000,000 of their territorial white neighbors. The former owners of primitive America, of her broad prairies, rich valleys and lofty mountains, are suddenly forced to live a new life, side by side with a more numerous and progressive race. The dictates of patriotism and justice demand that the Indian shall not be left to work out unaided the peculiar problem thus thrust upon him; and the nation that created the problem must assist in the solution. The solution of the Indian question is the excuse for the existence and maintenance of mission schools, day schools, boarding and non-reservation schools, the Indian agencies and the Indian Bureau.

The Indian American has something new and fresh to contribute. His noble traits ought to be, can be, and must be guided into national usefulness. Any faithful or successful attempt to interpret the Indian as a citizen in action, in the city or on the farm, in the army or in the navy, will have its value, so long as it is from the love or loyalty to the country. It is surely of the highest importance for the state that the very best civic virtues and most thoroughly equipped minds should be encouraged to share in the work of government.

Who is this Indian? What is he? Where does he live? Above all, why is he a problem? If these questions were asked of the average white man, the answers would be both inaccurate and confusing. In our early school-days, the Indian was defined as a savage who lived by hunting and fishing; who lived in a wigwam or tepee. He was a fierce, ferocious, cruel, crafty, treacherous, blood-thirsty red devil! Exterminate him! Exterminate him! Again, he has been described as a dirty, lazy, shiftless loafer, beggar and drunkard. No wonder "the only good Indian is the dead one!" Another, and the best view is that he "is a man and should be treated as such."

These facts show that "there is a string of philosophy in the Indian life upon which is placed a lot of jewels, some true and precious, and others false and valueless." The Indian is human. He is God's handiwork, and God has a more beautiful method of solving the "Indian problem" than by the bayonet, the sword and an ignominious extinction. Slavery was first tried, but Indian slavery did not thrive and died a speedy and a deserved death. Indian slavery did not pay. The policy of war and extermination was next tried as an experiment. But under this process the Indian in retaliation killed and scalped a lot of white men and women and children. He set fire to houses, and tomahawked and warwhooped; in short, he fought like a fiend. What else could he have done? What would you have done? He defended his lands, his people and his tepee home.

Forty years ago the native ward was turned over from the war department to the interior department, and General Grant's peace proclamation was put in force.

Friends of the Indian rose up and began a steady campaign for his uplift. They agitated on his behalf, and a humane and just policy was inaugurated and pursued. Certain Indian schools, such as Carlisle, Hampton, Haskell, Chemawa, and Sherman Institute began to turn out hundreds of educated Indian young men and young women who became the leaders of their people and were employed in all branches of civilized industry on the reservations, and became teachers in mission schools, government day schools, boarding schools and non-reservation schools. The young Indian has also gone forth into the army and navy, into civil life and federal employ. In following up the peace and educational policy another decisive step was taken when the Dawes Land in Severalty Bill was passed and signed. The bill provided for allotments of land and paved the way to individual ownership of land and a fixed home for the roving native. Before that date the Indian had been only localized on the reservation. The law has been modified since, but it opened the way to United States citizenship and it placed the Indian in a position to meet the enlightened and united races of America on an equal footing.

To-day, the civilized Indian has entered every phase of the national life; we have the skilled laborer, the farmer, teacher, clerk, lawyer, legislator, physician and clergyman. In the past he has shown his loyalty to the government as a soldier in the army, as a scout in the frontier campaign, and as a policeman on the reservations. And, if he is ever called to shoulder the musket for the service of his country, he will march and fight under the inspiring folds of her banner and willingly offer his life upon the altar of the Constitution. In tribal and inter-tribal affairs, in times of peace and war, the race has provided the most gifted orators, generals, patriots, diplomats and statesmen. The virtues of our Indian forefathers are worthy of emulation and as our heirlooms, these virtues should be encouraged and accepted for high service to the country. We rejoice to think that in the happily changed relations of to-day, from what they were fifty years ago, the Indian is free to repeat in a new way, the achievements of his renowned ancestors in devotion and patriotism.

The rights of the American people, the rights of the nation consecrated to freedom demand that both the unrestricted citizenship of the United States and the fair flower of liberty shall be extended to the Indian and shall be his sacred heritage as they are to other men. The larger number of the race is learning to read, write, and speak the English language, and nearly three-quarters are known as Taxed Indians, and as such, have advanced a long way toward complete citizenship. With increasing freedom he must continue his progress and strive for a full share of civic privileges, political duties, and federal responsibilities. Within our lifetime the Indian was not even allowed to become a citizen, but a revulsion of feeling in his favor has come and the great heart of the American people aims to give him every right and privilege in the national life. It may be in the eleventh hour, but we are glad that the hour has come when the Indian can stand before the world and say in its broadest and best sense: "*Civis Americanus sum.*"

AMERICAN INDIANS FOR THE HONOR OF THEIR RACE

Red Man, March 1914

I have been on this platform before.[2] I mean, in this building, but not on an occasion like this, but it was similar in that it was in behalf of emancipation. The Indian must be made free. It sounds funny to me to say that because this land on which he lived from time immemorial has been the land of the brave and of the free, and my people enjoyed that freedom and they were monarchs, not slaves. They have been placed by this nation on reservations, and reservations are very much like prisons to these people who are so used to freedom. And the result has been that this independent, free, noble race has deteriorated until they are a caricature of what they were before they were placed on the reservation. I was here three times before this trip, and those three times have been the beginning of a new movement to me personally, and I might say to my race.

I first had my start, of course, on the land where I was born. I was born in the state of Wyoming. As I told my friends of Columbus from this platform before, I was born on Goose Creek, and I looked up Goose Creek on the map of Wyoming and I saw that there were two branches of Goose Creek; one was called Little, and the other Big Goose, and I don't know on which I was born, but the Indians told me I was born on Goose Creek; my wife suggests that it must have been the Big Goose.

I have gotten my start here, as it were. When I first visited Columbus I came here as a boy of about 7 years of age. At that time I could not speak a word of English. I knew "yes" and "no," and sometimes I put them in the wrong place. I used the sign language to make my wants known at that time. The sign language is a universal language among the Western tribes among the mountains and plains, and it is so natural and simple that anybody can learn it in a short time. A white man married an Indian woman one time, and learned this language from the Indians. He says it is so easy and so natural that anybody could learn it; even a bear could understand it. Why, I said, Frank, how do you make that out? "Why," he said, "I went out hunting one day and I saw a bear, a silver tip, and I wounded him, and it displeased him and he took after me and I dropped my gun under a tree and climbed the tree. He then came to where I was and picked up the gun, turned it over, looked at it, smelled it; finally he picked it up and cocked it and pointed it at the tree and pulled the trigger, but it didn't go off. He threw open the chamber and looked at me."

What has that got to do with whiskey? It has this much to do with it. I went to New York and went to school there as a boy and learned the message of the gospel as we find it in the Bible. After I had attended the Presbyterian Sunday school a while I came away from the boarding school and my friends asked me: "What are you going to be when you get to be a man?" "Why," I said, "I am going to be a minister and take the message of the Bible to my people." They smiled and said: "Why, Sherman, who put that into your head?" I said: "No one." While I was playing in the streets of New

York there came news from the Pacific Coast that General Canby and Dr. Thomas were massacred by the Modocks among the lava beds, and the cry went in the newspapers throughout the city and throughout the country to exterminate the Indians. I knew then that the Indians did not understand the whites, and the whites did not understand the Indians, and that I did not think it was right to exterminate the Indians. I had lived several years among them as a child, and I knew them to be a peaceable and peaceloving people. I knew there were Indians who were friendly to the whites and whites who were friendly to Indians, and I also knew that there were a great many good white people, especially in the East. Many of those in the West were not of the best class of the white race. I made up my mind then that I would devote my life not only to preaching the Bible to my people but also in trying to make those two races understand each other.

Several years had elapsed from the time of my first visit to Columbus—when I could speak only the sign language—to the time of my second visit, when I was asked to give an address before the students of the Department of Sociology and Economics at the Ohio State University, and for the same purpose two other Indians were called to this city. They were Dr. Carlos Montezuma[3] and Dr. Charles A. Eastman.[4]

Dr. Carlos Montezuma is a full-blood Apache, and was bought from a band of hostile Indians by a white man who brought Montezuma east, where he was educated. The Doctor has degrees from a university and a medical college in Chicago, and is now a highly respected physician practicing in that great city.

Dr. Charles A. Eastman, a Sioux, and now a resident of Amherst, Massachusetts, is also a graduate of a medical college and a graduate of Dartmouth College. He took advantage of an old, obsolete clause in the charter of that college, which required that college to educate free of charge every year an Indian youth. In this way he was able to get a college education.

During the Spanish-American War, while in Washington DC, on business for my people, I first met Dr. Charles Eastman and his brother John, who is a Presbyterian minister. We went to President McKinley, who was a very busy man at that time, with a proposition which we thought would give the Indians a better education. We asked for a better standardization of our school system. The President listened to us and assured us that he would do everything he could to bring about what we desired. It was while we were in Washington that we three Indians talked of the great good that could be derived by forming an organization of Indians for Indians, but it was too soon then.

Several years later Dr. Charles Eastman, Dr. Montezuma, several others, and myself met in that city for the purpose of forming an organization which is now called the Society of American Indians, and I am proud to wear its badge. It is a badge with an eagle. The tribes call it the "thunder bird." It was universally believed in by the Indians, and it was dug up in one of the mounds of Illinois. It was engraved by our forefathers. We don't know whether it was done centuries ago or thousands of years ago, but we adopted it because it was so universal.

Now that society is working for the uplift and welfare of the race, and their motto is, "For the honor of the race and the good of the country," and everything must be subservient to that motto.

My friends, the Indians are human beings. It took a long time for the American people to find that out, it seems to me, but finally they found it out and made a law in 1887 by which an Indian can become a citizen of the United States. These Indians and their white friends have formed this organization to redeem the race and to serve, whenever they can, all humanity. They have formed this organization and they are making and writing a new history. We wish to avoid the errors and mistakes of our forefathers.

Three centuries of irrepressible conflict have been going on, three miserable centuries, and, my friends, I read yesterday that all these troubles came from the white man—they came directly or indirectly through liquor.

Red Jacket,[5] when he was talking to Christian missionaries, said among other things that "The white man brought liquor among us. It was strong and horrible and has slain thousands." It was true at that time; it had slain thousands, and it has been true from that time to this. It has slain thousands of this noble race. It seems that the white man was not content to take away our country and our land, our firesides and our homes, but they must also try to exterminate us with this demon of the centuries, this one great curse of mankind.

My friends, I have felt that I was free and independent; that I was strong and could regulate myself and my life, and I believed that I could use this beverage without hurting myself, and I have used it very, very moderately.

I thought I had a right to do it, but I don't think so anymore. This is my maiden effort at temperance speaking.

This is the first time I have joined the forces of temperance, and I mean to stay that way. There is a citizen among you by the name of Johnson[6] who is responsible for this.

My friends, whiskey, if it is bad for the Indian, is also bad for the white man. They have legislated to prevent the whites from selling or giving or bartering whiskey or liquor to the Indians. All this time the Government has had that law, as far back as I can remember. Why, when I was 10 years old—oh, less than that, I was only 7 years old—I saw a man in Montana in 1870 at the Crow Indian Agency, in the southern part of Montana, who was there to suppress the liquor traffic. He told me it was hard work to fight the liquor traffic in Montana, but he finally succeeded as a Government official and suppressed it and broke up the whisky ring at that reservation and at that agency.

Why, I remember when I first saw this beverage; when I first tasted it. My brother and some other young friends had a little, just a little, and they allowed me to taste just a little drop. It was a curiosity. It has ceased to be a curiosity and has become a curse to my people.

From a civil and political standpoint, I have helped to start a movement to redeem my race in forming the Society of American Indians, and I am glad to come here and start in another movement to help suppress the liquor traffic among my people.

One thing we are trying to do to uplift the Indians is to revive and cherish race pride, pride of origin. If a people does not have this, it will become dispirited and progress is impossible, and if liquor is brought among the Indians they will become a menace to their ten million territorial neighbors, the whites or whoever they may be.

No diseased or drunken people, no diseased or drunken race can develop, and we want the Indians to become efficient, peaceable citizens of these United States. So, my friends, I am here to help you to redeem the past and to join, in a small and humble way, this tremendous movement not only for home and country and for God, but also that we may redeem this race, one of the great races of this world, that has been looked upon as a vanishing race. There are three hundred thousand Indians who are living in this country, and we want them to have a chance, and they will take the Anti-Saloon League platform, or any other platform, shoulder to shoulder with you and march on for progress or anything that is for the betterment of mankind.

One boy in a public school was asked: "How did it happen that you got ahead in your conduct prize, got ahead of your friend Sammy Jones?" "Why," he said, "I am half Indian. I am just that much ahead of Sammy Jones." That is the kind of spirit we want revived among the Indians. A Chinaman speaking in Minneapolis the other day said: "You must eradicate whiskey from your land if you want to preserve manhood and womanhood in America." And I heard the other day that there was a man in China who came down through the country shaking hands with everybody, smiling, and he seemed to know everybody and had plenty of money. He said that "You missionaries will drive out opium from China. We are going to replace it with whiskey; we are going to make China the greatest whiskey market in the world." Shame upon such manhood as is shown by such a statement. Some people must profit by the weaknesses, the follies and depravities of their fellow-men. God help such men, and God help us to help them and drive out this curse.

THE AMERICAN INDIAN OF TODAY

Speech to the Denver University Student Body at the Third Annual Conference of the Society of American Indians, *Quarterly Journal of the Society of American Indians*, January–March 1914

One of the speakers last night said that the American people erected a memorial in New York City to the Indian in the form of a big statue of an Indian. He said, "They do not need that memorial. The Indian is not dead. He is very much alive, and needs greater things than statues."

Now, we started out with a new life staring us in the face—that which was brought over from Europe, therefore we have had to adapt ourselves to an entirely new mode of living. We have advanced to the present condition in fifty years. Up to that time the nation in general pursued the policy of war and extermination.

It may be of interest to you to know that we have among us today in this room one of the officials—if not the most important official—of our organization, whose name is Arthur C. Parker, State Archeologist of New York and Secretary-Treasurer of our Society. There was another man by the name of Parker—Ely Parker, I believe, was the name of the General. General Parker was Military Secretary to General Grant when Robert E. Lee surrendered, and it is in the handwriting of that Indian that we have the terms of peace that brought the North and South together, and that same General Parker was appointed Commissioner of Indian Affairs under General Grant, and it was General Grant that issued a proclamation of peace to all the tribes of the United States. And from that time on the nation has pursued the policy of peace and education, and in fifty years two-thirds of the Indians are called "taxed Indians," which is a long way toward complete American citizenship.

Another speaker has reminded us that there were thirteen of mid-Western Indians who took part in the Revolutionary War. There were Indians in every war that we have had, including the Spanish-American War, and not only that, but we have had Indians in the army in all our frontier struggles. We have had them as soldiers, we have had them as scouts, we have had them as policemen on the reservations, and they have not held back when they were in duty bound to arrest friends, relatives, and even to kill them for the welfare of the citizenship of the United States. Faithful to their duty, they were not found wanting when it came to a fulfilment of duty. That is the American Indian, and if ever, as a citizen, the Indian is called upon to shoulder the musket for the service of his country, he will march off under the aspiring folds of our banners and as loyally offer his life upon the altar of the Constitution as does any American.

We are banded together for the honor of the race and for the good of the country; everything must be subservient to that. That we are enabled to do this shows the advance we have made, and it is due especially to those who had the unusual advantage of schools and colleges and universities.

Why, when I first started out in life all I could do was by sign language to make my wants known. There is a universal language called the "sign language" among the Indians of the Western mountains and plains. I remembered that language; I understood it. I was among the Crows and the Sioux when I was taken away from the Arapahoes. One white man who had married a Sioux woman learned this language; he could speak it as well as any Indian. In fact, he said it was so easy and natural that even a bear could understand it. I said, "How do you make that out, Frank?" He said, "I went out bear hunting one day, and seeing a great big silver tip, I shot and wounded him. It displeased him so much that he chased me, and so I threw my gun under a tree and climbed the tree. He came over to the gun, examined it, smelled it, turned it over, and after awhile he picked it up and looked at it, cocked it, looked up, and pulled the trigger, but it didn't go off. Then he looked up at me, made signs of putting a cartridge into the chamber and told me by signs to (indicating throwing motion)." Frank continued, "I knew what the bear wanted, but I wasn't going to throw him any cartridges that I had in my belt."

I was taken by an army officer who was once stationed at Fort Logan, and I was taken up to Montana when I was a boy. He was stationed at Fort Shaw, and the children gave parties that winter, and I was invited to all of them, and finally I asked Mrs. Coolidge if I could not have a party and invite the children who had been inviting me. She said, "Yes, Sherman, I can give you a party. What kind of a party do you want—a birthday party?" I said, "Yes, that would be all right—any kind of a party." She said, "I cannot give it to you just now, but how would the twenty-second of February do?"[7] I said, "I would just as soon be born on the twenty-second of February as any other day." So I was born in Wyoming and had my birthday in Montana.

Up in Wyoming I worked twenty-six years as missionary among my people, the Arapahoes, and one day I happened to be in the county seat—it was the Fourth of July—and a man by the name of Coolidge, having the same name as myself, was the orator of the day. I met him with several friends on the street, and he introduced me very nicely and politely to these friends, and one of these friends looked in a rather queer way at him, as much as to say, "How is it you both have the same name?" So without any further ado he answered the man's glance and said, "Why, it is all right. We have the same name. That is not strange. But," he said, "of course, I'm a real Coolidge; my ancestors came over in the Mayflower." "Yes," I responded, "but mine were on the reception committee when they arrived."

I am very glad indeed to have this chance to speak to you about our race, and to tell you that it is very much alive. Many think it is vanishing, but it seems to be increasing, and I believe that if you give the Indian half a chance he will shoulder the responsibilities of State and church, and shoulder the burden like a man. General Grant said that the Indian is a man, and should be treated as such. All honor to General Grant! He seems to have been the first great champion of our human rights.

Instead of roaming all over the country as once, we are beginning now to settle down in town and in community, and we are becoming well aware that the responsibilities of life must be shouldered by us as well as other people; that we must not remain dependent children; that we must not be a burden, but that we must take off our frock and become productive, useful men and women.

THE FUNCTION OF THE SOCIETY OF AMERICAN INDIANS

Quarterly Journal of the Society of American Indians, July–September 1914

The aim and scope of the new race movement as embodied in the Society of American Indians is the revival of the natural pride of origin, the pride of race. If people become dispirited, progress is impossible. It is easily within our memory when public opinion viewed the Indian as lacking in capacity for advancement. To the white man he was a degraded savage, blood-thirsty, treacherous, and brutal. The superior white alien accepted as truth the teaching that by Divine Will and manifest destiny the aborigine must be exterminated and driven from the earth; "it is the logic of migration, the law of human movement." So this imperious white man decreed: "The Indian must go!" The necessity of driving the Indian away from the spot he called his home and of marching him out at the point of the bayonet were both sad and needless blunders in a land where there is room for all. The white man misunderstood the Indian and the Indian misunderstood the white man. A war and extermination policy was started by the whites and the "irrepressible conflict continued for three centuries. The white invaders introduced a new mode of life, and the native type was to be supplanted by civilization. It was thought that the Indian, for his salvation, must be pressed into the white man's preconceived mold. As a matter of fact, most Indians do not want to become white men. From the first contact between the two races the Indian was considered inferior, and not at all a fellow man of like passions, infirmities, and aspirations; different only in mental texture, hereditary influences, and environment." And therein is the deep-seated disease germ of the whole

Indian problem. The reservation system has fostered and accentuated the terrible ills resulting from the misconceptions of the white race concerning the red brother, and consequently the Indian has so deteriorated we can hardly realize him as the same proud monarch of fifty years ago.

To use Dr. Eastman's words: "The North American Indian was the highest type of pagan and uncivilized man. He possessed not only a superb physique but a remarkable mind. But the Indian no longer exists as a natural and free man. Those remnants which now dwell upon the reservations present only a sort of tableau, a fictitious copy of the past." On the anniversary of the discovery of America, in the year 1911 a conference was opened at the Ohio State University to organize the Society of American Indians, whose primary function is the revitalizing and cherishing of race pride. Once this task is accomplished the rest will follow. The organization furnishes an annual conference to which delegates of every tribe may come with equal rights. Representatives now do come from the east and the west, from the north and the south. Here, they meet face to face in national council with common language and for a common purpose; here, each Indian can see that he is not alone in the fight against the peril of being utterly crushed; here, the members gather for mutual encouragement, interchange of views and for consultation upon the live issues of the peculiar problem thrust upon them. The best asset the Indians can have is a united body of altruistic men and women of the race, and the Society of American Indians is composed of just such people, anxious to serve and who have lost no time in applying themselves to vital problems and grasping the essential features of the Indian question. The permanent program as outlined by the first organizers is found in the following statement of objects:

First. To promote and co-operate with all efforts looking to the advancement of the Indian in enlightenment which leave him free as a man to develop according to the natural laws of social evolution.

Second. To provide through our open conferences the means for a free discussion on all subjects bearing on the welfare of the race.

Third. To present in a just light the true history of the race, to preserve its records and emulate its distinguishing virtues.

Fourth. To promote citizenship and to obtain the rights thereof.

Fifth. To establish a legal department to investigate Indian problems and to suggest and to obtain remedies.

Sixth. To exercise the right to oppose any movement that may be detrimental to the race.

Seventh. To direct its energies exclusively to general principles and universal interests, and not allow itself to be used for any personal or private interest.

The existence of the Society of American Indians means that the hour has struck when the best educated and most cultured of the race should come together to voice the common demands, to interpret correctly the Indian's heart, and to contribute in a more united way their influence and exertion with the rest of the citizens of the United States in all lines of progress and reform, for the welfare of the Indian race in particular, and all humanity in general. Obviously, this noble movement is a tremendous undertaking, but it was ushered in amid general good wishes of church and state. It is at once a bold and a most praiseworthy step. The Society is managed solely for and by the Indians, and no one without Indian blood can be an active member, yet the white friends of the cause are welcomed most cordially as associate members. The membership at present is more than a thousand, over five hundred from the best of each race. A hearty co-operation with each other will produce splendid results; and, while conscious that he must do his full share in bringing order out of chaos, the red brother does not forget to remind his white brother that the nation which created the problem must assist in its solution and that the motto shall be: "The honor of the race and the good of the country shall always be paramount."

We were overjoyed by the fact that we could assemble so many civilized and educated men and women of vision from our scattered tribes who were in dead earnest and who were willing to pay the price of hardship and self-sacrifice as pioneers of the movement. We were not without our foe who said: "Don't listen to those blind dreamers!" "Don't lend yourselves to their false dreams!" "Their hopes are over-rosy." But some of our dreams have already been realized far beyond our expectations. Our suggestions, proposals, and advice have been received with kindly consideration everywhere. We aided in liberating two hundred and sixty Apaches who had been held in bondage as prisoners of war for twenty-six years, and persuaded Congress to appropriate $300,000 for land and homes for them. We helped the Cayugas in getting $247,000 due them from the State of New York. The murderer of Desota Tiger is in irons, thanks to some of our active and associate members and to Hon. Cato Sells, Commissioner of Indian Affairs.[8] Desota Tiger belonged to the Everglade Seminoles of Florida and was a respected member of his tribe. An Indian woman out west tried to get her money through the Indian agent and was put off time and again by some excuse or another for a year or two, and finally wrote to our Society for its service and received her money in three weeks. The fate of a $50,000 item in the last Indian appropriation bill was uncertain; it was for the education of about two thousand Papago children; but the bill passed, including the $50,000 item for the Papagos, and with our assistance. Then, too, the Society is advocating the passage of the Carter Code bill and the Stephens amended bill, both of which look to the solution of the Indian problem.[9] Nor is this all.

The foregoing statement of things achieved is only a glimpse of what we have done and what we desire to do in co-operating with the government. We must work in harmony in order that we may succeed in performing our mutual supreme duty. The Government has charge of $900,000,000 worth of property for the three hundred thousand Indians under its care; $100,000,000 worth of timber land, but will this timber be turned into lumber for the use of Indians, or will it be turned over to some corporation? Again, the Government holds $60,000,000 in cash for our national wards. What shall be done with it? These subjects are of vital interest to the Indian. Besides all this there are millions annually appropriated by Congress for our civilization and education. The Society of American Indians asks: "Are we getting a proportionate good out of this vast expenditure? Is it doing full justice to the tax-payers?"

The Madison meeting was the Fourth Annual Conference of the organization, and it re-affirmed the platform of the Third Annual Conference which took place at Denver, Colo.

The Madison Conference placed the financial situation of the Society in a better light. Up to this time the Society was kept in motion apparently by a few who supplied more than their share of energy and much of the sinews of war; our treasury was forever in sore need of funds. We lived a from hand to mouth existence, and our financial inability was almost the death of us. We thought of Uncle Sam with our $60,000,000 in cash, but by our principles we could not ask for one cent of it for the good cause; and by our principles we must not deviate an inch from the trail we are following and must ever look to the "Goddess of Liberty" to play the role of fairy godmother. It is a comfort to know that we are free to go forth and create Indian public opinion among the white people and the Indians. The past is beyond recall. But the present offers opportunities for redeeming the past and for redress. We are writing and making a new history and we can avoid the errors of our forefathers and plan a new day for the Indian American. Let us so shape our policy for his education that it will cease to be decultural, but become constructive; and blame him not if he refuses to become an imitation white man; if he bows not the knee to commercialism, or fails to admit that the white man is the ultimate model of the best citizenship or of noblest manhood.

CONFERENCE EVENING AT HASKELL INDIAN SCHOOL

Quarterly Journal of the Society of American Indians, October–December 1915

I would like just to say a few words to you tonight about my recent trip to San Francisco. It was a trip made primarily to give an address to the returned students at the Returned Students' Conference and at the request of Mr. Dagenett[10] who is a member of the Society of American Indians, and vice-president and chairman of membership. Twice my sympathies were drawn to the returned students. Twice I have made a trip for their sake this year. Once I received a letter from Wisconsin saying that there was a little group of returned students who were trying to keep together to learn the same sort of news in regard to the world and in regard to their race by having a library established at their boarding school at Lac du Flambeau, Wis. I made a special trip to have a talk with those students, and I enjoyed the trip very much, and also my stay there with them. And then came this request from Mr. Dagenett to go to California, to San Francisco, to make an address to the Returned Students' Conference, and I went. But before and after that Returned Students' Conference I also attended other conferences. I attended the Indian Government Service Employees' Conference. Perhaps you have heard that. I took part in it, saying a few words here and there during the discussions, and I was glad I was there to do so. And then after the Returned Students' Conference, I attended the National Education Association's Conference where there were thousands of people from all over the country and all over the world. Then after that I attended a conference of the Episcopal Church of the Pacific Coast States, and the Hawaiian Islands, Alaska, and the Philippines, and I gave them an address. I made an address to the clergy and to the laity. Then I made an address to the laities in another place and I told the laities that I had learned that there were more California Indians than I had dreamed of. My idea of the California Indians—the number of the California Indians—was taken from Helen Hunt Jackson's beautiful story "Ramona." I thought there were just a few Mission Indians in southern California, but when I heard there were 11,000 Indians in California I was surprised. I was very sorry also to hear that there are still 2,000 Indians in that State who are landless and homeless, and some of them so poor that they are eating grasshoppers to keep alive in a State bursting with plenty. And I also told the laities of that church conference that I would like to have them give some attention, give some kindness and help to the returned Students of California and Nevada; that returned students often went back home among people who called themselves Christians and who turned a cold shoulder to them.

I was quite busy attending these conferences, but still I took time to go out to the exposition spasmodically, and when I went there I passed usually a band of Indians who played on the grounds. They were from Nevada, and perhaps some of them were California boys, and they attended the conference of the returned students.

After I had heard a paper read at one of the meetings of the Government Employees' Conference, when the man who read the paper said to give the Indian the white man's chance, I went out that day to the fair grounds and I said to these boys, "One of your friends said to give the Indian the white man's chance." One of them said, "Yes; give us half the white man's chance and we will take the other half." And those were Paiute boys; Paiutes that I have heard called Diggers in my life. Looked down upon by humanity in the United States, and yet one of those boys was the one who said, "Yes; give us half the white man's chance and we will take the other half." That is the spirit of those Digger Indians. We must take a stand.

And besides seeing the Returned Students' Conference and the fairgrounds, I also took the trouble to go up to see that wonderful man Burbank,[11] who invents so many new kinds of vegetables and fruit and grass, and who invented the spineless cactus, making a good food for man and beast. Think of a man doing that. I was allowed to go and see him by the kindness of a friend, a member of the National Education Association. Those people who teach the young people in schools and colleges and universities were given the privilege to go and see that man for the sake of the young people of America; and because I represented the Indian race my friend got me the privilege of going with that party to see this wonderful man. His time is priceless, yet for the sake of the young people of America he gave us the whole afternoon and was willing to do or say anything for us. On that trip he showed us all those different things in that wonderful garden. I was so impressed that when I returned to town—it was a very warm day and I was very much heated—I stepped into the drug store and asked for a lemonade, but I said, "I want it a spineless lemonade."

I believe I have used my ten minutes, but I wish to tell you that we old people are looking to you to help us in this great work of uplift for our race, and we don't bar anybody from this society. We are nonpartisan. It is a society for no sex, sect, or section, and we want to do all we can for all branches of our race in the United States. We are looking to you for our future. I am working not only for the little missions that I sometimes have been visiting in Minnesota. This audience reminds me a little bit of that congregation that I have in Minnesota. The congregation is a mixed congregation of whites and Sioux Indians. The whites sit on one side and the Indians on the other side when we have service at the same time.

I am glad to be working for this Society of American Indians, and I am asking for your help and inspiration, and I hope we will give the same to you.

AMERICAN INDIAN DAY

Papers of the Society of American Indians, September 1915

Know Ye All Men by These Presents:

That I, Sherman Coolidge, President of the Society of American Indians, by virtue of power vested in me by the Executive Council of the Society do hereby declare the second Saturday in the month of May each year henceforth, American Indian Day, and call upon every person of American Indian ancestry to specially observe this day as one set apart as a memorial to the Red Race of America and to a wise consideration of its future.

In the judgement of wise and impartial men, the heroic struggle of our fathers against forces which they had no means of measuring or appreciating, yet which they fought against for homes, for family, for country and the preservation of native freedom, has no parallel in all history. Yet while we consider these things we are not unmindful that they made upon occasions the same mistakes, that have been common to all human kind, of every race and age,—and yet were virtuous men. Now that the glory and the shadows of the past have become a part of historic record that has been written, we are not to forget the present and the future of our people, that we may henceforth live in greater fullness. Let us now move forward and acquire all those things that make races and nations more efficient and more noble; let us reach out for a larger life, through brotherly love, purposeful action and constructive service to our country, not only for our own welfare, but in order that the American people and all humanity may be uplifted because we have performed, and strive to perform, our full duty as men. Let these things, and the means by which they may be accomplished, be considered upon American Indian Day.

Likewise do we invite every American who loves his country and would uphold its honor and dignity, to celebrate this day and to consider our early philosophy, our love of freedom, our social institutions and our history in the full light of truth and in the balances of justice, in honest comparison with the annals of other races, and to draw therefrom those noble things that we believe are worthy of emulation. But we call upon our country not only to consider the past but to earnestly consider our present and our future as a part of the American people. To them we declare our needs now and tomorrow as those primarily of Americans struggling for enlightenment and that competency that is consistent with American citizenship. We do avow our hopes and our destiny inseparably united to that of the people of the United States of America and that our hearts and minds are now and forever loyal to our country, which we would serve in our fullest capacity as men and Americans.

Unto this declaration I do set my hand and seal this 28th day of September in the Year of our Lord Nineteen Hundred and Fifteen. Done at Lawrence, Kansas.

STATEMENT BEFORE THE SENATE COMMITTEE ON INDIAN AFFAIRS

Hearings before the Committee on Indian Affairs of the United States Senate, Sixty-Fourth Congress, 1916

The Wind River Indians are very much concerned about the land that has been taken up by the white men on the ceded portion of their reservation; my impression is they would like to have such homesteads, not yet paid for, canceled and reverted to the Indians for their use and benefit. Then too, their chance to secure water rights from the State of Wyoming will expire December 1, 1916. The water right in Wyoming is a most serious question and probably many allottees need departmental or congressional help, or both. Such allottees are doubtless among the aged, widows, orphans, minors, and persons who by force of circumstances are absent from the reservation or otherwise unable to personally handle their land. Many of the allotments are under the management or authority of the agent, who may be too busy to attend to them properly, for instance, to lease for the sake of the water right; he may also face the difficulty or the impossibility of getting anybody to lease the land, yet it is his duty to protect the allottee whose land he controls. And again, the terms of the lease contract and printed requirements scare many a man out who might be seeking to work the land and make a beneficial use of the water on it, thereby securing and maintaining the water right of the Indian. And then the lease must be approved by the department which might mean delay and disapproval and disappointment. It is discouraging to the parties interested. I hope the bureau is looking after the water rights. The homesteads on the ceded portion are perhaps those not paid for and unoccupied.

Yes; Indians have been known to eat dead stock in the past, and it would not surprise me, if some of them are doing it at this writing. It is an old story on the Wind River Reservation, and might be just as true among other tribes on other reservations. It is my opinion they did so because they were both ignorant and hungry—careless of the cause of death. You state that, according to your recollection, on two occasions I have admitted the truth of statements to the effect that my tribesmen, driven by hunger "ate sheep and stock that had died from disease." One of the cases I admitted as true was the eating of drowned sheep by some of my tribesmen. Some thousands of sheep were drowned by an overflow of the river caused by the break of an ice jam. They ate the sheep they could fish out. It was winter; they were hungry, and it was a godsend to them.

OPENING ADDRESS OF THE PRESIDENT AT THE SIXTH ANNUAL CONFERENCE OF THE SOCIETY OF AMERICAN INDIANS

American Indian Magazine, July–September 1916

In speaking to you this morning I would like to announce the fact that at the conference of last year at Lawrence, Kansas, indeed all the conferences previous have been indications of the fact that we are still an experiment, an unfinished experiment, as an organization, that we are in process of formation and that while we are we must be patient. This organization came into existence and it was hailed with welcome and hope, by both the Indians and the whites. By it the Indians and the whites joined forces, banded together, one as active members of Indian blood, and the other as friends of the Indian cause in this country to work for the uplift and welfare of the race, the honor of the Indians and the good of the country. Each association has had its problem.

Each association faces a very difficult condition, from the time we organized in Columbus till this date, and what will happen and will be done at this session I do not know, but I hope it will not be to the destruction and shame of the Indians or the country. I hope that it will be for union and strength and harmony. I hope that we will work to better effect, as we must work harder each year for the existence of the Society of American Indians, and because we are young we have been running in a crude sort of way. Many things have been done, many things have not been done which ought to be done.

Both the white race and the Indian race have expected a great deal more from us than we are able, either through money or by workers, to accomplish.

We are not yet rich in money; we are not rich in members who will take hold of the work, for the most of the members are working at some calling, at some office, in some field, so that they cannot come to all the conferences, much as they might desire. But a few of us must come together. Those who can get away, whose hearts are in the work must come. Those who are in the distant part of our country, are unable to come for one reason or another. Therefore, we who are here have the tremendous responsibility of interpreting this internal movement of the race to the world.

I asked one of the members in our early days, "How dare we to enter this enterprise?" We have practically undertaken to do work that the Indian Rights Association, the Indian National Association, and indeed the United States Government, as well as the different denominations of religion in our country have tried before. We have in this endeavor tried to do the work of literary people, of people who write stories, legends, history, and indeed who write music; and also to study the handicraft of our people, and, what is more important, to see and understand, if possible, the problem into which the race has been thrust by the white race and our nation.

As a race we are in a state of chaos. We told that to President Wilson. That is the only term we can use to express the legal status of the Indian today, and we ask the white race to clarify the atmosphere, to make a better condition for the Indian in the upward trail toward citizenship, self-support and self-responsibility.

So in this Conference it behooves us to do things more according to parliamentary law, more unitedly, in cooperation, not so much in destructive criticism, muck-raking or abolishing. We are not so much out for that as we are for *co-operation*, "to co-operate in all movements tending to the uplift of the race," and work patriotically, for our Nation and country.

In this conference I hope to do what I can to limit the speakers more directly than in the past; those who come up on the floor and those who have papers must be prepared to be limited as to time. It seems to me ten minutes is enough for members who stand up and give an extemporaneous speech and twenty minutes ought to be enough for persons who have boiled down whatever they have written to present to this conference on any subject, and along that line we must have and for that reason try to adhere to the program; and I am hoping that all resolutions will be discussed by this body before they are put before the House to act upon.

I would like also to speak about what some members have suggested in regard to voting. One member at least has suggested that we ought to allow the association members to vote in some cases, for instance, in case of the officers. They have tremendous interest as to who represents them as well as those who represent the active membership. It is of vital interest, we want to know we have the proper officers to represent the Indian race before the world, to do the work, that is laid out by our settled principles, the fundamental principles on which the Society is based. These principles are general and are as wide as humanity and not only confined to the red race. It is unselfish devotion to our fellow men and we must guide ourselves according to the seven principles, not to allow or lend this Society to the use of personal interests. We are founded on unselfishness and we must keep in mind the fact that selfishness has no friends and that this existence of the society, whether we believe in any certain policy or opinion or not, that we must be loyal to the Society, and give up all selfishness and stick to the Society. For that reason we have got to put our pride and private opinion on various subjects in our pockets and hope for better days and better things. I think they will come in time.

Now the other thing that I would like to suggest is that we vote by ballot for officers. I for one would not care to know who voted for me or who does not vote for me. I like to vote as I think best and not unduly influenced by somebody else. Therein is our liberty; therein is our strength to maintain our independence and our liberty; that is what we are fighting for, to restore the Indian freedom of the Indian that is inherent in his soul, as well as the racial pride. This, my friends, will be our safeguard. I think I have said enough this morning and I hope again that we will stand shoulder to shoulder on the firm foundation of which I will perhaps have further to say, upon which our organization is founded. (Applause).

OPEN DEBATE ON THE LOYALTY OF INDIAN EMPLOYEES IN THE INDIAN SERVICE

American Indian Magazine, July–September 1916

The question was raised by Dr. Montezuma that Indian employees in the service of the Indian Bureau could not be loyal to the Indian race and to their real interests. His argument was that the Indian Bureau did not conserve the best interests of the Indians.

President Coolidge desired to defend the loyalty of the Indian employee, and calling Vice-President Roe-Cloud[12] to the chair, he took the floor.

THE PRESIDENT: I do not know how many times I must get up and say that I believe an Indian who is a Government employee can be loyal to his race and at the same time be loyal to his Government. Is the fact that I am a clergyman of an Episcopalian church to keep me at the same time from being loyal to the Government?

DR. MONTEZUMA: The Indian Bureau, not the Government.

THE PRESIDENT: The Government is represented by the Indian Bureau.

DR. MONTEZUMA: I think not.

THE PRESIDENT: I think it is.

DR. MONTEZUMA: It ought to be, but it is not.

THE PRESIDENT: The Government ought sometimes, as a Government, to represent the sense of the American people but it does not always represent them as a whole, the American people as a whole.

DR. MONTEZUMA: Let us start right out on that. It puts me in a very embarrassing position to place me in a position that I am saying anything against the Government; I am not. I explained that to you when I started out; that I have nothing against the Government—it is the system, it is the system we are after, the Indian Bureau, not the Commissioner of Indian affairs, or anything of that sort, it is the Bureau, it is the *system*, my dear brother.

THE PRESIDENT: I am not talking about the Indian Commissioner or anybody except you and perhaps myself as we differ in regard to occupying a position as Government employee and being loyal to the race and the Government at the same time. I think it can be done. I don't think I was disloyal to the Government when I was in the Government employ in the Indian service; neither do I believe that I was disloyal to my race.

DR. MONTEZUMA: A hireling only that is to do service. As a hireling he is not himself, he cannot be. There are Indians in the service, and that is what I am trying to express—they are not supposed to do anything that will embarrass the Indian department, not only the whites but everybody. If I went into the Indian service I would shut my mouth on a good many things.

THE PRESIDENT: I think so. You would not dare to say some things. It is about time we are setting you right. You say you cannot mix with the Indian Bureau any more than water with oil. I think you can mix with the Indian Bureau. I mixed with the Indian Bureau a good many times. They have the Indian Bureau there so I could mix with them, to help me to do the work on Indian reservations as a kindness to my people. By giving me work I paid my expenses as a missionary to my people. I have an obligation to them and every Indian in the United States has an obligation to them in that sense. We are facing *conditions* whether they suit us or not and we are to use our manhood in facing those conditions and try to help ourselves out of it and help others if we can; that is what we are here for.

DR. MONTEZUMA: You help the Bureau that is holding you in that condition?

THE PRESIDENT: The Bureau cannot hold me any more than it holds you. I am not hired by the Bureau, it has no hold on me. I am a clergyman, I am a subject of this Government and this country and I am a member of the Church but that does not say that I am a slave.

DR. MONTEZUMA: I am talking about the Indians, not you or I. You get pay from your church.

THE PRESIDENT: I do not; that is all you know about it. That is about the way you look at everything perhaps. I say I came into civilization in 1870, before Dr. Montezuma's time, I think I am older than he is. I think the Indian Bureau has its work to do and we have our work to do and I would like as much as possible to cooperate with it as I would like to work with any other organization or institution that is trying to do anything for the Indians. I do not like to be handicapped. I do not like to see the Indians handicapped. That is the reason I joined forces with this organization. That is the reason I am in its service. That is why I work when I can in favor of the race, at all times. Not a day I have not done it since I was seven years old. I worked as an Arapahoe Indian, a full-blood—just as full-blood as Dr. Montezuma ever dared to be—although somebody got up before this conference and said I was not a full-blood. I have not suffered for nothing, for I have suffered for my race. Perhaps I have suffered for myself but I have also suffered for my race. I have lived the life in the wild camp, you people call it. (I never saw it was so awful wild.) I was born there. I lived that life until I was seven years old. That is when I was taken among the whites, in 1870, and since that time I have not ceased to do everything I could to work for myself and my race and tribe and I have not forgotten the things done for me and my people by the American Government and nation. I know it expects me to be law-abiding and to be loyal.

REV. GORDON:[13] I want to say a few remarks. The question of the Indian Bureau, as far as I see, to state my opinion, I disagree some with President Coolidge who says a member in the employment of the Government is at the same time loyal to this Society. I do not want to cast any personal reflections but speaking generally I do not think that is possible.

MR. COOLIDGE: I did not say this Society; I said the Indian race. The race may be helped by this Society. That is not what I am talking about. Before this Society ever existed I was a Government employee. *I assert* a Government Indian employee can be equally loyal to his race and to his Government.

REV. GORDON: It is not possible for an Indian in the employ of the Government to take a step so he can get rid of the Indian Bureau.

MRS. BALDWIN:[14] My friends; I am one of those Government clerks that my brothers have been speaking of today. I do not know where at any time the Government clerk does not dare to say just what he thinks about the Indian Bureau, or if he should or wish, as they put it, that they do not dare come out and say it. I do not know where anyone got that idea. *I am sure that very many times I have told Indians that I know that I feel and I want the Indian Bureau to be abolished, but I do not believe that it ought to be abolished on the instant.* I think the Indians know that there are many Indians who are not ready now to be put out in the world to take care of themselves. They are not prepared to compete with the people that surround them in a business way, or in any other way. You may not know it, but it is a fact that the Indian Bureau is striving to that end, when someday there will be no need of an Indian Bureau. (Applause).

MRS. BONNIN:[15] I just wish to make a very few remarks. It seems if I would sit silent it might indicate to people I was afraid to take a stand or express an opinion. In justice to Indian employees in the Indian service I must say one word in their behalf. I cannot sit here and hear it said that just out of consideration of holding a job and getting a very small salary they must keep their mouths shut. I do not think that is true. *I am intimately acquainted with certain Indian employees who are prepared to enter the world at large, to compete with people in the different lines of occupation, to make a livelihood and get better things, who, from a sense of duty and by all the ties of the heart stay in the wilderness. Why? Because there are human beings there today that need their sympathy, and their kindness, just the kind of help that money could never buy, and that the salary from the Government does not pay for. These are to be found among the Indian employees, working under the Indian Bureau and among their own people on the Indian reservation.* In justice to those Indians who wish to be citizens of our beloved America, to be true to the Government of America, to be civilized men and women, to be loyal to their own who are not so far along as they are, these Indian employees are glad to work under the Indian Bureau, to hold their jobs; but that is the least that is pointed out, that it was only from the commercial point of view, that it was only because of a salary that they would not speak. I want it understood that it is not always so. And I want it understood that I know what I am talking about. (Applause).

MR. PRESIDENT: Is it right for us to act this way? With the consciousness that we are trying to attain the same end, it seems to me we misunderstand one another. We should try to understand "where we are at," to speak in the language of Texas. Some of us are more radical; some want to take the radical method of solving the Indian problem, and others have a notion that this Indian question is in a state of chaos, jumbled. We told that to the President when we brought our memorial before him and he gave us audience. We want to do right in all these things; but I do not like to have our discussion seem to show the employees of the Government as disloyal. That sort of thing as a general accusation has been used in regard to the Government employees many times. We have tried to get Congress to pass certain bills and to clarify the atmosphere for the Indian because it is in a state of chaos. Let us go right. Eliminate the antiquated rules, regulations and laws, by which the Indian Bureau is run and which might be used by some incompetent agent who has got a grudge against us. Get rid of all these old laws and clear the atmosphere for a new start, get ourselves on our feet as soon as we can and then abolish the Indian Bureau, but take care and do not abolish the Indians. That has been tried many times and it has failed. There were Indians on one reservation who wanted me to come and address them and I did, but before I made a speech one Indian,

> a member of our Society said, "These Indians want to remain Indians as long as possible so they will not have to pay taxes," so I told them that I would like to have them remain Indians as long as possible, to die Indians, be Indians in the Beyond, but I did not want them to shirk their full duties as American citizens and as American men. (Applause)

ESCAPED MASSACRE TO BE TAKEN BY WHITE FOLK AND EDUCATED FOR MINISTRY—STORY OF AN INDIAN BOY

Papers of the Society of American Indians, ca. September 1916

A long time ago a tribe of Arapahoe Indians went to Camp Brown in Wyoming to obtain their rations and their annuities from the federal government. The Shoshones and the Bannocks were traditional enemies of the Arapahoe. Though a treaty of peace had been signed between the warring tribes the Shoshones and the Bannocks were not averse to breaking it when there was a chance for blood and scalps.

On that quiet summer evening while the Arapahoe were setting up their tepees they were startled by the yells of their ancient enemies. The little band was surrounded and many of the men and women slaughtered. Three women and eight children escaped. Among the number was an Arapahoe boy seven years old, and his two brothers. They were taken to Camp Brown, and the seven-year old, black-haired, black-eyed Indian boy was adopted by Lieutenant Charles C. Coolidge, who had just brought his young bride to the camp. The lieutenant and his wife kept and educated the boy and fourteen years later that Indian boy, now grown to sturdy manhood, went back among his people as a missionary to tell them of the ways of the white man, teach them his religion and ask them to accept their pale face brother as their mentor, as their governor, and as their protector.

Mr. Coolidge Answers

That Indian boy, now grown old with the years, is in Cedar Rapids today, as a delegate to, and president of, the Society of American Indians. He is the Rev. Sherman Coolidge of Faribault, Minn., for more than thirty years an Episcopalian clergyman. Mr. Coolidge with all his civilization and his education, still is an Indian and he will die an Indian, because he believes in his people, glories in their past and sees a bright vision of their future. This Indian believes in the white man's civilization, the white man's government, and it is his best effort to teach his people to believe as he does.

He sat in the parlor of Hotel Montrose today and lived again his boyhood days when his father was killed by hostile Indians on the Tongue river in Wyoming for the benefit of an inquisitive reporter, and when he finished those who heard the interview were better impressed with them as a people than ever they had been.

Mr. Coolidge recalled his boyhood days in the Indian camp: the fight which deprived him of his Indian home and sent him to the whites for succor. He told of his education and of his trip back to the Indians to teach them the ways of civilization.

Civilization Almost Complete

"And the civilization of the Indians is almost complete," he said. "Many Indians have won their spurs in life. Many of them have been made citizens by the government, which has placed them on equality with the white man. The Society of American Indians has worked with the government to bring about all that has been accomplished in educating and civilizing the Indian.

"The European found the Indian with his own civilization, but the European looked on the Indian's civilization as different from his, therefore inferior. He looked on the Indian as inherently inferior in manhood to him, although that manhood dated back to the glacial period. The European said to the Indian, 'You take my mode of living, my manners, my customs, my education, my religion; be an imitation white man.' The white man with his civilization of thousands of years expected to make over the Indian in two or three generations. That is the way the white man goes after everything. He tries to, and does, force his manners and his customs on those whom he conquers, and that is perhaps why the Indian is not satisfied all together with the white man's civilization. We have crumbled ruins of a high civilization in South America and in some parts of North America which must have existed at the time of the early Egyptians and the Assyrians. We do not know whether this was an early Indian civilization, but we do know it was there before the white man arrived. We do not know how and when the Indian originated.

Some scientists say that he descended from the Mongolians and others that he did not. I do not know, but he is here and the object of this society is to write a new history of the Indian with honor to himself and the nation."

STATEMENTS FOR *SUNSET*
November 1918

A pure-blooded Arapahoe Indian of wide culture and distinguished bearing is Sherman Coolidge, an Episcopal missionary living at Reno, Nevada, and an ardent American patriot. In a public career lasting thirty-six years he has received many honors, but he says that the proudest day of his life would be the one permitting him to go to France as chaplain of an all-Indian regiment.

From his seventh year Coolidge was reared as the only son of General Austin Coolidge, who saw him graduated from the Shattuck Military Academy and the Seabury Divinity School at Faribault, Minnesota. He traces his ancestry back through four chieftains, Sharp Nose, Cut Finger, Little Wolf and Black Coal. The life of this notable specimen of the first Americans has been threaded with romance and adventure. When he was but a copper-colored papoose his grandmother was killed in the western onrush of white men. His tribe roamed on down into the Wind River country of Wyoming, where the lad grew into the name of Des-che-wa-wah, Swift Runner.

Tribal wars broke out and Des-che-wa-wah's father, Banashda, the Strong Hearted, engaged thirty Shoshone enemies while his confederates escaped. In honor of his bravery the old warrior's captors left him his scalp and killed him with the arrow. Little Des-che-wa-wah remained a captive until General Coolidge was sent to quiet the Indians, when Mrs. Coolidge begged for the child. He was re-christened Sherman Coolidge, after General Sherman and his foster father.

General Coolidge hoped that the boy, who made friends so readily and had been graduated with honors from the military academy, would follow his own calling. He planned to send him to West Point, but yielded to the youth's longing to be a missionary to his own race.

"They say the Indians are by nature cold," remarked Sherman Coolidge. "When I was first taken away I cried every night for my own mother and my own people. When I became a man I went back as teacher and missionary to the Arapahoes in the Wind River country of Wyoming, and there was my mother. She knew me and I knew her instantly. She called me her son and was proud of me, and I was able to help her till she died. Now I go back to see my foster parents and they call me their son and are proud of me. I am very glad for it all."

Soon after he became a missionary, romance invaded Sherman Coolidge's life with the coming of Grace Wetherbee of New York to visit in the family of Bishop Talbot's. The talented Indian had by this time lost his native skill at dodging arrows and fell a victim to the archery of the little blind god. The rich society girl and the handsome missionary were in love ere either thought to guard against it.

"And so we were married and have lived very happily ever afterwards," said Des-che-wa-wah Sherman Coolidge. Then he added, with a smile, "When we were first married, both sides of the new house were humorously dignified, my people boasting of my chieftain ancestry and Mrs. Coolidge's remembering that they were Wetherbees. But those things pass when there is a true mating. On the great Happy Hunting Ground we are all going to be surprised at the racial diversity of the chosen."

The Coolidges lost their only son but they have two small daughters and an adopted daughter of the Shoshone tribe, who is studying to be a Red Cross nurse.

The Indian patriot is said to be the hero of the dramatic story called "Strong Heart" by a distant member of the Coolidge family; is fifty-five years old, more than six feet tall, erect and vigorous. He thrills with pride at the way his people have rallied to the cause of humanity in the present conflict.

To show that no discrimination was made between the earliest Americans and their "pale face" compatriots, the government has scattered the three thousand Indians now in the service among the different camps and training-sheds. Many Indian educators, among them Brigadier-General R. H. Pratt, founder of the Carlisle Indian School, have felt that an all-Indian unit might create a feeling of race stigma. Only recently has there been a tentative movement in the direction of what Sherman Coolidge calls a "Noble Red Man Regiment."

As four-years' head of the Society of American Indians, and as foster son of General Coolidge, Sherman Coolidge was appealed to for support of the Indian movement. "Our race is proud and high spirited. They are naturally warriors," said the Indian minister. "This is not the first war in which Indian blood has been shed for the Stars and Stripes. We have many veterans of the Civil and Spanish-American wars. Numbers of us have education and athletic training equal to the Anglo Saxon. Would not a volunteer regiment of Indian braves add glory to our history, just as regiments of the Scottish Highlanders do to theirs?"

A Sermon and a Protest

YE CANNOT SERVE GOD AND MAMMON

Coolidge-Heinicke Collection, ca. 1920

This, I take it, means that there is no compromise between the love for God and the love for riches. Every man must decide for himself which he shall serve. In America it seems we must live the Europeanized method of life which is dominated by competition. Let every man gather in all he can for himself, never mind the other fellow. This is what European civilization demands, and it is a cut-throat principle. Competition is the soul of trade, but it is also a breeder of cruel strife among men with its attendant greed. The proudest militaristic nations of the world took a pacifist Jewish peasant for their guide and easily reconciled His teachings with bombs, poison gas, secret treaties, and all the lies of official propaganda. If Jesus of Nazareth is to be followed today, in business, politics, and society, His European interpreters must undergo a radical change. The commercial world would be better off if it would cast its net on the other side. European civilization is commercialized and materialistic.

At the same time, it presents the challenge of Him who said, "I am the Way, the Truth and the Life." "Love your neighbor as yourself." "All things whatsoever ye would that men should do to you, do ye even so to them." St. Paul also said: "Bear ye one another's burden." This is *brotherly cooperation*. Man *must* dare to *believe* and *live the Jesus way*. Then, and *not until then* can he say: "I believe in a Christlike world. I know nothing better. I can be content with nothing less." Man needs the vision to trust his destiny to the wisdom of Jesus. Follow the European economic system and you will be tempted to steal and rob and murder. The Red Man might kill from anger, for revenge, in battle, but *not for money*. He finds it difficult to adopt the European method of life. For instance, if he tries to advance in that direction by trying to be thrifty and accumulate money and property, he becomes distasteful to his fellow tribesmen, and is described as "stingy like the white man." There *is quite a difference* between the *Europeanized* man and the *Western Hemisphere aborigine*.

A writer has said that the Indian's religion is "interwoven with every phase of his life." The Indian *lived* his religion. He believed that religion is *vital* and must have an *immediate application*. To him it is *most sacred* as it has been to all men, *civilized* or *uncivilized*. For twenty-five years I held Sunday School services for the children of the Shoshones and the Arapahoes. Sometimes they came with the older people to morning and evening Prayer, and to Holy Communion. In my early childhood, the Shoshones and the Arapahoes were deadly enemies. My father was killed in battle by the Shoshones. I have married and buried some of the Shoshones. I have baptized many of the Arapahoes, presented them for confirmation, administered Holy Communion to them, married and buried them. I officiated at the funeral of a Shoshone man who was a hundred and thirty-eight years old.[1]

Three summers ago during the annual convention of the Church in Wyoming, I addressed a large audience of white people, Shoshones, Arapahoes, and visitors from the north, east, south and west; among them was a graduate of William Smith College, Miss Marcella B. Clarke, of West Field, N.Y. It seems that it was Miss Clarke's first experience among the Indians on a reservation in the West. I told my cousin, the Chief, that Miss Clarke studied at the same College where I had studied and I wanted her adopted by the tribe and given an Arapahoe name. He said: "*Wait!*" He disappeared behind a large building and returned with a crowd of Arapahoe men who said: "We are ready." I called Miss Clarke and we gave her an Arapahoe name and took her into the tribe. So, you see, William Smith College has an Arapahoe graduate and probably does not realize it.

I made my address at Sacajawea's grave. Sacajawea was the Shoshone girl wife of the official French guide of the Lewis and Clark expedition; but Sacajawea did the work. She successfully conducted the expedition from St. Louis to Oregon and return. She died and was buried, a few months before I arrived on the mission field, by the Rev. John Roberts, the veteran missionary to whom I went to assist. I know Sacajawea's children and grandchildren. On one occasion I married a Shoshone young couple at my house who could speak English; the young man not so well as the young woman. When I asked him to repeat after me the words: "And with all my worldly goods I thee endow," he said: "And with all my *worthless* goods I thee endow." These words have happily been eliminated from the marriage service, also the word *obey*. My very dear friend and diocesan, Irving Peake Johnson,[2] said that when they struck off the word Obey from the marriage ceremony, they did away with the only piece of humor in the Prayer Book.

The *Indians* are national wards of the United States, under the protection and care of the *Department of Interior*. Body, mind and spirit are *under* the absolute control of the Government. Yet this *is*, and should be, the province of the Church. The Church should teach the Indian the doctrine of the Blessed Trinity and the forgiveness of sins. He knows nothing about them, he never thinks about them, they don't bother him. He believes in God, in the hereafter, in right and wrong; in fasting and prayer and praise; in thanksgiving and thankoffering. The missionary can build on this good and natural foundation as I have tried to do for 32 years.

Brethren, you know, and I know, that "Uncle Sam" is a good moral man and a good citizen, and *believes* in teaching good morality and good citizenship to his native ward, but *he is not* what you might call a baptized and a communicant member of the Episcopal Church. I am sure that all thinking men would agree that if our modern commercialized civilization is to be squared up with the teachings of Jesus, revolutionary changes are ahead. Let us not lose hope, however, but press for the best that lies locked up within the universal human breast.

STATEMENTS AT THE COLORADO SPRINGS OPEN FORUM ON THE AMERICAN INDIAN

Colorado Springs Gazette, June 1927

"Altho the Indian has fought in every war this country ever engaged in since the war of the revolution, he is deprived the privilege of citizenship, and it was not until I was 50 and had proved up on 360 acres of land that I was allowed to vote in Wyoming because as a boy I had lived on an Indian reservation," the Rev. Sherman Coolidge, pastor of the Church of the Good Shepherd, said in an address which he delivered at the Open Forum meeting, held in the courthouse yesterday afternoon, on "Christianity and the Indians."

"The Indian is a subject foreign to most of the American people for they are so engrossed, in material things that they don't give much thought to other things," Dr. Coolidge said, "Even religion, the most important thing is put in the background. I was born a little savage, but I always resented that term being applied to my people because I know they are peace-loving, hospitable, generous and deeply religious. Yet they have been called 'Red Devils.'"

Befogged by Sect Squabbles

The Indian cannot understand the religious difference of the white people, for all Indians have the same religion, and to them one religion is just as holy as the other. The Indians have their sun dance and just because Indians say their prayers at sunset, and go through their sun dance at the break of day the white people take it that the Indian is a sun worshiper. But that sun dance is a deeply religious observance. By the Arapahoes it is called the sage hen dance.

If you will look at the pottery, and basket work of the Indians you will find worked in the pattern the figure of a bird. By the Indians that bird is known as the thunderbird. To him the thunderbird is the agent of the Almighty, and when it thunders that is his voice. When an Arapahoe is under oath he says, "in the presence of the thunderbird may he strike me down if this is wrong." The Indian does not take the name of God in vain, to him that name is too sacred. Doesn't that show the Indian is more religious than the white man? There is no synonym of profanity in the Arapahoe language. If the Indian wants to be profane he has to borrow the English language. They very soon learn swearing from the white man, and they do it very artistically.

In God and Hereafter

So when I was sent as a missionary to my own people I knew they believed in God, and the hereafter, and that they believed lying was wrong and cheating was wrong. I knew they had a religion that was somewhat like that of the Jew who believes in an Almighty and Ever-living God. The Indians also have a tradition of a universal flood. When I went as a missionary I built the Christian religion on their own religion. I knew they had a lot of foolish superstitions.

I told them what those superstitions were. I tried to follow St. Paul's policy, "I do not want what is yours but you," and "to prove all things and hold fast to that which is good." To test all things of the white people to leave some of them out, whisky and things like that, but to hold fast to that which is good.

Whenever war came the Indians have always rallied to the colors and fought the enemies of this country. Seventeen thousand three hundred thirteen Indians went to the front in the World war. To you perhaps that will not sound many, but you must remember they were drawn from a population of 700,000 or 800,000. Three hundred fifty thousand Indians are now under direct control of the government. Washington and Jefferson knew it was a good thing to have the Indian friendly to the United States. During the Revolutionary war Washington used them as scouts. At the time of the World war Indians were in every branch of the service, they were used both as scouts and snipers. Indians knew how to cross No Man's land and bring back a prisoner without firing a shot. I had an Indian boy visit me who was in the marines during the war. In one of the fights of the Revolutionary war an Indian chief mobilized his men and aided materially in that fight against the British, and the Daughters of the Revolution have caused a tablet to be placed on the spot where many of them were killed.

Uncle Sam Holds Purse String

People who have done what we have done should have the privileges of citizenship. The government has millions of dollars belonging to the Indians. If it would let loose of that, many an Indian man and woman would be glad to attend a college and university, and this money could be put to no better purpose.

PART 2

Grace Coolidge — *Writings, Letters, and Poems*

Articles for the *Spirit of Missions*

AN ARAPAHOE CHRISTMAS TREE

Spirit of Missions, January 1903

I wanted to call this article "The First Christmas Tree on Wind River." It was the first the *Arapahoes* ever had there. But a few days before ours, the field matron had one several miles above, at a settlement of Shoshone mixed-bloods, so, as that was also on the river, it spoiled my title.

The idea of getting up a tree was an impromptu one. Mr. Coolidge and I had very little for it but candy and peanuts, in bags which we made out of pink mosquito netting, and a few little toys left over from a Christmas sale we had had the week before, for the benefit of the Agency (white) church.

Our ranch is on Little Wind River, about fourteen miles from Wood Flat, as the Arapahoes call the place where they camp in winter. Mr. Coolidge's duties for the First Sunday after Christmas left us free to go over to Big Wind early in the day; so we loaded the tree—a little one, which we had got from Crooked Creek Canyon, ten miles above us, and which had already served at the fair and among the Agency's Christmas decorations—with the toys and peanuts, our bedding and "grub," as we say out here, into our spring-wagon, and started off in a howling windstorm.

We were to spend the night at the cabin of a friend, a young Arapahoe, who vacated it for us. We forded Little Wind River and followed the road, which struck off east through wide sage-covered hills toward Big Wind. We could see, on the edge of the plains, three snow-covered ranges of mountains: the Wind River Mountains to the west, the Owl Creek range in the north, and the Beaver Hills to the south. There is a line of Browning which might have been written of Wyoming: "So wonderful, so wide, so sun-suffused."[1]

Finally we turned down a cut in some sandhills, and came out upon Big Wind Valley. It is long, winding, narrow, two miles wide, perhaps, with Big Wind tearing down its eastern side, under the bluffs. The river was frozen, all but a dark, wicked-looking stream at its centre. On either side of the river stretch wide bands of timber, cottonwood trees, tall and thick enough for any country, and the sage brush grows higher than one's head, always a sign of fertile land.

We saw a good-sized camp ahead of us—several cabins and tepees—and we made for it to ask the way to Herbert's.[2] It turned out to be Mule's place, where we were to have the tree. Mule came out, and told us that Herbert had gone to his cabin to make a fire for us, and that we should find him there about a mile up the river. He had gotten a big armful of wood, and insisted on our coming in and warming ourselves, but we were too cold to get out, and started at once for Herbert's.

I wish that those who ascribe unhesitatingly to Indians those attributes familiar to us all, of laziness, dirt and indifference, could have looked into Herbert's cabin, which he had built himself. It was of logs, had two rooms, and was nestled under the big trees and close to the river. He had told us to bring only our bedding and food, that he had everything else we could need, but we had thrown in a few little extras, not being prepared to find dish towels, toilet soap, and even a whisk broom. And the house was so clean that you could—what is the old saying?—eat off the floor! Herbert and Bruce Goes Back, a schoolboy home for the Christmas holidays, son of a blind woman and a vanished father, whom Mule is bringing up along with four orphaned girls (distant relationship being their only claim on his care), had built roaring fires in both stoves for us.

Herbert was very anxious for us to see the irrigating ditch the Arapahoes had put through the valley the summer before, which will make it possible for them to raise abundant crops from the good soil. So, in spite of the wind, we drove four or five miles up the valley, to the head-gates of the ditch. On the way, at a crossing of the river, we passed several loads of baled hay, and halted while the men tried to extricate a wheel which had broken through the ice. Herbert apologized to us for "our boys," because they were working on Sunday; said the same accident had happened to them the day before, as they were going up to the ranch where they got the hay, and prevented their loading up and returning to their camps the previous night. These young men freight baled hay from the ranch of a white man on the reservation, to the sub-Agency—a day's drive at the slow gait of the freight team—unload their hay, go the next day to the coal bank, owned by a Shoshone mixed-blood, load their wagons with coal, and the next day freight it to Fort Washakie, returning home the day after, thus making a profitable round trip.

The ditch was a splendid one, and means possible plenty instead of hunger—it is often as bad as that—for this group of Arapahoes and for their horses. It is six miles long and seven feet in depth and width. It strikes out of the river first above an old beaver dam, which turned the water with great force into the ditch. The beaver is gone, but his friendship for the Indian persists! Herbert told us that twenty-five of the young men (Herbert was the "boss") worked on that ditch twenty-nine days last summer, without wages or outside help, save a few boards granted them by the Agent for the head-gates. They sang, joked, talked English as they worked, with never a quarrel. Herbert fed our horses with fine oats he had raised since the ditch was put through. That night we cooked our supper by the light of Herbert's lamp filled with oil which he had dipped from its spring, near the coal bank, literally into the lamp. It gave as good a light as ordinary kerosene, and did not smoke.

The next morning Herbert came for us early, and we drove down to Mule's. Mule has a big cabin where Mr. Coolidge is to hold services once a month this winter. It was empty, save for a stove in the centre and blankets spread around the walls. We brought in our tree, which had travelled over twenty-five miles by this time, and hung our candy-bags on it. I went out to talk to some of the school children while we were waiting for the late ones to arrive. There was a tepee beside the house, where the little children seemed to be waiting, for a great variety of giggling little faces poked out of the door, and dodged back again. As Sallie Sitting Bear, one of the schoolgirls, said: "I should think there were about a thousand children in that tepee!"

At last we went in. There were some sixty people there. First Mr. Coolidge made them a little Christmas talk, and then we gave out the things. When everything was off the tree, we found a beautiful pair of moccasins with Mr. Coolidge's name on them, hidden in the branches. They were from Mule.

Many of the Arapahoes are very poor, but they are a progressive people. I remember the wise principal of the school I went to as a girl used to tell us over and over again that no change could come to any individual or people from without. The feeling, the desire, the conviction, must first exist within us. So it seems to be with the Arapahoes. Their ideals have changed. Herbert showed his ditch with, I think, as great pride as ever the men of the generation before his told their war stories or danced their scalp dances. The same energy and strength which made the Arapahoes of thirty years ago a terror to the people of this region are now thrown in the direction of improvement of themselves and of their land. With a little wise guidance and help, this generation should be able to accomplish much. The ideal is there; the material result is sure to follow.

Much can be hoped for a people whose one, heathen, sacred code reads: "Be true to your friends; be brave to your enemies."

A CHRISTMAS TREE THAT BORE SOULS

Spirit of Missions, April 1905

Two years ago a little Christmas-tree gathering was held in a log cabin, chinked with wood, in the interior of this Wind River reservation in Wyoming. The tree was the result of a sudden inspiration, and bore very little in the way of presents. This is inevitable with sudden inspirations when one lives a hundred and fifty miles from even a single-track railroad. But the tree brought together about sixty Arapahoes, afforded many of them their first sight of a Christmas tree, and gave occasion to tell over again a story, which came as new to some of the old camp people, of the wonderful birth of the Saviour.

After Christmas we wrote to the Church Missions House, and asked if we might be sent a few presents for the next year, and were fortunate enough to fall into the kind hands of the Woman's Auxiliary of Ohio.

Not long after the holding of this first tree Mule, the man at whose house it took place, said to Mr. Coolidge that he wished to be baptized, together with the children belonging to his camp. On several occasions afterward, Mr. Coolidge asked him when he wished to receive the Sacrament, and he would always answer, "I am waiting for some great occasion, when a great many of the people shall be gathered together. They will all see what I am doing. I will talk to them and tell them what it means and why I am doing it. I think it will influence others to take the same step." These were, perhaps, not Mule's exact words, for I expect he talked in the expressive sign-language—hand talk, they call it—of the Indians. But that was the gist of what he said. Mule is the head man of a settlement of about a hundred people on Big Wind River.

When the next Christmas came around Mr. Coolidge and I were East, but on our return home, the first day of February, we heard that on the following Saturday, the 6th, there was to be a meeting of the Arapahoes in the council house, about two miles below our place. This council house is a big, rough log building, built and owned by the tribe, as such. It is probably a hundred feet square with an opening in the center of the roof, under which a fire burns, built to warm the building when in use.

As soon as it was decided to hold our second tree at this council, Mule came at once to Mr. Coolidge and told him that this was the occasion for which he had been waiting. We had but little time to make preparations. Two of the young men went up into the canyons and brought down a tree and set it up in the council house. We trimmed it with the presents from Ohio.

On the great day there must have been nearly four hundred people seated in the council house; the women and children on blankets spread on the floor, massed together on two sides of the house; the men, the young and unimportant ones, sitting on their heels in an opposite corner: a bench fashioned along the rear wall held the old men, chiefs and council men, and in still another corner sat the dancers, for Indians, like King David of old, on all great occasions, "dance before the Lord with all their might." The women with their smiling faces were gay with beads and blankets. Many of the little girls wore black velveteen dresses trimmed with elk teeth.

The ceremony opened with a brief service, then those to be baptized came forward, Mule, leading his two grandnieces by the hand, his wife's sister with her boy in her arms, and a young man.

The council house contains no furniture, so our font was a silver bowl we had brought with us standing on the candy barrel over which we had thrown a decent gray blanket. Five persons in all were received into the Church. They were almost the first of the camp people to ask for baptism. Most of our baptisms and all, I think I may say, of our few confirmations, have resulted from work among the children of the Government school, who are under Christian influence from six years of age, when they enter, to eighteen, when they may leave.

This christening made a striking picture! The old log building with its dirt floor and the sunshine streaming in through the hole in the roof; for background, the evergreen tree, the only one in all Little Wind Valley, the bright groups of attentive people, the dancers, jingling with every little movement, every now and then a new one stalking in, wrapped, even to his head, in a long blanket; the clergyman's white vestments contrasting with the riot of color around, and the solemn groups about the improvised font—it seemed to me I had never seen so impressive a service.

That was last year. There were a few, perhaps half a dozen, scattered baptisms during the ensuing year. Then came this last Christmas. Meantime more boxes and barrels arrived from Ohio, and, all through the summer, helped by other friends, we moved and enlarged the Little Wind Church, Our Father's House, and built a new church in Big Wind, the Holy Nativity, as it, too, had its birth at Christmas time. Nor were our white friends the only ones who helped us in this church work—Mule gave the land for the church on his river, and Yellow Calf that for the church on his, five acres each. Indeed, Shovel Foot and other men offered land, but we chose what we thought to be the two most central locations.

This last Christmas we had two trees; first, the one on Big Wind on a twenty-below-zero day. It happened to be, appropriately enough, our first service in the new church, the seed of which was planted two years before at our first Christmas tree. The school children took upon themselves the responsibility of the singing. We had the old Christmas hymns, "Once in royal David's city," and "Hark, the herald angels sing." At the end they wanted me to let them sing, "Jesus, tender Shepherd." I am sure no sweeter "little lambs" ever sang that sweet child's prayer. First at the christening came ten camp children, standing in a solemn row, a little shy, a little awed; only small Richard Wanstall, aged about four, would fidget and keep sitting down on the chancel steps, much to the indignation of his small neighbors, who vainly tried to restrain him. Then came two babies, cousins, and sisters of Mule's great-nieces, baptized the year before; then one young man.

The day the school children were returning from their Christmas holidays we held the last tree at the Little Wind church. The crowd there was so great that we had to take out the seats. The church will not seat more than sixty or seventy, and there must have been close onto three hundred people there. The others stood outside and looked in at the door and windows.

There was the usual service before the distribution of the presents. Then Mr. Coolidge came to the front of the chancel and called on those to be baptized to come forward. Yellow Calf stood by and marshalled the children to the front of the church. There seemed to be swarms of them.

On account of the crowd in the church, Mr. Coolidge had to take the children in groups of five up to the altar (we were using the old silver bowl again, as the font for this church had not yet reached us), and then had them stand in the chancel, facing the altar. Sometimes a father or grandfather would come up with a little one who was too shy to be induced to go up alone. Nannie Grass Hopper clad her baby, Yellow Calf's granddaughter, in the daintiest little white muslin dress, and Lottie Willow's baby was in the prettiest of beaded baby cases.

Afterward, when we counted up, we found that fifty-nine souls had been born that Christmas time into the Church. Surely Mule instituted for us a most fitting way of celebrating the Birthday of the Blessed Lord. Some of the parents and one old grandmother have expressed their intention of being baptized also when next the Bishop visits us.

This mission has been in existence a little over twenty years. Some of its original workers are still working here; some are dead. Things, especially things spiritual, move slowly with Indians, but we believe they move surely; and it seems as though this past Christmas-tide has shown that real growth has been going on, and that results are beginning to be visible.

And may I take this occasion to thank once more, on behalf of these Indians, the many friends who have been moved to send them presents, little and big, food and clothing, money for the sick, money for their churches, furniture to make these buildings churchly? And even more than for the things we, who are trying to help these people to a better life, thank you for the example you have set them with all your kindness. From unseen, unknown, to us as well as to the Indians, people, bound to them by no tie other than that which binds one Christian to another, all this generosity has come. You can be sure it impresses them and makes them think. And, more than any words of ours can do, it impresses upon them the reality of the truths we try to teach them.

My Sunday-school girls are learning the Catechism. Two Sundays ago we had the part after the Lord's Prayer, . . . "That we may worship Him, serve Him, obey Him as we ought to do." Worship and obey they understood, but serving God perplexed them a little until I asked them, "And how about the fifty-two dolls that came with your Christmas things? Who dressed them for you? And the hoods for the little children? And the candy? And the money to build your churches? What were the people doing who sent you all these things?"

"Serving God," they answered with one voice.

Now if only we can teach these Indians to serve God, too, in the same way! We had as many baptisms, nearly sixty, at our trees this year as we had persons present at our first tree two years ago. My hope is that in two years more we can send out gifts from these Indians to make sixty people, who otherwise would have no present knowledge of Christmas, feel it and its meaning, as the Christian friends of these Indians have done to them. That is what we now mean to work toward.

Writings for the *American Indian Magazine*

WANTED: TO SAVE THE BABIES, OR CAPRICORNUS AND A CORONER

American Indian Magazine, January–March 1917

Have you ever lived on a reservation? If so, you have probably sat of a winter evening, cuddled up by your stove and your lamp, cosy in your snug bit of a cabin, your book open on your knees,—the wide frosty mountain night all around you. And so sitting you have just listened to the stillness, broken only so little by the whispering and stirring of your fire. When suddenly, bursting across its peace, your ears have been assailed by a wild weird cry, something between the voice of the torn human soul and brute despair. You are upon your feet at once, of course, peace and reality shattered. Shivers rend you. For well you know what that sound is. Time and again on the reservation you have heard it before. But this time it has come so suddenly, and burst, so eerie and despairing, right into your own home.—

It is the Indian wail for the newly dead.

You rush out of doors, stumbling over your fallen book. In the bitter night cold of those high altitudes you wrap up your hands in your apron. Thus you stand listening, your heart in your ears. Half a mile over there across the valley lies the high road, there you can hear the rattle and clatter of an Indian "issue" wagon—the issue wagons rattle more than some—you can even distinguish the thudding of the ponies' feet on the iron ground.[1] Then that wail is lifted again, rising as high as the frosty stars; unreal, and yet the only real thing in the whole wide night; aspiring; despairing; trembling up towards that nebulous path on which tonight a new and shivering soul is journeying.

"Is it Betty's baby? Is it Sadie's? Both those little ones were sick; dying both of them, or is it little May?"

Tomorrow somebody will ride through the ranch with the news, the blind boy, He-sits-in-the-night, perhaps; or some woman will drop in to use your sewing machine, or some man to discuss the lease situation; then you will know. Tonight you can only stand alone and aloof, listening, and wondering.

So when the Commissioner sends out a pamphlet entitled: "Save the Babies," your heart jumps and you read it with hungry eyes.

Of course you have long known the death statistics, 15 per 1000 per annum among the whites, 30–32 among the Indians. Visualized you realize what these figures mean; that death among the whites is mainly confined to its own field, that old age, with only here and there serious depredations among the able-bodied and promising; while with the Indians it is not confined at all. It is everywhere; but mostly, perhaps, in the cradle. You know well that on that ordinary and typical reservation on which you happen to live that proposition means that not one family can you recall that has not lost a child!

Generally the little new-comers are born fat and healthy. For the first year, and over, their rotund, funny little noticing faces peer out at you from under the hood of the baby cases. Then suddenly they begin to change. As you notice them outside in the agency store they appear faded and thin. When next you see them they are coughing. You go down to visit them in the camp and to your great embarrassment you intrude upon a medicine making scene. The sick baby, scrupulously clean, and neatly combed and dressed, but limp and emaciated, the sacred red paint upon its brow, lies across its mother's knees. Everything seems to stop while you are there. An unwonted stillness prevails. All are most courteous, but, feeling yourself in an awkward situation, you hurry away.

Not long afterwards comes that bitter wail across the night.

Well, the pamphlet says: Teach, Urge, Improve, Extend. But as you read it you find yourself Wondering whether its author has ever lived neighbor to the Indians on any reservation, has ever seen the sacred paint on little dying faces or ever heard the cry across the night.

Teach! Almost all the mothers of today have been taught and for twelve of their first eighteen years, in the Government Indian Schools. Urge! Most of them have been most constantly and emphatically urged by teachers and preachers and friends. And many of them are anxious to follow the urging, but one young mother is so feeble to withstand the pressure of a whole tribe.

Improve! Most of them and their agencies, and even their homes, have been improved according to "white" ideas. And to many of them the services of some sort of a hospital have been extended, as also those of a field matron. Two generations of school girls, the mothers and grandmothers of today, are the fruit of this teaching and urging and improving; and yet you do not see much advance beyond the old careless—or rather, lawless—insanitary, futile ways of the past. Why? You ask. Why?

There are two deficiencies in Indian life that contribute, you decide, more than any other causes to the appalling degree of mortality, particularly amongst the babies. One is the absolute lack of a milk supply, supplementary to nature's own. So much so, in fact, that the Indian word milk—or "food-water," as he calls it—implies exclusively one kind. If he means cow's milk, he says cow's milk.

When at the age of a year or a year and a half, the first baby is supplanted by the new little brother, the fountain from which he has hitherto freely drawn of life and peace is suddenly denied him, he must go from that bounty to what? Cow's milk, as is the case with the white babies? But if the little brother happens to come in the late winter or early spring, when the camps and all that pertains to them are at their hungriest, no one will have any hay left to feed the cows. Also the Indian country is mainly unfenced, so, even if the cow is able to find sustenance ranging on the barren winter hills, she will be unavailable for a baby. Besides, the red issue cattle are poor milkers. It would be hard indeed, even under favorable conditions, to coax the milk of one of them to last on from one calf to the next. And again, many of them are just wild range cattle. You do know of one family, perhaps, who, in extremity milked one of their cows for an ailing baby. To do so they were obliged to drive the animal into the branding pen, secure it there with gates, and extract what milk they might from it from between the boards of the fence.

There is of course canned milk in plenty at the trader's store, but in these stores, although a form must be gone through in order to obtain a license to open one, after that is once successfully done, prices are absolutely unrestricted by the Government or other control; many articles are charged for at one hundred per cent higher than the universal prices elsewhere, and canned milk is among the luxuries beyond the Indian purse.

So the camp babies are forced to go from their original plenteous fare, to the meagre larder of the camps, to boiled meat and fried bread and sweetened coffee, a desperate menu for the semi-toothless. The one-time fatling grows gaunt and peaked and by the time its second birthday comes round, more often than not it is sleeping in some sunny fold of the hills, snugly wrapped in its beaded and beribboned baby case.

But that babies should die for the sheer lack of milk seems certainly unnecessary. It appears to you that there must be some milk supply adaptable to the Indians' mode of living. And indeed, such is the case, for nature has provided a wet-nurse, the friend and partner of the poor the world around, the saviour of countless peasant babies; one whose rapacious appetite and stomach are appalled at nothing, to whom winter grease-wood and rabbit-brush and bare willow twigs would provide a feast, whose glassy eye could spy out the belated blades of grass among the sagebrush; the faithful, though much ridiculed Harlem Goat.

When camp was moved a goat or two might readily find place to travel in the tail of an Indian wagon. Often have you seen the weak colts transported thus. The goat could live and thrive where the camp did. And also, beside it, might survive, even through the perilous second year, under the benevolent sign of Capricornus, that most precious fatling.

But not all Indian babies are precious. Not all—the Indians are advancing in civilization—are wanted. And of those who are really cherished, many must yield to the unchecked demands of custom and precedent. You know of one tribe at least whose custom it is to send its mothers, at the hour of childbirth, out from the warm accustomed cabin or tepee into a small frail lodge hastily erected, often right upon the snow. There she and her new born must stay for a period of two weeks or longer. Many mothers have died from the exposure this custom imposed on them. You have talked to the young women, the ex-school girls, about this. "We don't want to go out there to have our babies," they say. "It is cold, and the bed is thin and hard. And it is wet in the spring time! Louise's mother died that way, and the baby too. They had to put the tepee up right on the snow, and there came the Chinook wind and melted it, and water rose up over the quilts and wet them both. It was in the night and she was alone out there. We don't like going out there but the old women make us. They tell us that nobody would think we were nice if we stayed in the house. They say that our husbands wouldn't think we were, and everybody would talk about us."

And so, in this case, the twelve years of teaching in the Government school, although they have indeed in a sense taken root, have through outside causes failed of their ultimate object.

Of the not wanted babies there are lives among the Indians as among the whites than can only be saved through the intervention of the law. At present *deaths on a reservation are absolutely unquestioned.* There exists indeed in the West the Coroner, and plenty of him. But always he lives outside the confines of the reservation. He is always the Coroner of the whites. Their business is his business, not the Indians! He drives about in his old dust covered Fremont buggy, behind his pair of rangy cayuses. Many is the distant place to which his grim duty calls him, many the miles of broken Bad Lands he lumbers across, many the creek in flood that he negotiates. Often in his meanderings he must pass over a bit of the reservation, but never does he stop there—except in the case of the death of some white man or negro or Chinese laundryman. No, he drives on, leaving Death squatting, satiated and at home, within the boundary lines that mark the Indians off from the rest of humanity.

You often, do you not, wonder whether the tax payers of this country, they who vote a sum of four million a year to run the Indian Bureau, and incidentally the reservations, realize this fact, that death in the Indian country exists unchallenged. In fact as things stand at present it is decidedly to the advantage of the Indians to hide from the agency the knowledge of a death—for some of their dead have drawn rations and many have shared, to the benefit of their surviving relations, in the disbursement of the per capita tribal funds.

Here is a list of cases, of which you happen to have personal knowledge, which a coroner might have investigated to the advantage of justice and humanity.

(1) A little boy, in his mother's tepee, was accidently shot by some white men out hunting. He lived for a week after the accident. During that time he was attended by the most powerful medicine woman of the tribe. Among other ministrations she probed the wound with a willow twig, probably prepared with some special "medicine." What the child finally died from—that is, whether directly from the wound or from a later infection—no one knows

for no one competent to judge ever saw the child, although the case made a great stir and took place close to the sub-agency where the Government doctor had an office.

(2) Two little souls in succession slipped out from their bodies, one one year, one the next and this almost before they had established a separate existence from that of their mother. This was at White Buffalo's camp, and happened simply because at the difficult moment of birth they found no hand competent to help them. An old and doting grandmother, with a pride in her own ability, would not listen to the pleading of the young mother and send for the Agency physician, fearing to see her methods superseded. So the poor mother might only tragically endure, and later weep for her lost babies, her lank hair falling loose in mourning about her anguished face. Both of these births took place close to the Agency.

(3) Then there was the little girl whom nobody wanted. Her young mother married after her birth, but a man other than her reputed father, and, as the Indians so poignantly express it, "threw her away." She found asylum in the camp of an austere and indifferent man and his equally hard-hearted wife. On one bitter cold night as she slept alone—which in itself is most unusual in the case of a child—insufficiently covered and in the chilly front part of the tent, the camp dogs crept in and snuggled about her for warmth. In the morning it was found that they had smothered her to death. No one was ever held responsible.

(4) Another case was that of the child who died within a few days of its birth because it was administered to with infected scissors. Again by a grandmother who refused to have the doctor in—until too late. Afterwards the mother herself explained to you about it, "What could he know about it. My mother has had eight children. Has he ever borne a child?"

(5) Another is that baby who, at the moment of difficult birth, loses all that life has offered it, its mother. For even before its first cry, her soul has winged its way out from the misery of the smoky tepee. Afterwards, amid the tears of the camp, the little new-born orphan, is swaddled in its bright calico squares—neat with its mother's stitches—unwashed, but with face and head anointed with the sacred red paint, and is laid on the hard breast of all that remains of its earthly mother. And so, wrapped in new bought quilts, the dead and the living are hidden away together in a shallow grave.

(6) And there was the baby who, because "fatherless" was not wanted, and who when it died, as conveniently as mysteriously, was by its own shameless mother, thrust into a rawhide, parfleche case and cast forth among the rocks, and but scantly covered by them. Then the coyotes came nosing, and dragged it forth. The agency doctor knew of this case for in her extremity the young woman had called him in, because in her case no fond grandmother intervened. He reported that the child had been born healthy, and, when word of its premature death reached him he asserted that he would at once take up the case with the Agent. This, however, he failed to do. On being questioned later he stated that he felt that reporting the case to the Agent would do no good as it was really nobody's business to prosecute.

(7) And last of all this sorrowful list was the baby of some mixed bloods who died at the Agency of diphtheria, as also nearly died of the same disease a young white girl, the daughter of one of the agency employees. This because the Government school authorities grew tired of maintaining a long and troublesome quarantine, and finally sent all the well children home, holding the affected ones at the school. No choice as to receiving the children was given to the camp people, for these were not sent for to come and fetch the pupils, as was the custom. Instead, the youngsters were dispatched afoot, distributing themselves and the contagion broadcast over the fifty square miles of the reservation.

You could of course prolong this list almost indefinitely, did you not fear that it is already too long. What you want to show is that, as with the whites, both teaching, and laws, are required to be effective. The Indians suffer from too many laws, as things stand, but they also suffer from the absence of certain laws. Just as the children have been compelled to attend school and now, generally speaking, do so universally—barring a few very remote tribes, such as the Navajo—so a death certificate should be obligatory, as should some reputable doctor's attendance at childbirth. These requirements, together with the restricted practice of the medicine men and a closer supervision from headquarters of the way the laws are applied at the agencies; with the support of Capricornus before, and the backing of the coroner afterwards, would in your opinion based on your years of experience, do something at least toward really lowering the present abnormal Indian death rate.

THE CARPENTER WHO HAD NO ONE TO SET HIM STRAIGHT

American Indian Magazine, April–June 1917

Daniel Blind Bull was building a house (one must call it a house because it was nothing else) but had it been any less than it was it would have failed of its intention. Daniel had driven but a little way into the mountains for his logs; he might have gone farther and fared better, but he was not particular. As a builder of houses his imagination ran but a little beyond his skill. So he took what fell readiest to his hands, thereby saving work to both himself and his team.

Having unloaded his logs at the site of his intended dwelling he drove up to the Agency store where he bought nails in two sizes and half a window. Hammer, saw, and spade he borrowed from a more prosperous neighbor. Then he began the work of construction. His hands he guided by his eye, being altogether innocent of the science of measurement. From a dirt floor, slightly levelled, in a form which he believed to be a parallelogram, he began to erect his weak-kneed structure. He carried on the piling up of logs until the walls reached the least possible elevation compatible with safety to heads. Then he quit to raise his roof beams. These he covered with poles, eventually heaping earth to the thickness of nearly a foot upon the whole. In his roof he had left a square hole, faced with an old split five gallon oil can. This was the place through which the stove-pipe would protrude. In the walls likewise he had made two openings, one for his door, the other for the half-window. These he framed in axe-hewn logs. The chinks between the wall logs he stopped with chips and bits of stick, and finally with mud. To apply this last he used, in lieu of a trowel, his spade or a bit of board.

The most difficult feat to accomplish next to the making of the door, itself a triumph of ingenuity, was the fitting of it and of the window into their bossy frames.

At last, however, the thing was done. It had consumed an undue amount of time in the making. The cold weather was already upon us. On all sides I heard talk of this house; from girls coming in to sew on my machine, from mothers seeking advice and medicine for ailing children, from neighbors running in to borrow baking powder or coal oil or to pass on to me some bit of gossip.

"Dan's got his house done."

"So I heard."

"The door's awful crooked."

"So's the window."

"He's banked it up all around but it's cold."

"His wife, she says she goin' to put her tent up 'long side that house an' stay in that, cause that house it ain't only fit to live in in summer, she say."

"But didn't he chink it?"

"Yes, he try to but them holes they so big the mud wouldn't stick. It's all awful crooked."

"Why didn't he get somebody to help him?"

"Who could have helped him?"

"Well, the Agency carpenter might have told him some things."

"He did ask him. He asked him to come down." In their eagerness they both spoke at once.

"That's the right thing to have done."

"But he wouldn't come."

"He said nobody never asked him to do that before."

"Was he—was he busy?"

"No-o."

"They're making some repairs on the agent's house, maybe—."

"No, he wasn't doin' nothin'."

"Dan likes to build. He's always wantin' to learn how."

"Simon Little Dog helped him some."

"I expect Simon doesn't know much about carpentry, though."

"He don't but he's willin'?"

"And the Agency carpenter wasn't."

"I guess it was cold for him to drive way down to Dan's place."

"It's only five miles. Wasn't cold for you to drive up here."

They laughed.

Later Dan's wife came. She sat by the stove warming fingers and toes and peering curiously about my room. I saw her eyes travel from window to door, from door to corners.

"Are you living in your new house?"

She snuffed a little contemptuously, settled her fat baby more solidly on her knees.

"No," she said. "It's too cold for the baby. That ain't no house. It's just a shed. We keep the harness and saddles in there, and the plow." She looked at me a little disagreeably. "They don't mind the wind," she said. Then she repented. "But Dan he work hard, only he don't know how, and there's nobody around here to tell him nothin'. Some day I guess we'll be taking them logs down and burn 'em. They'll do for fire-wood anyhow." And she gave a little sigh, straightening up the sagging baby.

THE WHITE PLAGUE

American Indian Magazine, July–September 1917

He came back to us from a non-reservation school whither he had gone at the price of great sacrifices, and coming he brought with him a wife, an alien wife, an Indian girl but of an Eastern tribe. To a people as clannish as are the members of his tribe the fact of her strangeness was most disconcerting. She could not speak their tongue. She was unfamiliar with their ways. She could not be proud with their cherished pride of race. But he wrote that he was coming and with her. His letter was passed about the camps.

He had learned a trade at his non-reservation school. He was a baker, and that position at our school being left unexpectedly vacant, he was coming home to fill it.

But when he came we saw that it mattered little whether or not she was alien for soon she would be even further removed from us than she was by the fact of her birth, by, indeed, the grasping implacable hand of Death. Her days were numbered. The shadow lay upon her face.

The position of baker is one of the least in point of honor and of pay of all those in a government boarding school. On account of the latter fact this couple could not very well join the school mess, costing as it did from twelve to fourteen dollars each per month. Double this sum was expense not to be thought of for them.

They went to the superintendent begging a couple of rooms, one room even, anywhere—there was none of the few school cottages vacant just then—neither were there vacant any possible house-keeping rooms.

The young baker stared helplessly at the superintendent.

"There are two rooms in the bakery, the one where the ovens are, and the mixing room . . ."

"You mean that you think that your wife might cook in the mixing room?"

"I thought of it."

"I think I could find you a stove."

"She would be very glad."

And so the matter was arranged. In the mixing room where stood the tubs of rising dough they set up their little stove and table. Here while the young baker directed the efforts of the boys of his "detail," the young wife cooked and coughed.

The Winter slipped by. Spring came. The young wife approached her end, or rather the fate that awaited her surged up out of the abyss to engulf her. They could not take her to her husband's people, to dingy cabin or huddled hut to die, for she knew nothing of life as these "blanket" Indians lived it. And also if she had not the pride of their race she had at least that of her own. So he left with her at last as he had come, travelled with the frail wraith of her to the home of her people.

And he buried her there. After a while he wrote and told us of her end.

A Tale of the Boy Who Coughed

The little boy sat on the steps of the boys' building and coughed and smiled and coughed again. His clothes hung awkwardly upon his lean little body. His thin hands were clutched about his skeleton shins. The sun of Spring beat down upon him and the little boy turned an eager back to the warmth of its rays.

The matron followed my lingering glance.

"We've sent him away three times, and three times he's come back. He says there's nothing to eat at home. And he's got a little shaver of a brother here. He seems to think the small chap needs him. He doesn't go to the school-room. He can't. Indeed he doesn't do anything but sit in the sun or up against the steam pipes, and eat, and go to bed."

"I think I never saw so thin a child!"

"He shouldn't be here. If an inspector were to see him he would certainly make trouble for us. It is against all the regulations to keep a child in his condition with the other children."

"Does he—does he sleep with them?"

The matron made an impatient gesture. "We have only the one dormitory."

"Of course, I know."

"We are as full as we can be. Anyhow, we've tried to send him away. He just won't stay at home."

"What will become of him—in the end?"

"In the end? They will send someone horseback, flying, for his people. And they will come and carry him out (his parents are not living) and before they will have reached the Agency we shall hear them crying. That's the way it was with Minnie Badger and little Nancy; you remember her. They died in the wagon, both of them."

"Can you not send him home again? Should you not do it?"

The matron looked over her shoulder at the little shrunken bundle backed toward the sun.

"I don't know what the superintendent could do," she said. "I couldn't."

A Family Reaping

We had a way of staring at her with incredulous eyes for she was the luckiest one of us all, the pampered of fate, the immune one, the sole triumphant mother. For she had had two children and they were both living. And even as we stared at her we turned our own eyes to the hills, the engulfing hills where we had laid our own. And if we were at all lucky, we reached out our hands toward our spared little ones. But some of us could but fold our hands, keeping our eyes upon the ground.

Then her first child, a little girl of nearly two, fell ill. She with her family had spent a part of the preceding winter with an old friend, a woman of middle age, the mother of one son, and whose only son was dying. They had gone for but a little visit, but seeing the distress of the mother soon to be torn from her one living child, they had remained to do for mother and son what they could.

He was a gentle young man, patient in his distress, his eyes very touching because of the little rebellious flame of hope that would burn in them, even to the very end. The little girl of nearly two was a great solace to him. On the ground, at meal times, she sat beside him, while he fed and tended her; dressed her even, assaying to smooth her downy hair, rebellious in its miniature braids. The young mother whose arms were full with her new born, was thankful for the help, for the young father must needs be absent the greater portion of the time earning money to feed them all, his hosts as well as his own.

At length the young man died, and the camp was broken up.

And then we heard that the child, the one that was nearly two, was dying. The disease in her had travelled with the consuming rapidity of flame. She lay a fluttering pallid thing upon the mother's arm, her great eyes resting upon us; not shy anymore, she was past that; not even interested, and so nearly dead that but one desire yet persisted in her, the wish to be by day or night upon her mother's arm, her great eyes resting upon us; not shy anymore, she was child on one arm, the new born on the other. But always her eyes were upon the face of the dying one; steadily upon it, patiently, but with despair.

We came and looked upon her, we who so recently had envied her. We saw the child, we saw her look, and seeing we crept away, our hands reaching again for our own.

Then the little one died. And the young mother, patient and despairing, did not shift the new-born into the other's place, and sat as before, still staring, still patient.

Suddenly the littlest one grew ill. Pneumonia we judged from what we heard, though the Indians do not differentiate diseases. And in three days of staring, of patient, of augmenting despair, in the mother's arms, the baby also died. They carried her, snug in her "beaded" cradle, gay with red flannel and purple ribbons, a silk handkerchief drawn across her face, and laid her in the obliterating ground.

Then again we went to see the mother. She who had been so busy, so harassed, now sat idle, her futile hands hidden beneath her shawl. She looked at us, she spoke to us, she even roused herself to a semblance of her old manner. She laughed a little.

It was three months after that that her grandmother came with her into our place. It was summertime and as I happened to be outside she did not go into the house but sank down upon the ground in the shade of a wagon, leaning back against a wheel. She spoke, but only in a whisper. It was the grandmother with signs who told us what had happened.

It seemed that they had been on their way on foot up to the Agency when just outside of our fence she had been seized with a hemorrhage, her first one. Watching the talk of the old hands, I understood only too well. It had left her breathless and voiceless, her hair clinging to her clammy forehead.

Behind the wagon the old woman wiped away her furtive tears.

In a half hour's time the young woman felt better and together she and the grandmother walked slowly down the valley toward their home.

A year, almost to the day, from the death of the young man, beside her babies with tears and lamenting they laid this young mother upon the warm, all-embracing bosom of the earth.

JUSTICE ON A RESERVATION: A STORY OF AN ACTUAL HAPPENING

American Indian Magazine, Spring 1918

He was a young man of roving eye and taking ways, of ardent, rather obvious glance, and—though this latter fact was of course incidental—he was also a member of the Indian mounted police force.

Now it was the custom, during the term of office of a certain school superintendent who experienced difficulty in controlling his ill-understood charges, to keep one of the police force stationed on the school grounds to watch, to report and to restrain. So he of the roving eye was delegated to that work. His name, by the way, was Harry Little Dog. He was allowed to place himself where he pleased about the plant so long as he kept himself in evidence, and the large tin star upon his breast proclaimed to curious student eyes the authority he represented. If his clothes were unduly vivid, if ribbons adorned his hat, if sheepskin shaps decked his person; if, and most of all, his roving eye went forth constantly seeking encounter, these were decidedly incidentals which concerned no one but himself. And if the girls—the older girls—passed frequently down the steps of the dormitory building on their way to or from the school room, or on household duties bent; if their eyes, roving also, met his, why—youth is youth, and life at a government boarding school for pupils and policeman alike is uneventful in the extreme.

After several days of these visual encounters, Pauline, the pretty one, issued forth from the dormitory door and passed on down the steps into the basement, a steaming bucket of hot water in one hand, a mop in the other. Her sleek braid was looped up with a big ribbon bow and as she walked, slowly, she peered back over her shoulder. It seemed as though it was not of his own volition that he, looking at her clapped his heels to his pony's sides, so that even as she disappeared within the basement door his horse gave a great bound in her direction. Then, strangely enough as the horse leaped he recollected suddenly that that very morning he had been instructed to go at once and see to something—let me see, was it—about steam pipes? Just what was said to have been wrong with them or where the trouble was to be found he really could not recall, but obviously the basement was a likely place to which to go to find disordered steam pipes. He swung down from his horse and, straight, vivid, and jingling he strode up the terrace steps two at a time and down the basement ones with equal speed.

Now the superintendent sat at his office window and gazed vacantly about him. His eyes ranged the dusty, crude room, the sunlit valley without. He looked because he had eyes, but having little above the eyes he saw not much more deeply. But he noted the direction taken by pretty Pauline, and later by Harry.

In one corner of his office the steam pipes rattled and dripped spasmodically. A tin basin caught most of the spurting flow. The sound of the falling water recalled to him that he himself that morning had told Harry about this leak which needed instant repairing. He had also instructed him as to the whereabouts of the tools that he would need to mend it. And Harry had listened, seemingly, though his roving eyes were questing about somewhere in the region of the superintendent's back. The man noting the young fellow's careless attitude, a sort of fury, dumb and impotent, had shaken him. Of course it was in no wise the duties of a policeman to turn plumber—but lines are not drawn too finely in the Indian service. The superintendent demanded at least obedience. Subsequently he had noticed Harry for a good three hours sitting his horse in idleness while the steam pipes dripped and a little black tongue of water licked out over the office door. And then suddenly the policeman had come to life and had leaped from his horse and sped away to be engulfed by the basement door, whither also had gone that child, Pauline, (the superintendent used another noun) the prettiest and most troublesome girl in the school.

The man was constitutionally better at glowering than he was at reprimand; but this time he decided instantly that he had stood enough. He got suddenly to his feet. He was a heavy man but his tread was light as though he was one who would preferably go without attracting attention, and come without warning. So now on speeding, soundless feet he descended the basement stairs.

What happened after he arrived there has probably never been correctly told. The three who took part in the scene gave subsequently each a different version of it.

Before Harry was finally arrested by the civil authorities the whole affair was threshed over in the presence of the agent. At the investigation Pauline admitted that when the superintendent had come upon them—they had not heard a sound of his approach—she and Harry had been "skylarkin'." When further questioned as to what she meant she had ducked her head, laughed out of the corners of her eyes and elucidated: "Oh! kind of gigglin.'" Then further asked whether she had been a witness of what the superintendent claimed Harry had done to him she replied at once that indeed she had not, in fact in her own opinion Harry had done nothing of what was alleged. Her testimony though clear and positive enough was considered—and not unnaturally—to be prejudiced.

Harry's version was that he—Harry—had been made mad at the very moment of the superintendent's entry, at something the man had said—in fact, at a certain name that he had called Pauline.—The girl listening flushed a little.—When pressed Harry refused to repeat it. He had then strode up close in front of the older man and had bestowed upon him, in retaliation, an ugly epithet. Then the superintendent had lifted one of his fat hands—Harry turned supercilious eyes upon the offending member—and had struck him upon the side of his face. On receiving the blow involuntarily his own hand had flown to the gun upon his hip, though he had not drawn it from its scabbard. He was very insistent upon this latter point. And as soon as he had realized what he was doing, or seeming to be doing, he had recalled his impetuous hand.

The young policeman stood straight; he was exceedingly good-looking in his gay clothes; he spoke in a fiery, nonchalant manner, withered the fat superintendent with an occasional contemptuous glance. Pauline's eyes were continually busy seeking his, then fleeing away only to be lured to him again.

At last, ponderously and with unction, the superintendent told his story. He first spoke of the incident of the leaky steam pipe, magnifying a little the extent of the damage, repeating his curt command to Harry as though it had been a sort of urgent appeal. Then he had gone on to say that soon after he had noticed Pauline, mop in hand, going into the basement and that the thought had come to him that perhaps some further pipe trouble had been discovered and that the girl had been sent there to mop up the flow.

Pauline interrupted him at once. "But I had a bucket of hot water in my hand." Her glance was on him, contemptuously also.

"Did you, my dear? Well? I didn't notice that."

Pauline's eyes sought Harry's.

The superintendent continued. On reaching the basement he had been somewhat horrified to see—to see—"Well, I won't say they were embracing."

"What will you say they were doing?" asked the agent.

"Skylarkin'," murmured Pauline.

"—that they were seemingly near to doing so," continued the unctuous voice. "This young girl is temporarily at least in my care therefore I confronted the man at once, remonstrating with him."

"What that word mean?" put in Harry.

Several glances silenced him.

"I suppose I spoke with undue vehemence. I know that I shook my finger in his face—"

"Not my face," remarked Harry.

"Silence! Silence!" said the agent. "You've had your turn."

"—then quick as a flash he whipped out his gun from the scabbard and aimed it at me. His finger was on the trigger, his eyes looked like those of a maddened beast. I confess I was thoroughly frightened."

There followed a moment of silence. Then from the back of the room a voice spoke. "If Harry pulled his gun on him at all I'm sure it was in rather a bad jest. He—he's somewhat of a 'Smart Alec.'"

"He probably never did pull it on him, as he—Harry—said," grunted someone. "Mr. Hodges was excited. He says as much himself. Pauline, did he pull his gun on him?"

The agent rapped loudly on the table. "I beg your pardon but I am under the impression that I am the one conducting this inquiry."

"Oh! All right. You are. Excuse me."

Thus the affair dragged, or was jerked on. In the end the agent not being able to arrive at any satisfactory conclusion turned the case over to the local authorities. That move culminated in Harry being arrested and taken to Rawdon, the county seat, fifteen miles distant, to jail. Court was held in Rawdon twice a year, therefore for five months did Harry remain immured in the small stale lock-up with its shifting, uneasy tenantry, no white man being willing and no Indian able, to go bail for him.

At last his case came to trial before a jury of his so-called peers; old-timers whose memories reached back to the days of frontier warfare and constant Indian depredations, or younger men living on ranches neighboring to the reservation, who looked constantly with green-tinged eyes upon the Indian farms across the border lying untilled, and of course, untaxed, while they on their side sweated to support themselves and the state.

The testimony, given this time without side-remark, was repeated. Harry demanded an interpreter and got one, though of what particular benefit his services were is not plain. The trial resulted in Harry being sent to the penitentiary at Rock Creek for fifteen months. Just before Harry's actual arrest we about the Agency were being thrilled by the fragmentary reports that reached us that a murder had been committed in a certain distant part of the reservation. At the Agency office little seemed to be known of it. What I gathered of it I learned mostly from whispers going stealthily about the camps.

Whittington was the name of the Indian who had done the killing. He was not an Arapahoe but a member of the other tribe living upon the same reservation. He was an old, evil, cynical man, a mescal eater, a gambler, a man possessed of an evil old wife whom he seemed neither to condemn nor to drive away; a careless, misanthropic, secretive old man who did not seek nor give friendship.

The story was that in a certain "draw," in the remote Bad Lands, he had come upon an old man called Rides Last and between them a discussion had ensued relative to a horse ridden by Rides Last but claimed by Whittington. In the quarrel Rides Last—so said Whittington—had pulled his gun on him and he, Whittington, had been obliged to shoot in self-defense. Incidentally the old man had been killed.

At last Whittington came and reported the happening to the agent, but not however until long after the story was in every mouth in the camps.

After some delay and a few weak efforts on the part of the agent to obtain evidence the matter was turned over to the county officials. It really would seem almost an empty formality even to arrest the man. He asserted that there were no witnesses to his deed and common sense confirmed his statement. The old man who had been killed was almost without friends, no one seemed to take much interest in his side of the case.

Then a very adventurous person whispered something in my ear. "There *were* witnesses. Two 'Rapahoe women seen it. They were gatherin' wood that day, a good way off of course, but they seen." These women it seemed believed that the old man had not drawn his gun first—nor indeed at all. They had been, naturally, very much shocked by what they had so advertently witnessed, and after the nature of their kind were all for keeping the fact and their relation to it hidden. Not a word indeed had they spoken till the story of the crime was being told broadcast.

I passed on this bit of news. Finally some white person reported it definitely to the agent.

"Indeed," said he. On a scrap of paper he jotted down some sketchy notes. "Unfortunate these alleged witnesses did not make their connection with the affair known earlier. Of course now that the investigation had been conducted and concluded by me, it seems hardly justifiable to reopen it—at any rate they must have been at a great distance off. Then Whittington, you know, is really one of my best and most reliable men, head of my police force and all that. I rely on him greatly. And the women who claim to have seen the event are Arapahoes. Now would their testimony against one of the other tribes with whom they are known to be at constant odds, be of value? Really I can't think so. And after all the affair was entirely between Indians—there was no white man in any way involved. That being the case I should hardly feel justified, as I said, in taking the matter up again. You understand."

I remember the day the sheriff came for Harry. The buggy containing the two men stopped before the Agency office. The sheriff handed the reins to the prisoner and jumped down to go inside. He was seeking an overcoat and arctics to borrow for his charge who had neither. The weather was very cold and the drive of fifteen miles could not be accomplished in less than an hour and a half. During the wait quite a group of Indians had time to gather. They were all mounted; there were guns in evidence. There seemed to be very plainly visible a good deal of excitement and dissatisfaction. It almost looked as though there was going to be trouble; a flash in the pan, to be followed to those responsible by the usual consequences.

But nothing untoward did happen. For a mile or two the Indians scampered and crowded about the sheriff's buggy, naked rifles held across saddles. Faces were grim, eyes hard. The prisoner's roving glance strayed from friend to friend. But no word was said. Finally the low hills about the valley being reached, one of the riders swung his horse about and started homeward, a little uncertainly. Others followed suit. Then doggedly in a long irregular line they all loped back into the valley.

Just before the group of riders left the prisoner, however, they had all passed close in front of Whittington's camp. He stood before his tent bareheaded, shading his eyes with his hand; lean, slouching, unkempt, bold, sardonic, cunning; his willful, disgraceful old wife beside him, staring likewise after the flying group.

All of us who were about the Agency at the time rushed out to see the excitement. A man's voice at my elbow spoke to me suddenly. "The old fellow over there by the tent is the one that's said to have done that killin', ain't he?" I glanced around. The voice belonged to an old mule-skinner of some local reputation. "And the young man ridin' with the sheriff is likewise said to have pulled his gun at the wrong time. An officer using his authority against—well, against authority. Say, they most generally picture her with a blindfold on, don't they?"

"What? Blindfold? Who?"

He laughed a boyish, hearty laugh. "Why, Justice."

"Justice?"

"I've worked a long time with a pack outfit, mules, you know. And I savvy all about blindfolds. We most always have to blindfold the mules before we can pack 'em. If we didn't they'd kick every blame thing to smithereens. May be that old girl, you savvy who I mean, well, may be around in this Injun country anyhow, you got to treat that old girl Justice the same way."

Letters

DEAREST REDDY, 1896–1901

July 4, 1896

HOTEL MANHATTAN, NEW YORK CITY, NEW YORK

Dearest Anne,

I'm nearly bursting with delight for I don't see any reason why I shouldn't start for Wyo. a week from next Monday or Tuesday!!!!!!!! This statement warrants even more exclamation points, I think. To say I am glad is so inadequate, it is absolutely foolish. My dear, since last I wrote you, I have even had awful misgivings about being able to come at all. Doesn't this sound ominous? You see when I went home from Boston in the first part of June and came down here after Kate Sanford's wedding, I found my uncle really awfully ill. He has kidney trouble and has been getting steadily worse for about a year. Of course, for a man of his age this is pretty serious. My aunt was all alone and in a dreadful state of worry. Nobody knew what was going to happen next, or when it would come. You can imagine Auntie's frame of mind. Well, I stayed until Gussie Brown's wedding, June 17th, and then came back the day after instead of going to Cooperstown to the Gregorys as I had expected to do. I stayed a week then went to the Gregorys for that time and expected to go from there to Schroon Lake in the Adirondacks for the same amount of time. Just the day before I was to have started I got a letter from Evie Breslin (I was going to Schroon with Madge) saying that Madge was very ill with malarial fever. It seems they are afraid of heart failure and Madge is in a very critical state. I was thunderstruck! as you can imagine. I feel awfully worried about poor old Madge. You know she has been very delicate for a couple of years past. Well, I came home from Cooperstown in consequence of all this and can therefore start for the good Laramie all the sooner. Uncle is certainly better. At any rate for the present, and Auntie is very much cheered up, so I can come with a clear conscience. As for Pacci![1] I don't suppose I shall really bring him when it comes to the point, but how I shall even get along without the angel all that time is more than I know!! I think you will probably see him tumbling out the car behind his mother, but I am not sure. Anne, dear, I *know* you would love him now. He never does any naughty little thing even in the stable! And he minds before you have spoken to him thrice! He is a perfect sweet, and his mother's heart grows large within her when she thinks about him. I really am afraid he'll come. Pompey was sweet to be so glad to see you. I had a dreadful shock when I got back from Boston. I thought Pacci didn't know me. Being an undemonstrative child he didn't say anything when he saw me, but he didn't wish to leave me for an instant. Just now he is sitting outside the window looking mournfully in. Enough of Pacci! As for seeing you again, words simply are not to express any sentiments on that subject. Until I read yr. letter I didn't know what it was my innards were craving for. That's just what I want, "a good summer in my in'ards." And after the summer work, with a capital "W." We must talk things over a lot. Next winter sees me settled of something, it doesn't make much difference what. Lou and I talked a good deal about going to Germany. Of course, it was only *hope* on both sides. But Anne we all feel that we *must* do something and now it only remains to decide. *Don't* speak to me with such scorn about *gooseberries*! Indeed, Anne, I really hoped for that which you *didn't* write me. I am most anxious to see "Francis (Bennett!)." He must be a very sensible person, at any rate. I judge *a-priori!!!!!!* I feel quite idiotic today, so you mustn't put the dullness of this letter down to my fault. If I had had ink and paper on the train yesterday I could have written you in blank verse. I felt like it. "'Twas ever thus, from childhood's hour!" More's the pity. Now, do write me again, *here*, and tell me you still want me and that you are *sure* you want the Thunder Bolt.[2] I am sure Pompey was never better than Pacci reformed. By the way, I got an awfully nice letter from Nellie Hart[3] a little while ago, asking me to come up to their place near Denver, Grand Lake, I believe. Wasn't that nice of her?

Give my best love to Mrs. Talbot and the Bishop. If ever you saw a chuckling person, it will be G. D. as she tumbles out of the car at Laramie.

Monday or Tuesday a week after next; that will be the 13th or 14th from New York. I will telegraph you anyway the day I start.

Joy!
Grace

Kiss Pompey's black nose for his Auntie Grace.

April 2, 1897
HOTEL DEL MONTE, MONTEREY, CALIFORNIA

You darling old thing I thought of every possible reason (but the right one) to explain yr. silence. At last, to shake from my mind the horrible idea that I was being neglected, I decided to believe whether it was true or not that I had forgotten to give you my address. In fact I had fully made up my mind to write you and tell you for pity's sake never to undeceive me. You old silly to get ill, and poor Gracie way off here and just aching to pet somebody. (You'd do.) There are moments, even, when the aching gets so pronounced (usually at night) that this foolish child pretends with the maddest glee that Annie is just on the other side of the bed. And what is the good of poking out yr. hand to feel for her when you know she is not there? It's a lovely game. And there's never any end to it! As for meeting at San Francisco we shall be gone long before you arrive and also too soon to catch Mr. Yardley up, at Salt Lake. Mother has taken state rooms for the 12th May. I think I shall go to Russia. Bessie Donner has written Mother to say that she won't be able to get to Europe for a year at any rate and is counting so much on seeing somebody from home this summer (meaning me). So I am beginning to feel convinced she really wants me. She says things are awfully primeval and I would just revel. So I think I'll go. I have to go for 6 weeks to a horrid German cure with Mother. Manheim near Frankfurt. Annie Talbot, what do you think Mother wrote me the other day??? It seems the Bishop lunched with them and cheerfully announced that you and Mr. Yardley were *going to be married!!!* Mother remarked cheerfully that she didn't suppose she could write to congratulate you as things weren't announced yet. I gasped! I shall certainly have to write my congratulations to Mr. Yardley as soon as I get home. Not a word from the Tanbark. False, perjured Clarence! I don't know what to say about that wonderful book (6 Women, *not* Tanbark!) It was just like our trout fishing. All the fish I had dimly seen and vaguely fished for, suddenly landed in full sight upon the bank. It is certainly the best thing on the woman question I have ever seen. It seems to me I feel just like every word in it. As for that chapter on Duse[4]—it was simply seeing Duse; nothing short of it. I discovered such a wonderful girl at S. Barbara. We went for a walk and she said everything you and I think way down in our remotest in'ards. Even to Peterkins.[5] I gasped—thinking how can she be in real life when I've rarely seen her out of books before? The worst of it is I think she is just a wee bit [illegible]. She doesn't sound so but she hasn't quite the right type for *our kind*. It grieved me so to think so, tho'! that I have to say it out loud to somebody. I once knew a girl, seemingly splendid, but she didn't look right. For two years I shut my eyes and believed. At last I had to see and I found she was only what I thought on top. It was the worst disappointment of my entire career. Naturally I've been a little skeptical ever since. This one's a wonder if she is what I fondly hope. I *loved* A Singular Life. Why did you say perhaps I wouldn't? That was rather horrid of you. It's an awfully compelling book. I'm not reading anything now as I've got away from the library. When you leave San Diego you can do the things up in short time. A couple of days driving about Pasadena, pretty but stupid. Then Santa Barbara. You must not miss that. I like it better than any place in Calif. It makes you feel so Peterkinsy and so *good*. I can't describe. I felt it as soon as I got there. And I was so agitated all the time, I was on the point of causeless tears. Do go up on the *mesa*. Take the horse car to the beach and then walk to the right from the park along the beach till you go up on the bluffs. Sit down on the grass on the edge where you can hear the waves break and think "the campaign with its fleece of feathery grasses everywhere. Silence and passion, joy and peace and everlasting wash of air."[6] You know, I needn't quote. I never understood before why I always thought "oh, if I could only lie down and die in it!! if I see a field like that, or such a blue sea," until I read Cleon the other day. I expect it's to get into a state where one can feel, *enjoy*, as much as one is bursting to do. You will go there, won't you? Oh, Annie, *how* I longed for you—it almost hurt—way down in my tummy. You know that place. What an Annie you are to me. And what an Annie you must be to Mr. Yardley!

We came over the San Marcus pass from S. Bar. It is a splendid drive but you have to stop over two nights and spend two mornings in trains which hardly pays. But for goodness sake don't go by water unless it is smooth. Some friends of ours went at different times and nearly *died.* It would be silly of you to go and get ill after yr. winter here. This place is maddening. If S. Barbara makes you feel good this makes you primeval and then when you are feeling like a savage it absolutely wipes you out, obliterates you. Of course I am speaking of the drive, the famous 17 mile one. It is all there is of the place. *Do* do it on horseback. It. is about as footless and so as to think of the Valkyries coming in carriages. Get *Polo*, the most heavenly creature in the way of a horse I have ever been on, *Bluey* (!) not excepted. You will write me often this summer, won't you? You see how I am improving about writing. As a matter of fact I feel as tho' I couldn't write you often enough. What *has* become of Lou? I haven't had a word from her since Jan.

Goodbye, you old sweet thing!
Gracie

Palace Hotel, S. Fran. till 12th. Brown Place Hotel, Denver for a week later, then home.
Annie, solemnly I say to you, do we like each other from the fullness of life or for a smaller reason? That is what the book, the book, says we should do.

June 24, 1897
KARLSBAD, BOHEMIA

My dearest of all Annes,

It is impossible to give adequate expression to my joy on receiving yr. letter (to say nothing of the enclosed one!). I had made up my mind with the fortitude of an ancient Spartan to expect nothing from you for several months—for obvious reasons. You said you would write often and I do so hope you will. It is such a deep down joy to get yr. letters and you were such an angel about writing last winter that you spoiled me. Well, you see (that is, you will when you get to the date) that I am in Karlsbad. Mother and I sailed on the 3rd June for Hamburg. We came from there here shopping a couple of days each at Berlin and Dresden just to break the journey and see these places a little bit as neither of us had ever been there before. You can imagine in that amount of time I did not get more idea of the places than I had before. My principal impression was of the hideous people. Actually I didn't see one good looking one, man, woman or child. I don't wonder Nordau wrote Degeneration. My only feeling is one of wonder at his having been able to wait so long before doing so. George Caramano says the plans for the Turkish campaign were sent from Berlin and followed by the Turks to the letter. Looking at the Germans I can well believe it. Think of the myriads of these degenerate little people it must have taken to build up a Goethe a Wagner or a Beethoven. It's incredible that the structure could ever reach such a lofty height. Which reminds me that I have discovered when struggling with cabmen, customs officials, etc., that the Wagner librettos are painfully deficient in traveling terms, and as all my German comes from that source you can imagine my embarrassment. Isolde only traveled with a medicine chest (so sensible of her) and as for Lohengrin I always had a suspicion that he borrowed his wedding clothes from the chorus. It is very pretty here in Karlsbad. The hills are pretty and most tempting. I went for a long, long walk yesterday, but alone, you can imagine it wasn't very gay. However it was nice sitting up in the pines and smelling the good earthy smells. There are heaps of untidy people here, not interesting (looking) enough to excuse the untidiness and I have to go out on the street looking respectable with gloves on and my hair curled. We shall be here a month. I found yr. letter here when I got here. I fear Mr. Yardley couldn't tear himself away long enough to post it, as you said he would, so I didn't get it before sailing. I had planned to go from here back to Berlin and then to Bessie Denver in Petersburg. But we found letters here from Alice[7] saying that she could not join us here as we had expected she would do, so I can't go wandering way off to Russia till I have seen her naturally. I expect we shall go from here to Switzerland. I found letters here from the Greek.[8] Several, *at last.* I thought I was the maid of Athens,[9] after all, such a long silence! But it seems he was ill with fever (as far as I can glean. He is a horrid, shut-up thing like that Mr. Yardley) from drilling in the hot sun and the frightful life they have to lead and he's broken-hearted about the way things have turned out and the treachery on every hand, of the government of the Powers, and of their own officers. It makes one's blood boil. He has to stay in Athens as long as the peace is not concluded. I have a faint hope of seeing him in Switz. in July or August. I dare say all this doesn't interest you at all. Now I'm going to go back to your letter. In the first place you made me wildly homesick for Wyoming. I want to smell the sage brush and *quite* sure till when I was in Monterrey. All of a sudden one night it came in to my head *quite* straight. I went to Dr. Lubeck directly when I got home. I know you'll be glad. I certainly thought I should never come to it, but I am *quite* straight now. I *couldn't* change.

I'm glad I've told you.

Please write me lots. I can't tell you how I love to get yr. darling old letters. Love to all the dear Laramie people. I suppose the Bishop is in England.

Always lovingly yr. old Gracie.

September 10, 1897
GRAND LAKE, MIDDLE PARK, COLORADO

Dearest Reddy,

There is a painful Sunday calm over everything, the last one awake. Mr. White (the man Edith Hart was engaged to) has a strained look about the eyes, so I expect to see him drop off at any moment. But as I have you, Reddy, I don't need them or their naps. Reddy, I must confess to you the most hopeless, tenderfoot trick I did last week. Thought I'd climb a mountain which stood up in the sky very temptingly in front of the house. Started about ten with the kodak[10] and two slices of bread. There was no trail and the timber was close and lots of fallen timber, but Bobbie

Harrington had been to the top so I saw no reason why I shouldn't go too. Climbed till four when I got well above the timber and found a snow drift. Hadn't had any water all day. Choked down my bread and started for home. Allowed myself three hours to get down in. Didn't get quite to the top as I didn't dare allow the extra time it would have taken. (Wish I'd gone now!) Came down, down, down through fallen timber. Finally got out on a point where I could get a view of the lake. Saw I was on the wrong spur and would come down way above the head of the lake. But there was nothing to do for it but go on. Found deer tracks and followed them down an old water course. Deer aren't particular about where they go, apparently. Down over rocks and fallen timber at a descent of 60 [degrees] at least, swinging downwards by holding one sapling then grabbing the next. Shirt torn, hand cut, head bumped. Bottom at last. Heard water. Listened. Found I was near the Upper Falls 5 miles from the lake and through the worst country in this region! It was then 6:30. Got down to the river. Long grass and swamp. Plunged along. Fell into holes. Butted through willows. Waded through the river. Got onto rocky spur of the opposite mountain. Lost my matches in the thicket. It got darker and darker. Kept getting into difficulties and having to go back and around. Had been climbing for ten hours and legs began to get revolutionary but I remembered the heroes of antiquity and struggled on. At last it got so dark that I fell down every step or two so I decided to make a night of it. No coat, no fire, wet feet, no gun and visions of Nellie worried at the other end. Couldn't even find a decent bed it was so dark. So lay down between logs on a spurt of rock with a few small pines nearby to climb in case of bears. Said my prayers, thought of you, remembered that certain seraphic individuals had once been lost not 15 minutes from home the other side of the lake, and went to sleep. Slept and shivered till 5 o'clock, when it was light enough to see a little. Then went on for two hours over rocks and rotten logs till I got to the lake. Prowled about a house, saw no one moving, so stole a boat and rowed the 2 miles home in frantic haste and landed on our beach in deep embarrassment. Three men out looking for me till 3 o'clock!! Now known about the lake as "the girl who spent the night out on the mountain." Now did you ever know of such an idiotic trick? Nothing to eat till 24 hours and sleeping out (the mud was frozen in the morning) without a coat doesn't sound pleasant but it really shows you what you can do at a pinch and it was a fine feeling of independence and, if I had not thought of being such a fool and of worrying everybody I should have quite enjoyed myself. There were moments, however, when I fully expected to be wakened by the tickling of whiskers of a mountain lion. But I had a plan! First snap the front of the kodak open in the creature's face, then make for the nearest pine!!

But I think I've talked enough about myself. Mr. White is up here, as I said, and yesterday he and I went off into the mountains after deer (never saw *one*, tho' I saw two not 30 feet off my day in the mountains) and had such a fine climb. Were gone all day. I do hope someday there'll be a little deaconess ranch for us (sounds as tho' I meant Mr. White and I, but I don't) in the mountains somewhere. Getting to be a much better climber, Reddy. There was room for improvement!

We are going over to Hot Sulphur Springs tomorrow (25 miles) for the night and the hot bath, then "out" on Thursday. The next Monday we (with Nellie) shall go to Manitou for two nights, and then home. I got Mrs. Stone's announcement cards and wrote to congratulate. Isn't that nice that it's a boy! Since last I wrote you I have read yr. two letters from Manitou and the last one from Belfast (written by the way, the afternoon I was tumbling down through the timber to my rocky bed). Didn't you rather like that Mr. Mills? There was something faintly suggestive of the seraphic about him to me.

I'll certainly hunt up Mrs. Rupp. I lost my Crucifix at the Mammouth and never discovered it till I got to Denver. So I wrote back to all the park hotels and—got it back!

How curious of the Sisters of the Good Shepherd to join the Deaconate. Of course it will be splendid for the latter. Anything to get out of the Grace grooves!

I think we shall start for home about the 22nd. So write me to the deanery until then.

Goodbye dear Reddy. Don't tell Mamma of my little adventure!! What would she say?!!

Yr. Gracie

What a fat old thing you are getting to be! Nellie sends love.

January 16, 1899
NEW YORK CITY, NEW YORK

Dear Reddy,

I have been wavering for some time between putting tonic on my hair and writing to you and have just heard myself saying, Damn the tonic! I have been a little bit afraid that I was writing you with such feverish frequency that you would be getting tired of my silly letters. But I have wanted to write you awfully! I'm sorry to say that I am still missing you most uncomfortably—I have been rather oppressed too, just lately with a sense of the uncertainty of things in general; this is due to the fact that I have been going through and *tearing* up a lot—oh! but *heaps*—of old letters—from way back in early days. It was rather ghastly to observe the fatal procession of my succeeding friends. I tore all yr. letters up with the rest—some that I would have given almost anything to keep. At first I was afraid I was doing it because I was haunted with a vague fear that someday I might be able to tear up yr. letters too, without a pang, but, after sitting in a heap of confusion on the floor and thinking very hard, I decided that my real motive was a desire—oh! a burning desire—to let go completely of things tangible. (I found that old photo I wanted you to have. I'm sorry that I seem to be sending you so many of myself.) I have been grubbing at the house. It is not nearly ready and Mamma is not well enough to hurry much and then so many things have not come from Paris. I have got my room almost altogether settled. The stuff on the walls is horribly dark, but it looks rather better now the pieces are hung. I don't think it will be *possible* for me to go over to Bethlehem the 25th,[11] which will be Wednesday week. But, oh! don't let's talk about that till we have to!

I went to the Rheingold[12] the other night as you know feeling awfully festive about seeing that Loki so soon. In fact I took out that red thing lying between the pages of the "Tommy" and gave it a kiss—just to let it know what was going on. But such a disappointment—it wasn't Loki at all but a sort of pink Mephistopheles with the Old Boy's eyebrows and—Moses's horns!!! Rather a shock! I believe to sing Wagner properly you must *first* love the gods and then music. If you begin the other way around, you'll never really sing it at all. Lilli Lehmann's[13] recital on Tuesday was nothing short of marvelous, you sat with the tears trickling down, tho' there was nothing on earth to cry about, and I suppose with yr. heart in yr. ears—that is, if it hasn't there you hadn't any heart.

You were very good to send me the calendar. At present I'd rather not look at it, tho', for I can see nothing but horrid last Friday (I shall hate Fridays until I see you again) and that 25th with a question mark hanging over it.

I asked Francis[14] to come up last night to go to the Philharmonic. He was very sweet. I think he wanted to talk about you and of course I wanted to have him, but he only said little things. I wish he would talk to me, tho' when I am with him I am constantly dreading his doing so. What can be so desperately tragic as almost having and then losing through yr. fault and yet not yr. fault!? I always feel when I am with him that I am standing by and seeing somebody drown knowing that if I jumped in after them I could not save them. Oh! dear me! I did jump in once. I tore that letter of yrs up with the rest without having the courage to read one line. (*Will you please forgive me for it?*) I expect there is nothing for Francis to do but live along until other things have accumulated enough to cover this up. They must in time; you know. In the meantime I told him to read Thomas Kempis and keep his spirit above water, or words to that effect—and dreamt about him all night! Don't you write to him anymore?

Don't think about Francis now, think about me! I don't want you to think about Francis when I am wanting to see you. When I see Francis and Tommy I feel, for the first time in all my 25 x 365 days, a sort of grim joy in being only a girl after all, for at least I can have a girl's part of you. Think if I'd been a possible Peterkins (no question about the capital letter, *there!*) How I would have punched Tommy and jumped on Francis with unholy glee, I finally died unregenerate and alone, I *hope*, still punching. As it is, I have a sinking feeling that there may be many Peterkins but there can be only one Annie. I see that this feeling bodes no good for the peace of the Peterkins ranch. I shall send Peterkins out to look on the eternal hills and feel ashamed but I shall be sitting inside and thinking "If I'd been a man—."

Reddy, I've always had a deadly feeling that to find a man as fine as a woman was impossible, is and ever more shall be—which reminds me that

I found a lovely church today, S. Chrysatonis (don't know how to spell it) a Trinity Mission, 39th and 7th Ave.

I'm going to send you something next letter that'll make you awfully mad. I'm sorry but I'm going to.

Why didn't you telegraph me Tommy couldn't come and you wanted to go to Tristan? *Idiot child!!!* I thought from the way yr. letters sounded you didn't want to. I'm *so* sorry. Oh! despair! I wish you were here. Why haven't you written me for so long? I generally wander aimlessly about thinking of you. Please tell me every letter that you love me—if you do. But I don't see how you can.

It's so silly to have had to talk so much about such a natural thing, isn't it, Reddy?

January 1899

NEW YORK CITY, NEW YORK

Reddy, I think you're treating me very badly. Why don't you write me instead of sending me incoherent telegrams? Of course I was obliged to say I could not come, not knowing what plans you were brewing, not even whether or not I really could. It was bad enough to come to the realization slowly that I should have to give up the long-cherished plan of coming to Bethlehem so soon again without you going and making me write the horrible fact down on paper and send it to you. If you don't come to me as I asked you, on Friday, the morning at that, to stay until that horrible Sally drags you back, I shall know—I don't know what I shall know. I hope I shall have brain fever or something deathly that will make you feel repentant.

As for what's in the envelope, if you knew the horribly uncomfortable hours its contents have given me, you would for once in yr. life give me some definite proof that you like me a little bit. I got them (in my mind which is the real getting) that day we were washing beads in the bathroom and I've spent miserable, horrible, hours of night over them. If you knew how miserably uncomfortable (I say uncomfortable in place of something stronger) it makes me to think of you coming over here for three days as you did before Christmas, which certainly cannot be worthwhile to you, and how much more miserably uncomfortable it makes me to think of yr. not coming for the three days! Can't you love me enough to take what is no more mine than *yrs.* as *you know?* If you don't want the horned things throw them away, never let me see them again. I've had them for ten days shut up in a drawer, the obnoxious things!!

Olga Nethersole[15] is here, and the opera is good, and maybe there might be another Schumann recital. In case you don't care about seeing me I'm holding out attractions. Mother wants me to ask you particularly to come; as I said in the telegram.

Please don't be angry with me! I'm very [illegible]. I hope you'll realize some fine day that I'd so much rather give you everything I have if there wasn't this absurd prejudice against giving people things. I have always believed there was a sort of affection quite above those little things. *Is* there, Redtop?

I cannot bear to think there is even a possibility of yr. not coming on Friday (*morning*) you know it will be weeks before we can see each other again (I don't count the Gotterdammerung time) if you don't come. We are going to [illegible] on Monday or Tuesday; are waiting now principally to get a cook.

Reddy, come! Think what a few years we have to see each other in before the long separation. It's a thought that haunts me all the time.

Of course the thing I wanted to say in this letter is what I have left unsaid, but you know what I have been thinking every time I have thought of you.

Oh dear! There are such things I want to say but I mustn't.

Lovingly,
Grace

March 30, 1899
NEW YORK CITY, NEW YORK

My own Reddy,

The Francia came tonight and is sitting in the blue chair opposite me while I am writing. I have wanted it for years, Reddy, and now that I have it I can't feel half as glad that I have as that it is from you. It is so resigned and so beautiful. It will go to the Deaconesses House with me and all that time and all this time before it will be a help and a comfort. I am still dimly trying to get used to the thought that it must be six months before I can see you again. It is true that we are not, either one of us, *right*, or when we are together we could not be, and feel as we do. And yet it is so horrible to think of wasting six months of these few, precious years. I almost ran back to you yesterday in the station, only the thought of all those strange people in the car, of Lou and of Siddy kept me back. I feel, for my part, as tho' I had come to the foot of the mountain where the real climbing must begin, as tho' all that had gone before had only been the easy approaches and I know that the one way I can possibly go is up the mountain side. I think just now that I have come to the end of myself. All that myself can give me it has given and now I want to make a place for something else, to annihilate this self. When a time comes when I really love you better than I do myself I want to go to you, to fly to you, Annie—only tonight what I most want to do is to kiss you and kiss you—Let us both pray for regeneration. But oh! to think that we—that I—have gone on all these years and yet have come to nothing.

That day after I left you I went down to Geissler's and got yr. crucifix. I looked at lots and lots and could not fine one that was just right when at last I found the one hanging up on my wall now and which I shall send off to you tomorrow. I am afraid, Reddy, it is not a very well carved one (but Mr. Geissler was not there so I could not ask his opinion of the work) but I got it because it seemed to me to embody the most beautiful moment of the crucifixion; the moment of the realization of the joy of sacrifice, the moment of complete self abnegation. It looks so exultant. And it suggests the Resurrection. If you think it is poor in workmanship I am sure we can go to Geissler's sometime and exchange it, but I saw none there which was half so fine in conception. I hope you will love it as I do the Francia.

Do write me as often as you can; unless you feel like cutting loose from even that for a while. You know I will understand.

I love you, darling, with all there is in me fit to love and if I have any good in me you know it is yours.

Gracie

April 16, 1899
NEW YORK CITY, NEW YORK

As I told you, Reddy, ever since the first time I was in Bethlehem this year I have been wanting you more or less regularly on Sunday nights. It's a very sweet time because, besides having time that day to sit quietly down and think how fond you are of people, you feel a certain courage for the rest of the week (which generally doesn't hold out till the end!). I sent you off the box of goods and ends yesterday and hope I haven't forgotten anything. You'll have yr. gaiters in a few days. I'll send them to Roanoke. The crucifix too. I packed it in the afternoon, I'm crazy to know if you like it. I wore it for two or three days while I was getting the chain. Reddy, I want to tell you two things about it; first, I got the chain long (a little) so it would reach down to a sweet little place and live there. (My chain has always bothered me by being too short so my cross rests boldly on the top of my breastbone!) and second, I left the crucifix at S. Timothy's for Mr. Cockcroft with a note asking him to bless it, or consecrate it or set it apart or whatever it is called, so it wouldn't be just like a store one anymore. There's a service in the Priest's prayerbook, I think. I'm awfully attached to mine so I hope you will be. When I'm a deaconess I shall wear it boldly outside my clothes. But, oh! Reddy, how I hate to send things off to you when I have to stay here! I've taken to reading Thomas Kempis every night and he says just what you did. I'm trying very hard to be good, Reddy. But you must tell me you love me in every letter. I feel, as I look back on the winter as tho' it had been very fine inward things for all the outward things have been very near failures. I believe I feel today past any fear of retracting, that the real life *is* the life of the spirit that renunciation *is* gain and that the eternal, the worthwhile, is not to be found here. If I believe truly, I think I *must* act someday, don't you? Oh! Reddy, love me in spite of everything. If you knew how it breaks my heart to think how

I have fallen short. But you do know. Having you here and at least the chance of trying for the great things to come I feel very rich, even in spite of everything.

I want to tell you all I have been stopping to think, here about how I love you Reddy; not how much, but how; only I think after all you know, and then how can I talk about it when you're not here?

Write as often as you can. I will try to find some decent books to send.

Your trying-hard Gracie

May 9, 1899

NEW YORK CITY, NEW YORK

My own Reddy,

I am seized with a desire to sit down with a large pad and a fine pen and say many things. Oh! I've had such an agitating week since last letter, that's why I didn't write on Sunday night as usual, that and incidentally having Peggy Hart for a few days. You know Peggy's tongue is hung in the middle and as mother and father were away, I seemed to be at both ends of it at once. She's gone to Orange with Marie now. Of course the trouble was about the Deaconesses' House. (Oh! Reddy, what *should* I do if I hadn't you to come and tell things to? I have so wanted to cuddle up and tell you everything. You always seem so much bigger and stronger than I am; which I never can make you believe and yet which I can't understand your not believing.) One day I, being alone with Mother, was prompted to speak and I served fiercely and spoke. Mother took it very well, seemed awfully sorry to think I should be away such a lot. Tried for the 99th time to make me see what a foolish way I was in, but said she saw no reason why I should not go and see Dr. McKim. I had to take a Henry Streeter to the Infirmary so after I got that off my mind I went to the Reverend Father, deeply embarrassed but firm. May I be spared many more such interviews! It was an attractive thing with a solemn look but a naughty little twinkle in the corner of its eye. Asked me most impossible questions: Didn't I think I'd find it pretty hard to study now? What! Graduated in 92 and hadn't done much studying since! Had I managed to pass my exams? Well, of course we couldn't tell how we'd feel a few years hence but—sometimes they get married, you know, we don't like very much to have our deaconesses marry; all this with eyes cast up toward the cornice, while I nearly busted within. Well, after all this had gone on for some time, he decided that I might get Dr. Lubeck to write him a letter and give me "a character" with a giggle. I fled the house and wandered vaguely about the streets, finally ending up at the Deaconesses' House, where I stopped to ask Miss Knapp a lot of things. I had thought that I could board with Alice at home and then go by the day—So the next day I told Mother about my various interviews. I supposed that was the thing to do. But she'd been thinking in the meantime and came down on me like a wolf on the fold. She said to begin with that I only wanted to do it because I wanted to do it and this sounded so much as tho' it might be true that I got scared. Well, we both lost our tempers. At last I proposed going by the day while Alice was here as an experiment and if Mama found that it took me away from home too much when Alice left I would give up studying. But I couldn't get even her consent to this. She said she would never give either her consent or refusal. So there we stand at present. After relationships being rather strained for a time we are now on friendly terms once more. But I am in despair, Reddy. Oh! the blackest sort. What I was going to undertake this week with the idea of giving myself up and then suddenly to be confronted with the idea that I was prompted by selfishness—It took me about three days to think myself out of that—You don't think it *is* selfishness, do you? Oh! Reddy, *do* you? Of course, that was all that really bothered me. As for giving up the going into the Deaconess order, I shall never do it, I think. If I cannot do it next year of course there is plenty of other work to do and other years for the Deaconesses' House. But I shall let things wait a little—and be sure of this, I shall *not* give up to just a whim of Mother's, if it is no more than that—I shall go. The whole trouble was started by my stupidity in wanting to board there. It is impossible. Father is so dull that it really would be disgustingly mean to leave Mother alone with him all the time. But I have a very strange feeling, stronger than I have ever had it before, that I want the consecration, the setting apart, the being obviously what you are inwardly; making the business of yr. life what you most want to because it is not only because it is *most* worthwhile, but the *only* thing worth; feeling and acting in fact, like a man, and choosing my own vocation. I can't see that that is so much to ask, can you? I do hope that

I shall do what is right in this for it would be more than horrible to spoil it by selfishness, wouldn't it? In the meantime my blank to be filled out by Dr. Lubeck, etc., is lying in my desk staring me in the face.

I'm sure you'll be charmed to hear that I'm driving with Sister Lizzie tonight, the occasion for which unprecedented proceeding is the last of the lectures for *men only* given at the Ch. of the Holy Communion, by Bishop Deane. This one is on the Church. Sister Lizzie says they only let men in (impossible!) but that she knows a gallery where ladies are still allowed to penetrate. I plainly see that I have been neglecting Sister Lizzie this winter! I should have known her sooner. She came to see Peggy on Sunday and they greeted each other with a holy kiss. The Dean says they are going to elect a coadjutor (I don't know how to spell it) for Colorado. He hopes to have things all under way as the Cathedral does most of the paying in Colo. Wants to get Bishop Courtney (the Canadian one) in. I don't think I see him coming! Also spoke freely of Dr. Grosvenor of the Incarnation! He seems to think anybody would *like* to be Bishop of Colorado!! I've about decided to go out in Aug. for a camping trip. I might as well, you know, Steamboat Springs. When I'm a deaconess (oh! oh! oh!) I'll go out to our Indians in the summer to do work!! Isn't that a fine idea? It woke me up the other night.

Oh! I *must* not forget this time to tell you that the dressmaker is very much dejected about yr. dress. I spoke in impassioned language on the subject. She says to tell you to send on a sample of the stuff and she will fly to John's and get enough of it for a new back and put you in one sufficiently long waisted next time. I think I have an excellent dressmaker now, a Miss Carney whom I once went to. She is at Altman's now, upstairs, was in business for herself but too delicate to do the handwork of managing the establishment and so. I always liked her immensely but she was too expensive. She made that green dress I had that hooked up the back.

Give dear Sam my love and think about my Deaconess bothers!

My own Reddy!

Grace

I really felt awfully bad. Quite gave up hope. I think I'll get my admission anyway. I can take part of the work anyway. Tell me you don't think I'm selfish in it and I'll go ahead.

June 10, 1901
EVANSTON, WYOMING

My dearest Reddy,

If you were only here! I am sitting on a sage brush hillside, a sheepherder's outfit down in front of me, the sheep all over the valley, sage brush everywhere, and way off in one corner the Uintah mountains, the only thing between me and the Reservation! I can't believe that you aren't just back over the edge of the hill. Dear old Reddy, I am so thankful that you and this splendid West are practically all one thing; it would be so hard to have to love in opposite directions. As it is, I can't remember where it leaves off and you begin. Oh! how glad I was to see this big country again. It began to spread out about Erie where I woke about six and looked out of the window (at the top of the P.E. convention in that city!) and then it got bigger and sweeter till it turned into prairie dogs and paintbrush and till I didn't know what I was up to for joy. Just here the mosquitos got so bad that I came home and am finishing up in my room before church. I have so much to tell you. Such thrilling changes have happened to my plans. I got here Thursday morning (providentially I had bought a ticket no further) and found both the Huntings[16] at the station. They are really very nice and have got a sweet little house and have made me feel so at home and comfortable. Now listen. I was to have left yesterday (Sat.) to join the Bp. at Salt Lake,[17] but Miss Cammie was taken ill suddenly in Calif. and had to have an operation for appendicitis so he went on there and sent word I was to join him on Wed. next. I had to go from here to Salt Lake, 6 hrs., then a night on the [illegible] to Price and then stage for 36 hrs. Wasn't that a hopeful prospect, when I knew that there was nothing between me and the agency but this one range of snow mts. and about 100 miles of country? I kept saying, "if there was only a road or even a trail!" and finally I said it to a woman who said "Why there is a road! They freight ore over the mts., from the Ashley valley (near Whiterocks) to the U.P." If I didn't fly home and spread the glad tidings and then just rustle, gently but persistently, with the result that on Tuesday morning, having only telephoned the Bp., we (the Huntings) are going to start off in a buckboard for 4 days driving! (130 miles) The Huntings are going to take two weeks, how's that for luck! There's lots of snow on the mts., and I expect we'll strike drifts and a terrible road but hurrah for the great outdoors! I say, isn't that just sporty, tho'! I just feel like a different person since I am out here where there is room so that all yr. feelings and ideas don't come back and crowd onto you. Precious treasure, if it hadn't been for you I should never have known, there was such a place as Wyoming. The Huntings know Miss Carter[18] and say she is perfectly sweet. The people here are awfully nice for this kind of a town and so many of them know you all, or at least the Bp., that I feel quite at home. Oh! how I wish you were here, tho' I'm settled on coming West now for good and all. I just can't live in a shut up town anymore. I am going to locate here just as soon as I am done at St. Faith's. We'll have our little house yet, precious! It was sweet of you to telegraph me. Did you get my answer? I hoped to get a letter from you here, written last Sunday night, but I expect you didn't write. Tell me about the ordination. I caught a little tiny sage chicken out on the hill this afternoon. He sat right in my hand. But his mother seemed so agitated I let him go again. I'm taking such comfort in these big shoes of Jantzen. Do get a pair.

Reddy, get on with Parkman. The Montcalm and Wolfe part was fascinating. Wolfe is just like my Reddy, even to his red hair. You see if maybe you don't think so when you read it. If you get hold of any really good book, send it along. I will do the same to you.

Here's a piece of sage. Smell it and think of Wyoming and me. My precious treasure, I don't dare tell you how much I wish you were here.

Much love to Sam and the bishop and just heaps for you.

from yr. Gedy,

I know this letter will make you wish you were here!

June 21, 1901

WHITEROCKS, UNITAH AND OURAY RESERVATION, UTAH

My precious Reddy,

I did find yr. letter here after all, as I was late getting in here than I expected. I'm not going to answer all you said about our two selves. As you say, or imply, we have talked and written enough about our insides. I think we only make bad matters worse. They seem very bad to me. Instead I want to tell you about Whiterocks. *I* mean to write *you* every week altho' I did miss last Sunday, there was so much crowded into it but of course I don't want you to write me if you don't want to. Letters are so horrid anyway. Well, we left Evanston Tues. morning of last week, in an old buckboard with an old pair of horses and all our camp things piled in. There isn't much to tell you about the trip. We got to Ouray, the other mission, Sat. evening found the Bp. there. We were in the range two days and one night. We slept in a deserted old cabin with our horses in one corner. That night there was a snowstorm (it had been snowing and melting all day) and five inches fell, we snowballed each other all the next morning, from the snow that fell into the wagon from the trees. I happened to remember that it was the anniversary of the hot day we graduated. I'll send you my kodaks as soon as I get them. The next night we were rather dejected, as we didn't get out of the mts. as soon as we thought we ought to have done and the road apparently was going the wrong way, and we hadn't the least assurance we were on the right one. It was bitterly cold and we had to sleep out with just a canvas windbreak. The next day we met a sheep herder's outfit and he told us we were alright. Pretty soon we saw the valley below us, came down thro' a beautiful canyon and got to Vernal, a little town like Lander, for dinner. Then in the afternoon we got fresh horses and came on 40 miles to Ouray. I began work that night sleeping in the Infirmary with an Indian girl who had her leg taken off about a month before. After service we came on here, the Bp., Mrs. Hunting and me, I mean. It's about 20 miles from Ouray with the Post between. Then there is another agency 10 miles the other side of Ouray. It's all spread out, not like Fort Washakie. From Vernal on it's all desert but here, about 15 miles from the foot of the mts., it's the sweetest little green spot. Miss Carter came out to meet us dressed in her nurse's dress and looked very sweet and fresh. She looks a little like Miss George and is so awfully nice, Reddy. She isn't yr. good kind, a bit, tho'. She lives in an old school building and I have a room just opposite in the back of the doctor's house. It was all fixed up so prettily and neatly. I go in thro' the doctor's dispensary and the smell there makes me feel very much at home. (Oh dear! there are so many little things I want to tell you, I *wonder* if you mind?) There are almost a dozen horses here and we have such beautiful big trees in front of ours and have taken to eating outdoors all together. Sunday night there was a service here and a lot of little boys and Miss Carter's baby were baptized. The baby, Elizabeth Lee, is such a dear, 4 mos. old and just as sweet as they come, her Indian name meant Heap Hair. It's so long you could almost tie it up now. Monday we went to see the Sun Dance. Oh! Red, it was the weirdest sight. You know how the lodge looks and you can imagine the Indians. They were like fiends. They had been dancing for two days without food or water and were haggard beyond words. They were naked, almost, and barefoot. We wanted to go to the finish next day when they give away the ponies to the old men and visiting Indians, but a finger amputation case turned up. A man had got mixed up with a rope and a wild horse. I guess any self respecting hospital would have had a fit at the operation. A cat walked around freely, we had the doors open, and Elsie, the little girl whose leg was amputated, and an admiring group of friends stood around and watched the performance. Miss Carter only has two rooms, the back one is the bedroom and the front one divided with a curtain is the kitchen and hymn room. The operation was in the front room, of course, and that is really how we took to eating outdoors. Our patient hadn't wakened up by dinner time! He was a nice Indian and I think went to sleep singing the Sun Dance song. That afternoon the Bp. went away. We have been awfully busy and are still as the doctor's wife has been very sick for 3 days and we have had her 5 young hopefuls to look after. I had to stop in the middle of this to go and clean up her place a little. Elsie (she's a Shoshone) went away yesterday. Miss Carter hated to see her go and so did I. You ought to have seen the old Squaw who came for her. She has been with Miss Carter for over 2 mos. and was so fond of her, but she went off without even saying goodbye. These Utes are like the Shoshones. They are not very good Indians. They are dancing the Ghost Dance and we are going to try and go to see it. I was so homesick for you and especially when Bp. Leonard was here. He seemed so much like old Laramie days, somehow. I felt as tho' you all must be here. I miss you so. I just can't feel settled without you. I'll write you soon again when we have really gotten to work. Miss Carter had been down at Ouray till a couple of days before we got here so things are rather upset.

From yr. Gedy

November 24, 1901
NEW YORK CITY, NEW YORK

My dearest treasure,

I thought this peaceful time when I could actually sit down and write to you in a quiet was never coming. I got yr. sweet little Reddy letter just as I was leaving for Denver and carried it around in my pocket all the morning before I actually got off on the train and could read more than the first page. I can't write on the train for it always makes me seasick (!!), there wasn't one half moment's quiet and seclusion to be had at the Harts and since I have been back I have been fearfully rushed. (I am going to take up 3 kindergartening courses with one of the other seniors which will just fill up every spare minute. I think it will be very helpful with the Indians, sort of adapted, you know). I want to write you just then to tell you what distress I was in on account of the death of our baby. Lucy's letter had come just a few days before I left for Denver. Poor Lucy! It was all so pitiful. The poor little details and it nearly broke my heart to think of Lucy going through with all that alone. I wrote begging her to come to me in Denver and come home for the rest I know she needs so much, but she telegraphed and then wrote that she wouldn't. She is really very fine. I just can't think calmly about the baby yet. I know how poor Lucy must feel. You know what a darling thing she always was. I think I have never known such a sweet baby. And then again I was never anything to a baby before and she knew us both so well. Lucy always used to wish to keep her a *little* baby and she will be our *little* baby always now. I always meant you should see her, Reddy, and see how *sweet* she was. Isn't it pitiful? Perhaps you saw the little notice in the Churchman.

The wedding was very nice. I sat next to Bobbie at the supper and we talked up trails and things instead of giving vent to the usual wedding idiotics. It was a sweet and piousy wedding. The next day Marie and I hit for the hills, one spent all day in the region of Golden on two very decent ponies. The mountains were *beautiful* with the first snow on them and the foothills bare. You would have loved it. Of course I stopped at Erie coming back. Hugh has bought Gussie two horses and 250 incubator chickens, the latter are fenced in with trunks and "brooders" in the attic!! This is a large room, originally intended for a ball room. There is intense excitement in the night when one chicken escapes and goes shrieking around the rest of the room, and the air is musical all the time with the voice of, as it were, many sparrows. After all, why should we be trammeled by convention and keep chickens in the hennery instead of the attic? I think Gussie is nearly ready for her baby. Her lungs bother her a lot. I do hope nothing is wrong; somehow I feel kind of scary. Speaking of the Convention for the second time now I have heard the pastoral letter read from the pulpit of St. Paul's, Erie. It was a very nice letter but I had to take a train which prevented my going to Evensong—Did Erie make you feel terribly energetic? I think that's really why I hurried home to take on the kindergartening. I was wavering in my mind before. I am thinking of putting in two weeks at a maternity hospital during the Xmas holidays. I registered a solemn vow over my Sioux boy last summer that I would never inflict my ignorance on anyone else. Which means hospital work. But I dread it. I feel very happy at St. Faith's. It's most fearfully narrow and "sheltered" but I have found a real freak amongst the seniors who is a comfort to my soul. She *understands* at least, and hasn't pious prejudices. And she thinks she won't be a deaconess and I have almost made up my mind. At any rate, I shan't be ordered till I feel that is the only possible course to take. It ought to be like getting married; when you feel it's the only earthly thing you could do next! And really, how could a deaconess ride *à* la squaw[19] and you know I'm not going to get my pony's back sore with a saddle! It may be uncanonical but, by Jove! a horse is a horse.

If you don't know what I'm talking about in my letters (the one who peeked in at the door was the Goop, of course, idiot!) I can't read yr. writing, which is even more ignominious. "If it had been who I wouldn't have dared look him to afterwards?" and what is the type of the rector of the Incantation?

Oh, Reddy, this summer has taught me two things; first, that I can get along without you and second, that I'm "heap hungry" doing it. I used to think at Whiterocks that I could do without after all and I used to remember how bored you would be if you were there doing our stupid things and how you would wonder why I wasn't and then I would get so promptly. But when I came away I wanted you *so* and every day now I turn to you and want to feel so only *half* without you, so incomplete, everything is fine but always lacks point; just you, Reddy. And yet, you were the one who saw first and knew that we must break off, but I think I've seen at last, Reddy, and now I feel as tho' I never wanted to see you again if ever there was going to be one word more added to all that has gone. I mean it, sweety. It is myself that I blame as I should and I don't know whether I am sure of myself or not, I don't think I'm sure. The same things give me the same frightened feelings they used to. I forgot them in Whiterocks and at St. Faith's but coming back into this house is like hearing an echo of it all again. I am trying to be good and fit myself for all I hope to do but, you know it isn't natural to me and I've never been brought up to it; but this I mean to do if I can find the strength for it, and that is to put my work before you. You know I didn't do that, and you can't serve two masters. But oh! My Reddy, how hungry I am for you this minute. For the sweet feel of you. I only want to tell you frankly, I'm desperately afraid, and of the same two things that used to be all the trouble to me in you. Well, I want to throw all the responsibility on you and say you decide about our seeing each other. That is, the when and the how, for we must just see each other long enough to tell all the skipped things! We *must*, Reddy! I want to be just as foolish with you and argue wildly like at St. Faith's, only with you instead of just these months that merely happen to belong to individuals.

Write me soon, as *soon* as you possibly can. You have had nothing to do in the country why haven't you written?

I think, Reddy, (you *must* understand) that the only way I feel stronger about us now is that the horror of all that has happened has at last taken hold of me. I *think* that is all. But I'm your Gedy and nobody else's.

LOVE, MARRIAGE, AND DEATH AT WIND RIVER, 1902–5

June 13, 1902

FORT WASHAKIE, WIND RIVER, WYOMING

My precious Reddy,

I was very glad to get yr. letter and read all about the Convocation. It was nice of you to tell me all about it. I thought of you at Gettysburg the day I was coming thro' the state. Things are going on slowly here. We have been seeing the school girls about confirmation. Bp. Funsten[20] comes for Sunday. Yesterday we went to a camp to see a sick girl and we spent all the afternoon standing on our heads in missy[21] barrels. 123 pairs of drawers of assorted and abnormal shapes!!! And two other boxes on the way! This morning I wrote three letters of thanks for the 3 barrels of yesterday. I hope they had a missy tone. Mr. Roberts himself says if you don't stretch the truth, you hang the cause! We shall begin visiting the camps systematically after the Bp. has come and gone. I think there is a great deal to do but naturally it is very slow starting and I suppose, this is the hardest time. The most interesting thing is the house. I have at last after much politeness on both sides convinced Mr. Roberts not to plaster it. It is going to have a red cedar partition between the two rooms and ceilings and the walls will be just the rough logs. There is one big window in the bedroom and two in the living room, one east and one south. After much more politeness I got Mr. R. to put in a horizontal window on the west side of the living room. You ought to see the mountains through it. They are so lovely. It will be a sweet place to sit and sew or read. He thought a west window would make the house cold but I would rather be a little colder and see those sweet mountains, wouldn't you? Poke[22] has a black and white pinto which belongs to an Arapahoe named Sage which I can get for $25.00. I'm going to try him. I shall be glad when the house is done. I think we shall be in it in a couple of weeks. It is very noisy here; the Shoshone children wake us up at half past five and the food is messy and not nice. I don't mind so much for myself but I naturally have Mary more or less on my mind. She isn't used to roughing it. I have seen the Moores and they asked about you very particularly, especially Mr. Moore.

Annie is rushing a young man from N.Y., or the other way. We have our breakfast at seven, then Mary and I do our room and wash all the dishes. At nine the Indian children have a little service in the chapel. They are real nice children. There is one named Delia, a perfect fiend. I called her an elf in the missy letters, which meant the same but didn't sound so, I hope! She is only four but she manages the entire placc. She seems to have all the wisdom of all the past Shoshones in her bad little head and all the mischievous instinct necessary to put it into play, and then sometimes she is just a poor little baby. They say she goes [fragment missing].

June 25, 1902

FORT WASHAKIE, WIND RIVER, WYOMING

Dearest Reddy,

We certainly are not keeping our writing promise. It is two weeks nearly since I have heard from you, and ten days, anyway, since I wrote you last. Why didn't you write when you promised to? I keep waiting for yr. letter. Let me see what has happened in the ten days. Bp. Funsten came. We had confirmation at the school and thirty-one of the older children were confirmed. The next Sunday they had the Communion. It was real sweet to see them. The Bp. stayed till Tuesday night. He certainly is not prepossessing to say the least. Mary and I were bored to death by him and his pokey sermons. But I guess he is good. Ugh!

Last week we did Agency calls, trying to drum up the Sunday school which has fallen into decay, as it were. We went to see most of the half breeds around the Agency, too, among them Poke's sister, Mrs. Hereford.[23] Mr. H. is a Shoshone quarterbreed. She looks just like Miss Bennett!! only very pretty and attractive. She has a little Sherman who is going to be baptized soon. Named for his uncle. Poke hangs out in that big room where we used to see the Indians get their rations, does apparently nothing but keep his eye peeled for those who pass his windows. He comes to see us occasionally, but not as frequently as you might hope. I'm trying to get him to adopt me into the tribe so he can issue me a stove. I do just hate to go and buy one when I might get one for nothing. We are getting settled down and are having a very nice time. Yesterday morning Mary drove Buckskin[24] over to the Agency in Mr. Roberts ramshackle little cart (I being laid low with mulls[25]) to borrow Poke's very stylish cart to drive to North Fork in the P. M.[26] where we were to meet Mr. R. and make calls preparatory to starting a Sunday School at North Fork. That is the little ranch settlement just before you drive up on Boulder Flat, you savvy. The noble Poke sent Prince with the cart so we drove over in great shape. We are going over to N. Fork, 10 miles, every Sunday p.m. I have been down to the little Arapahoe church twice. It is so sweet there, and really piousy. Michael White Hawk is very nice, but not like Fremont. The Arapahoes certainly are nice. They seem *real* but these Shoshones are just like magpies. The little house, ours, Reddy, is done, all but a day or two of "chinking" inside, and is very sweet. Mary and I have been making curtains for the shelves today. Our school children went home last Sat., for good and life seems very tame without the war chief, Delia, who used to appear by the window, make a sudden sally, as it were, and carry off any little trophy she happened to fancy, and then have to be chased, shrieking, all over the place. You never saw such a witch. Of course she is much the nicest of the bunch. There was a big Wolf Dance on Sunday. Mary went but I went down to the Arapahoe camp. The Shoshone Sun Dance begins Friday, right, over there when the old lodge was. We have been to a few of the camps. At one two women were sick, and they died. And at another right near, really the same camp, and they moved when the first two died, there was a little sick school girl. We have been over a couple of times to take her things to eat. Last night I could hear the drums and the singing till way in the night and this morning we saw the funeral going by. They go into a decline, just the way wild birds or plants die. Isn't it too queer to think of nature, or the primeval, or something, having such a hold over them? I suppose it is a sort of general tuberculosis. This little Dinah was in school until a month ago and you ought to have seen her, her bones almost thro' her skin and just burning up with fever. I just couldn't keep asleep thinking of that poor little one and those medicine men. It sounded so ghastly in the night. Mr. Roberts seems so glad to have helped. This work is enormous and, as he says, no one man can lift it. He wants me to have the school next year. Of course I should love it. There is such a nice girl who takes care of the children. She would go on doing that and I would just have the teaching and bossing as it were. I could bring in heaps of kindergarten and have a fine time of it. Tonight is Commencement at the govt. sch. and after that we shall have visiting in the Arapahoe camps, to keep hold of the confirmed girls. I have a pony and what do you think, Red, he is the color you wanted, a sort of dizzy blonde, a lemon colored buckskin!! We haven't really bought him yet as the Indian who owns him says he is his squaw's and she is very deeply attached to him, but I guess we can persuade her. He is gentle and bridlewise and really very handy for the camps and we have a system of kicks which mean *lope*! and "bully up" as Delia says, and he just picks up his little legs and scoots. He's not much, but I guess he'll do. The master of Poky's black and white pinto accidentally shot himself in the eye the other day so that rather stopped negotiating in that direction.

Last week we almost perished with the cold and one morning the snow was on the foot hills right down to the canyons. But now it is warm and nice.

I hope there will be a letter from you tonight. Do write, Reddy. You know, you promised you would. It is so nice and comforting for me to feel, "Well, there isn't a letter tonight, and maybe there won't be one tomorrow or next day, but surely by such and such a day there must be one."

It's just lovely here, Reddy, lots of room and lots of Indians and lots of work, soon, I hope. I only want you, just to come and see how pretty my west window toward the mountains is. The Moores are so sweet and say it seems as tho' you must be here when they see me. It does make me frightfully homesick for you to go there. You know how that wet lawn smells.

I love you, so, dear Reddy, just as warm and sweet.

Yr. Gedy

Give Lou my best love.

Please send us the July Cosmopolitan. And do look up the Wyo. and Ida. records and see whether or not yr. father consecrated the Arapahoe church. I always thought he did but Mr. H. says not.

July 2, 1902
FORT WASHAKIE, WIND RIVER, WYOMING

My precious girl,

I meant to write you again right off in a day or two and I think it must be a week since I wrote last. It is almost indecent the way time flies out here. I got yr. sweet talky letter just a few days ago. It was such a dear one, Reddy. The telling ones are very nice but the talking ones make you so much nearer.

Reddy, I'm so glad about "the trouble." You see, I'm *so* happy out here and I wanted to tell you about it and I did so want to be free to be happy, too—and then I would think, "Oh! my precious Reddy, *maybe* she isn't," and I couldn't tell you or let myself go. And when you said you were going to stay in S. Beth. till on into July I felt sure you didn't want to a bit and were so sweet and fine you just did it. I expect that is true but I'm glad about the other, gladder than I can possibly tell you, you old sweety.

Do you mind if I just talk about myself, Reddy? It's disgusting, I know, but I haven't been able to feel the least interest in myself for so long that I do feel as tho' I had found a nice, new somebody to play with—and I want you to know. It's the Mission, Reddy. It all *bust* upon me one day and there's not a contenter soul anywhere than yr. Gedy. The only fear I have is that I'll get so I'll just spend my time grinning at the mountains and never do a lick of work! Things are working up slowly but the possibilities ahead! It's just like having (as we do 3 times a day—t.i.d.[27] as we used to say in the hospital) mountains of dishes to wash and knowing that all you have to do is to get at it to come out the other side. Excuse the homely figure. Talk about irons in the fire. Two Sunday schools, both weak, two parsons, with peculiarities, two tribes, heap nice, school children in school, school children in the camps, white people, half breeds, sick people, babies to be christened, *such* dusty churches—why I just dream of brooms! And it's so lovely to have them tell you they've been looking for a useful lady for ages and to be able to fall to, hit or miss, and take yr. personality with you. I feel about 20, wear corsets, and sit up as straight as a gopher, just for pure joy, *and* curl my hair!! Now could my own Red ask more of me? Our Arapahoe Cousin is docility itself. It is very nice to have him to work off yr. superfluous personality on, and he seems to have the same feelings himself. All I have to do is to order sermons on baptism and they come forth and wildly, suggest that services should be held at the agency church both morning and evening Sundays (they have been having them only on alternate Sundays) and the notice is straightaway given out. I do hope this docility will last. I wash out Poke's little stole collar things, you savvy, and write missy letters for Mr. Roberts, and they're both just as sweet as they can be, meaning the parsons! Last week was the Sun Dance (Shoshone). I only got there a couple of times as I was feeling rather seedy just then!! All the time I was writing you last time I was battling with a fearful desire to go out and harness my yellow pony to Mr. Roberts little cart and just see what would happen next. Mr. Roberts started to try him the week before but said the pony would smash things (you remember his contrariness!). So I sneaked out and got him and had the harness on by the time I was discovered. Of course, Mr. Roberts just roared. I tore around for a couple of hours just driving the creature without a cart. That evening was the school commencement and we put him in the buckboard with one of the old horses and Mary and I drove him down to the big school in great style. Aren't we dashing? Everybody laughed like everything when we told them. He's rather lacking in personality is the yellow pony! Reddy, I wish you could have seen these children and the audience, mostly Arapahoes. I could have wept the whole time. The children all had such pretty gingham dresses on their hair curled and tied so sweetly. There is a fine superintendent now and I am sure the school is quite equal to Carlisle or any of the big Eastern schools and has the great advantage over them in working almost entirely with fullbloods. You wouldn't have found sweeter more attractive or better behaved and more intelligent girls and boys, big or little, anywhere, I'm willing to stake all I've got on it. Lots of the half breeds were there. Mrs. Hereford, Poke's sister, among them, nursing little Sherman freely in the gaze of the public. Poke gave an awfully good address, written, I'm thankful to say. I was simply paralyzed for fear he hadn't given it a thought before he got up. I think he is improved, much more serious and *not* so conceited. Gracie calls him down on every possible occasion.

Anyhow, it's real nice to have him around. He's so human—and you know the atmosphere of the Mission is a little rarified at times! The inferior brethren are so much nearer my level!

Yesterday Mary and Marian[28] and I drove to Lander and got a stove and our furniture. Mr. Olson, the man on the farm, came down with the team and brought the things back. The house was finished the day before. I opened a bank account at Lander, Reddy, and now I'm a Wyoming girl for sure. When we go to the Oklahewahah, or however you spell it, I shall register, Shoshone Agency, Wyo. I give you fair warning! I have been putting up hooks this morning, but Maggie Havve, the old squaw who comes to scrub drove me out at the point of her mop, so she could clean up. We'll be in directly. I have so many plans which I can only carry out when we get in our own diggings. I guess I better wait till they materialize before I tell you of them. You know what my plans sometimes do! We have had an awful time about our trunks. It was exactly 3 weeks before Mary got hers and my saddle bag came, and yesterday my clothes trunk came. There is still the one with my books and blankets to get. We have got along very well without them but I certainly was glad to get my saddle. Our door in this room is so funny. There are things hanging on it; an epitome of the life of woman, as it were! A spur, a fountain pen, and a hot water bottle!!!

Oh! the mountains, Reddy. And oh! the sage brush. Sometimes I rush out and look at the mountains heap quick in the morning, and other times I save them up for hours. Of course it all taxes you. Nobody else can see how pretty they are, just like you can, and I feel as tho' I was stealing something from you every time I look at them and you can't see them. But they are just sitting up and waiting for you, the pretty things, as patiently. I gave Poke yr. message about Monte but unfortunately Monte has been traded off for a mothy creature, with legs like a cart horse. Poke says he wishes Mugsie[29] *would* come out, and I told him to write and tell you so. It was really Mr. Moore who got us our trunks. Wouldn't you know it would have been? Mrs. Moore has given me such a nice kitchen table with a sort of a sink thing fixed in it. I certainly am telling you the little things. *Everything* is so thrilling when Mary gets a registered package and when it turns out to be riding gaiters from Harriet Hyde. When Mr. Olson's mare has a colt unexpectedly and we all rush out and pet the sweet little thing. When a skunk gets after the chickens and Dewi rushes out in the night and demolishes the creature with dire results. Life is just one long, satisfying thrill. And I'm *so* happy. You know when I'm home with you and happy I always feel so hurty as tho' the least little thing would just hurt so. But here, they could slam me around like everything and I know I would come up grinning.

Oh! Reddy, I've just done nothing but talk about myself but this is one of those days when I feel like putting an exclamation point after every single sentence. I hope you will see Miss Bryant. And Reddy, if you can get any scholarships for us, *do*, $40 a year. Tell me if I could write to anybody. Mr. Carpenter ought to raise one at Senafly. I think I'll give Sid a jolly, too.

Could you send me two or three of those big book things that the Bp. keeps his letters in, files them I mean. I know I could keep Mr. Roberts' letters much handier for him than he does now. You could send them to me by mail and tell me how much.

Write me often, Reddy precious. *Please.*

yr. Gede

Dr. Rafter is a horrid gossip. Neither of those tales are true.

July 7, 1902

FORT WASHAKIE, WIND RIVER, WYOMING

My darling Reddy precious,

Don't you wish you were sitting by our own fireside? I do. Last night I got a very emphatic call down from Mary and Poke in chorus for saying that so often, so, in future, I'll have to whisper it privately to you. But, oh! my me, I do.

I've had a very chequered week since my last outburst to you. Do you think you *honestly* don't mind if I tell you all the little, tiny things? I do just save them up for you and then I'm so afraid you'll be bored by them. It's no fun telling anybody else but you anything and you know I just must tell! I wish I thought you would enjoy my little things as much as I do Lucy's. Maybe so you do! Anyway, I'll pretend you do.

Wed. night a Mr. and Mrs. West who have a ranch 65 miles N.W. of us, up toward the Hole, came to see us. They are great friends of [fragment missing]. Mr. West is awfully nice! He has been out here since the early days. They asked us to go "down below" as the Indians say to the Arapahoe Sun Dance the next day. Marian and I rode the ponies down and the rest came in the buggy. It was about 5 miles below the Arapahoe church. My eye! Reddy, but that Sundance was the real thing! The Ute and Shoshone ones just seemed like bravado compared. I don't know what they wanted but I'm sure they wanted it hard and I hope they'll get it. They don't dance to and fro from the pole like the others, but just stand still, and sort of leap up and down in a queer way. It was the third day and they were pretty well used up. One big man rode right into the middle on a crazy little pony with a little mite of a boy in his arms and they took the baby down and made medicine over him. They prayed over each other and blessed each other and [fragment missing]. It was a wild sight. The next day was the Fourth and Annie Moore got up a picnic for the canyon. Mary and I had been going off up there with the Cousin. So we went, 8 of us. A Miss Welty, the Agency Dr.'s daughter and her young man, Annie Moore and hers, and then we 4 leftovers, Mary and the field matron and Poke and me. I tried to divide Poke up with the other two but he refused to be divided and behaved very badly. He told me the whole story of Longhy. I think it rankles like fire. He's dead proud, is the Cousin. I have decided I don't like my pale yellow squaw pony. He is too mild, as Franklin would say. So I tried a sorrel one that day an Indian brought in in the morning. He was most frightfully rough and finally the noble Poke let me have Prince for the last few miles. It did just feel like heaven to get on that nice easy old horse. Mary has inherited the squaw pony. We haven't bought him yet. The Indian who owns him says his squaw loves him too much. But perhaps her heart will speak after a while. Now it doesn't say anything. In the meantime the yellow pony is eating our alfalfa and we are enjoying him.

Poke came up night before last when I was just raging over having to give up a kind of mean, black pony, which had been acting up a little so Mr. Roberts wouldn't let me get it and soothed my wounded feelings by telling me that he had found just the pony I wanted and to get my skirt on and come and look at it quick. I tried him and oh! Reddy, he's a dream. The old Indian told us he was a race horse, that he'd run away and was a "little bit crazy." Poke just doubled up with glee and said, when we got off the ponies that he knew Andrew had sold his pony when he said that. And sure enough, he's a dear, with a gait like a bird and a fine mouth and awfully free. I took him home that night and brought the money down to the Indian in the morning. I've had such a fearful horror of getting one of those perfectly safe Robertian squaw ponies with legs that don't work quite right and a little queer in the wind, but I've got the best pony on the ranch, now. We met Mr. Olson walking as we were riding home from choir practice last night and I asked him to get up behind me which he did after some difficulty as the pony won't stand still and that little gem just carried us home at a trot, a good bit over 300 lbs., I guess. Mary was riding double with Marian and, as Poke remarked, we looked like a lot of Indians!! We are trying to start an altar guild and have invited all the confirmed people, about 15, to the wickyup Sat. There is so much to be done about the church. The two Sunday schools are doing well. Both were quite full Sunday. We haven't begun to visit the returned school girls yet as Mr. Roberts thinks they ought to have a little time home first. Next week we'll start out. We moved into the wickyup Saturday night. It's so pretty and sweet. You ought to see how the logs shine when the lamp light falls on them. We light a little fire at night and it's so cozy and homelike. I sleep in the front room on what we hope people think is a sofa and Mary has the bedroom. It's been awfully cold until yesterday. Fresh snow on the mountains every few days and lots of wind. Mrs. Moore gave us Virginia's desk and a book shelf thing. Wasn't it sweet of her? Mr. Moore sends his love to you. I gave him yr. own blushing message. Can you spare the extra picture of us two? I think the ones of me are horrid. I put them all in the stove except one for the family. They look like mother. I like the one of us together and the one of you. I have Miss Bennett's photo up. It's the first time I've felt like having it up since I left school, but I expect she'd like these Indians, too. To-sat-see was in the other day, as sweet as ever and all dressed up fit to kill. He was one of the Sun Dancers. Speaking of those we have known and admired (!) I had to write to a lady in Francis' parish the other day to thank for a box, or something and I ventured to send my salutations to the rector. Also as we were riding up the canyon one of us spoke of Tommy and Poke promptly fished out a cigar case with a large and handsome T. H. J. on it. So you see there are hosts around in these foothills still! I think there are lots of Longhy ghosts. It really is very interesting having all these friends with haunted casts!!

I had a dark and terrible adventure on Saturday. We went to see the new baby at a halfbreed's house close to the agency and Mary went in to Mrs. Hereford's to ask about it. You know how I hate to go to half strange people's houses. Just as we were getting in the buggy to drive away, Mary said, "that poor woman has got a mountain of ironing to do and she is just nearly crying, she's so tired." So I rushed in and asked if I could help and she said no, in that way I always say I can't stay another day in Bethlehem, so I told Mary I'd stay a while. She irons for I don't know how many soldiers. I worked for 3 hours as hard as ever I could. I knew you would have had a fit if you could have seen me, when I remember yr. remarks about that little innocent washing at White Rocks. But the poor thing would have been at it till ten o'clock at night alone. It's Poke's half sister, you know. And to say that I enjoyed little Sherman is putting it mildly. I was just so hungry for babies for days afterwards it would wake me up early in the morning. He is a perfect cherub. But the point of all this tale is that in the middle of the ironing the door of the cabin opened and in walked,—Poke!! Talk about being embarrassed! First at being caught there, and then the way he must have felt about her. She calls him Coolidge half the time and says "for G__'s sake" and talks about things you don't exactly talk about in polite society. Well, I thought I'd die on the spot. I declare Poke's a gentlemen, Red. He just gave me one wild look and then said, "Hullo," as cheerfully as tho' it was the most natural thing in the world to find me ironing soldiers' stable jackets with the cats and the babies swarming. I stuck to the ironing and blessed Pokey for being such a dear. Little Sherman was sweet with him and we got thro' alright. I'm to be godmother on Sunday. That is, Mrs. Hereford asked me and I guess she wants me, I asked Poke last night and he said, yes, she did. But wasn't that ghastly, Reddy! I was dead glad I went the' for she was feeling real homesick and miserable and I did have such a good time with little Sherman. Indian babies are so much the nicest.

Are you at Lou's and did you see Miss Bryant? Do tell Lou that I will write her someday. Maybe so, but with 3 letters a week regularly and a few missy ones for Mr. Roberts, I don't get much time for other letters. Give her and all the family my love, and tell Tope the Indians are just fine.

You are a dear to read all this stupid stuff. I'm so afraid you won't know just what I am doing and I'm afraid of getting far apart. It's so sweet to have you to share things with. I feel as tho' I had the best the world had to give, you and Injuns.

Best love yr. Gedy has to give, Reddy! Mary brought me yr. last letter to Mrs. Hereford's but I didn't have a chance to read it till I got home. Oh! talk about embarrassment . . . !! Poor Pokey.

Yr. *heap* loving Gedy

July 21, 1902
FORT WASHAKIE, WIND RIVER, WYOMING

Dearest girl,

I'm going to write you early this week for I have got a lot of outside letters to get off Thursday and tomorrow will be taken up going over to North Fork for the ladies' guild meeting (!!). We are going over for dinner and to talk up plans for getting up an entertainment to raise money for their church fund. Time flies so frightfully here that, honestly, we never seem to get anything done. I had an awfully fool week, last week. Fell off my pony, for no reason at all and did other equally idiotic things. I must say the pony acted most sweetly. Mary's pony, called Mellin's Food,[30] on account of his fitness for infants and invalids (the yellow one) shied into him, we were going rather fast down the agency road, and gave me such a whack I lost my balance and went plumb over. Then my foot caught in the stirrup. We had just passed Andrew Bazill the old fellow I bought him from and, such is the weakness of the feminine mind, I never called the trusty Mary to the rescue, but "Andrew, come and pull my foot out" was what I heard myself remarking. The pony stayed with me and I only got a little bumped (I ought to have got more so for being such a fool) and have been spending my time hiding my wounds from Mr. Roberts' eye. I had to confess to the cousin for being such a fool, sort of punishment, you know. Mary fed me on whiskey and rubbed in turpentine most ably and I don't think anybody knows. The other fool thing was even fooler! Mary reminds me of Lou except that she is not N.E. She can't hitch up a pony right yet after nearly two mos. This is not to be taken in *direct* connection with the remark that went just before. We had 30 at North Fork on Sunday. The little school house was packed so that some of the boys had to stand up. That's not counting us and babies. We can see the school house and our faithful parishioners (!) buggies and ponies drawn up and tied to the fence about 3 miles off. That's the time you begin to wonder how much of the Bible lesson you know and when you wish you hadn't left it till 11 p.m. Sat., to prepare. Poke comes over in the evenings rather often, and altho' very much shocked at first, produced boxes of gold tipped cigs and we smoke behind lowered shades. It's a great thing to have a cousin in the field. Life would be far from the same without him. It was nice of you to send the notice of the Erie church. But honestly, it seems so much less important than whether Cousin Pokey has his little lace collar things sewed in, and whether Lucretia sweeps the church out before Sundays, etc. etc. This world is little, but it does shut out the big one somewhat. We read The Virginian this week, Owen Wister's last. It's very western, have you seen it? There's a wedding trip in it that would settle my hash, if any one proposed it. There's one thing I do like about Owen Wister's books, he never forgets to water the horses and tighten the pack and build the fire to leeward, etc. etc. I'm so sorry yr. so bothered about Irvine.[31] The Bishop is too well known and too long at the business to really feel it so very much, I expect. And you really mustn't call Irvine's and his fellows' faults "the church." I expect they are what make it the church militant. I don't believe I'd try Methodism. It's open to everybody. Irvine might decide to do too. But I don't think I'll try defending the church to you. It might get to be like defending the Indians to Mrs. Roberts.

The services are getting so nice. We have abolished Gospel hymns, thank heaven, and other abominations of desolation. Poke is so sweet and docile and, you see, he being rector of the agency church, we have only to say the word. We have started a fine and enthusiastic altar guild and hope to do great things. Nobody was here to take the lead in those things and you know how everybody's business is nobody's business. We have choir practice Wednesday evenings and have got up nice music for the communion on Sunday. The Cousin did baptize that baby so sweetly. He hardly looks Indian, the baby, I think it's too bad.

I hope next letter things will be going better. Isn't there anyone to do anything to that Irvine? It makes you feel so dead helpless when common justice goes back on you. You are so sweet, my precious girl, and how happy I am and the Bishop must be to have you. I hope they won't insist on having too much of you. I'll have to get up something dire so you will just have to fly home. What do you think would bring you, Reddy?

I love you every second as you know directly.

Your devoted
Gedy

August 5, 1902
FORT WASHAKIE, WIND RIVER, WYOMING

My precious Red Head,

You misjudge both my pony, and my cousin. He *didn't* throw me, I just naturally fell off and if you were here (I wish you were, I begin to want you hard) you and Mr. Roberts would be reinforced so we should stand 3 against one in favor of caution. You see I went riding Saturday night up on that mesa which we crossed going to the place we went fishing that time. (Weren't you with us, by the way? Poke swears that you went with the buggy and he and I rode over the trail. But I can remember you there.) And just as it was getting dark an old rattlesnake went off like an alarm clock right under my pretty boy. Of course I leapt off like a shot and began firing rocks at it. When I had killed him I turned around and demanded Poke's knife to cut off the 5 rattles. But Poke coldly refused to give it to me. I said, "Reddy loves those little things to hang on her hat," then I got scornful and said he was just like those squaws we saw at the Arapahoe Council House that day, who were afraid to touch a bit of dead rattlesnake skin. Still no knife. Then I said if Reddy was here she would cut them off! I was told that I might want Mugsie to be bitten by a rattle snake but he didn't want me to be. We almost came to blows. I got the knife finally and having gained my point and it being so dark I could hardly see the thing on the ground and well, yr. rattles are up on the mesa still! But when we kill a rattlesnake, Reddy, we won't act like Injuns, will we?

I'm always so happy when it comes the middle of the week so I can write to you again. It's so nice, even in the act of killing snakes, to think that I can soon write you all about it. How lucky I am to have you and to have you want to hear. Mary went off to Dubois with the Wests Friday and I'm reveling in every moment of my solitude. Oh! it's heavenly not to have anybody to tag you! And I never have to decide a thing one second before I do it! I rode as far as Sage Creek with them (and Annie Moore) and then I turned my Fox around and loped home those 9 solitary and consequently heavenly miles, till the Post came in sight. Just the mountains, and Fox and me. (Erie, indeed! I thought of calling him Plato, but I was afraid it might have an ambiguous sound, besides, why name a nice horse after a mere man!) I told Sherman the other day it was worth coming out to Wyoming just to get such a superior pony. He jumps ditches and can beat long legged Prince running. And you ought to see him climb. He follows me all around, and doesn't bust fences anymore tho' I can't say as much for ropes. Honestly, if I'd make up a pony in my mind he couldn't have been nicer than my boy is.

I had a lovely time Sunday. Mr. Roberts goes to Lander once a month and this Sunday he stopped off at North Fork and took the service instead of having Sunday school. So I had an afternoon off. Poke can't get off weekdays so it was very nice. We went up Trout Creek Canyon, a heavenly place, prettiest canyon I've seen around here. We ate buffalo berries and choke cherries and Poke brought me home a *big* pine branch and a *big* cedar one, and then made my wickyup look so pretty. Prince looked like a Xmas tree. I fixed the horses up with white berries in their bridles and we looked very gay indeed. Got down in time for EvenSong. Red, the services and the congregations, too, I think, are improving so at the church. The Altar Guild and Sunday school are stirring people up a little and I think both the parsons are glad to have somebody to take an interest in things. It's awfully heavenly to be of use. We got some of the Arapahoe girls to the agency church Friday night. My! what nice girls they are. They had all come up for rations the next day. They only issue every two weeks now. The Arapahoes seem like real people, only nicer than most, but I can't make the Shoshones seem real. They arc just like sunflowers, round and foolish. Someday I'll go and live "down below" with the Arapahoes, in spite of myself. Nobody does much for them, almost all the work is amongst the Shoshones.

I don't see how you can like being with them, Reddy. I do so want to hold on to people when I am talking to them, I nearly have to sit on my hands to keep them where they belong. The other night, sandwiched in between wild jokes, our poor Cousin talked to me about himself, his Injun self, I expect, and oh! Reddy, he was the pitifullest thing. I wanted to cry awfully, and I wanted to go and comfort him so and I could only sit, half way across the room and stitch like mad on that old Arapahoe altar covering. I expect he has had a pretty hard road to travel, poor thing, I am afraid I treat him just about as I would you, drag him into these canyon trips and all that. I'm so afraid I'm unwomanly, it worries me to death. I'm afraid you'll think this letter has an Arapahoe tinge! But the way of it is that play is so much more fun to talk about than work. Poke and I have decided that we are just like Robinson Crusoe and as we've no one else to play with we might as well play with each other. I explained all this carefully to him the other day and he agreed with me perfectly. So if you think there's too much play, why just come out and play too? Don't you think it would be nice if we three all could go up to the Sioux country someday?

You darling, write me heap quick.

Yr. Gedy

August 20, 1902

FORT WASHAKIE, WIND RIVER, WYOMING

I was so glad to get your letter. I can't tell you. I thought when the week went by without one from you that you were hurt or cross at my letter.

I was so sorry I had spoken at all. But you weren't. Oh! you're a dear. Reddy, I don't know exactly what I'm up to. Don't you think you could come out and tell me? My, but I want you badly. Come out for September, October, or anytime you like, only come. You know you oughtn't to leave me out here with these Indians all by myself. I'm awfully mixed up, Reddy. Honest, I am.

Talk about principles. Did I ever have any? How far can you let them go when they don't mean anything serious and you don't? I never let anybody before hold my hand a whole evening, or even a few minutes. I'm so afraid it seems flip, then I explain that I never did this way before, and I am convinced that makes it worse. I do get so horribly tangled. Every night that goes on and it was after midnight last night when it stopped and the yellow puppy (the children gave him to me and he's such a foolish dear) and I got to bed. And *you* don't mind they're kissing you, do you? But I haven't reached that point—I won't say *yet*. Why should I? I had a narrow escape, but I tried the power of the human eye that Helen Copill used to bank so on in oral exams and it worked pretty well. But then the poor thing sat down and called itself a fool so many times that I almost did it myself after all. I feel sure if we had then reached the present hand-holding stage I would have. Say, Reddy, I'm old for this foolishness, doesn't it make you chuckle? I expect I am just lonely and I know Sherman is. But is it undignified—oh, unwomanly I suppose I mean—to act this way? Is it, Reddy? And what shall I do about it. If I only had your little white hand to hold I shouldn't have to go around borrowing other peoples'. I explain all those things as I go along. I feel pretty sure we are both playing not with each other as objects, but together, each being subjects. Do try to savvy me! Do you think I had better stop? He is too old and has been burnt too often to have to be much considered, but I don't want to be, or seem either, to myself what I said—that horrid word—unwomanly. I guess I could stop but it would be kind of lonely. We had an awful time a week ago Friday night. He thought I had meant something awfully mean and heartless by just some little thing I had said—put me right down with all those people who say mean things to him because he is Injun and all that. It hurt like fire. I told him he would never have a chance to hurt again and I meant it by Jove. You don't know how frightfully careful I am *not* to hurt him, he is so absurdly sensitive. And it isn't natural to me to think twice. That made it worse. Well, I sent him flying. I was pretty nearly sick for three days after. Then I felt horribly good—that is, I guess it was that—as tho' he had had about enough of that kind of thing and I could stand it (being hurt) better than he could. Then I heard Prince was sick and he was walking from the Post to the Agency so Wednesday morning I got my courage up to go down to the office and offer Fox. Whew! But I guess you can do about anything you have to.

August 25, 1902
FORT WASHAKIE, WIND RIVER, WYOMING

My own Precious,

Do you believe you would love me any less if you heard that "the power of the human eye" had failed, or rather had failed to be turned on in time, for the last three nights? Your Gedy has been feeling like Adam and Eve after the fall. (That reminds me, did you know they were Arapahoes? Sherman says so and has a very plausible story to prove the fact.) For heaven's sake write me quick and tell me if you think twosing without any prospect of ever getting beyond that stage is very promiscuous. You know how I felt about you and Tommy and with Francis after *his* fall, when it had turned into only twosing. But honestly it feels so natural and comfortable I can't think why I ever did anything else. All but the first night and then he almost scared me to death, but since then I have drawn the line at a certain point. It was all so funny, except that scary kind. I kept wishing you were there so. I've got a box fixed outside the sitting room window where we roll up in blankets and sit. There were the sweetest moon right up in the sky in front and a whole bunch of coyotes howling up in the hills. That Mrs. Geddes that I was going to take care of (she has got a nurse by the way, so I won't have to do it) is awfully sweet and sporty and as she is awfully late and feeling pretty rocky I brought the babies home for a couple of days. The family are away camping so Mary and I are cooking for ourselves and Mr. Snyder, such a nice Pi-ute halfbreed who works on the ranch. I had the two little redheads in my bed that night and bunked on the floor myself. Right in the middle of the excitement, Mary having gone to bed in the back room, one of them began to cry with the toothache and I had to roll her up in a blanket and bring her out and comfort her. They were the goodest little things. But what with all the work and not getting to bed till nearly morning and up at six or so, and the rest of it, I all but went to sleep in the middle of things last night and had to send the Injun home and get to bed. Red, do you think I'm an awful fool or maybe worse than that? What's happened to me, I wonder? My convictions are, I *think*, the same, but it does seem so comfortable and natural I might as well buck at kissing you. But is it wrong to Sherman? I honestly can't make myself care about him like he says he does about me and I tell him so every few rounds. Maybe we both like just the twosing. I guess it is because he's Injun that I feel so at home. They always have seemed more natural than just white people, tho' I don't tell him that. Oh! yes. I did too, partly. And he said, well, wasn't he one? I said, yes, but how about the quarter of a million others? And he said something silly about the seventy million other whites in the country. You have to get up early to get ahead of these Arapahoes. All of which is very silly and not to the point at all. I guess Prince wonders if Langley[32] has come back!!! I wonder what Sherman expects with Langley and a half dozen others besides behind him. You can't have your cake and eat it too, as I tell him when the subject comes up.

I wish you'd tell me what I'm doing, Reddy, and say a little prayer for my perplexity. I have been using that word for the last week and I don't think I ever heard myself using it in my life! You thought you liked Tommy, you see, and that changes the whole case. I wish I could fool myself but I can't. Don't you believe you better come out and take care of me? It looks like you had to me. My but I wanted you that first night, I'm awfully green for my years. But I always thought men were just about like women. Indians don't seem to be, anyhow. Well, if I hadn't you, I never would dare go as far as I have. If you tell me to stop, I will. But it's awfully nice to have somebody to say good night to.

What is that harmony of yours? Sherman wants one and I told him to wait till I asked the name of yours. And here are the blank cheques I forgot to put in. Do write me, soon for I don't know what a day will bring forth or don't seem to know. All that agitation the other night started by

Sherman saying something to Mary and me about what he and some other Indians did and what some whites did. And when Mary went in I said I didn't like to be called whites, and with that he went off half cocked and has been absolutely bronco ever since.

For heaven's sake, say something, Reddy. I wish I liked him like I do you. I guess there's something wrong with me. I want to like and I just plumb can't, only you, you old red headed sweety.

Your perplexed Gedy

Honestly I most hardly felt fit for church yesterday.

Sherman told me to give you his love every time I wrote so here goes. I guess he's got plenty to spare whenever there is a petticoat in the question. It looks that way to me.

The littlest Geddes "Wilhelmina, only but they call me Willie" aged three, calls the Agency, the Injuncy. I laughed after and she thought I was laughing at her pronunciation so she said with great dignity "Indiancy." She murmured to Mary in church yesterday, "Doesn't Mr. Coo-coo-coolidge look nice like that!"

September 1, 1902

FORT WASHAKIE, WIND RIVER, WYOMING

My precious Reddy,

The Indian man,[33] Indian if he is Eastern, came last night but I didn't have time (!?) to open him till this morning. I have built a shelf outside my house on the East side, as the West backs on nothing and I'm sure he will be able to do wild things with his arms soon, as the wind comes up just tearing about almost every afternoon. I love to have any kind of Injun things and further I love to have anything from you, so this present combination is a very sweet one. You feel so near to me these days, I love to know you are thinking of me. Your N. E.[34] letter came the other day, and read Sherman the first about the cramped position for three weeks and the war whoops and we just roared. Mrs. Geddes' littlest girl "only but they call me Willie" is just like you. Both our Cousin and I have decided you must have been just like that and we like her just heaps in consequence, as you can imagine. I want you to write me so I can hardly wait. I think I've gone in circles since I wrote you. *How* can you tell if you like them? The other night Sherman asked me to marry him and I was so glad, Reddy, I almost died right there and then, but I told him I'd have to have a long time to think. I haven't the vaguest idea how I feel about him, except just dead comfortable and happy when he is here, but I guess that's because he's Injun, they always make me feel that way.

Honestly, just coming home from North Fork on Sundays it gives me the sweetest shiver the first Indian we meet on the reservation. It was an Arapahoe yesterday too. He's an awfully sweet old Injun, anyhow. *What* do you think of me? I can't write you very fully till I have had an answer to those two last letters of mine. Does all this bore you I wonder?

Your-not-half-so-much-perplexed-as-I-was Gedy

I know it means more slaps for him, poor thing, and he has certainly had his share, and I guess he knows it, too.

I needn't ask you not to breathe a word of this to Lou or anyone. Let me have peace till I have thought it out.

I read your letter to Sherman and he said he thought so too. I think you might send your love to him! He is going to write you today and I think and Mrs. Coolidge too. It's awful these important letters that we have to get off.

Your very much blissful,
Gedy (and Sherman's! Yes, I am too!)

Do send us something to read. How do you expect me to pass my time on that honeymoon? Do read Nathalie Blayne in the Sept. Harper's. Don't talk about articles on Arizona and books—then never send a thing. Sherman's reading Tommy [and] Grizel but he doesn't get much time (!). Reddy, that's a wonderful book. I feel more and more like Grizel every day. I expect all women do. And we make wonderful new discoveries every few days like they did. Did you and Francis or Tommy? Did you? But the one last night was the deepest down one yet and just went to the spot, that spot where you get glad, when you are very thoroughly glad. Mary couldn't get any white stuff but she sent to Lander for it and we will work on it Saturday. I have a skirt pattern Harriet Hyde gave me. It's wonderful how helpful the Deaconess School has been!!

I said last night we could have a hymn at our wedding and I got funny and asked Sherman if he would prefer Peace, Perfect Peace or Fight the Good Fight or The Voice that Breathed on Eden, in memory, this last, of Adam and Eve—Arapahoes! But he squidged his eyes up and said he'd like Abide with Me!!

What's your favorite season of the year, Reddy? Mine is Indian Summer! Ha! Ha! Ha!

And when I'm married, Reddy, I'll be half Arapahoe which half, Reddy? My better half!

Etc. I ask Sherman these things in the evening. Well, we have to do something to pass the time away.

September 10, 1902
FORT WASHAKIE, WIND RIVER, WYOMING

I thought I should just bust till your letter came—nearly two weeks! Honestly, Reddy, I thought you didn't like the idea and I guess Sherman did too. Last night we were sitting out on some logs under the west window enjoying the moon and the Shoshone songs going off in all directions, when Mr. Olson and Dewi came with yr. letter. I didn't read it till after Sherman went, but oh! I was so relieved that you didn't buck. Unfortunately this letter of yours was only an answer to my first one. "Hand holding in the dark" seems a trifle passé just now!! I wish to heaven you were here. I want to know how you did it and more than that I want to know what to do. The Injun has been very good and patient until last night and then he got rambunctious and wanted to know what I was going to do next. Just what *I* want to know. It would all be so nice, feel as tho' he was so much realer than any (man) body I have ever known and it is so much more natural to be twosing with him; I'm just crazy to stay out here the rest of my natural days, and Mr. Roberts hardly gives me any work to do—I guess if it hadn't been for Sherman I would have been off to Whiterocks before this, there is a fine opening for work amongst the Arapahoes in Big Wind about 18 miles below here. They are asking for a church and a day school. I couldn't very well go alone, and besides it needs a man and he's just as dear and sweet as they come—only I just can't open my mouth and say the word. I feel just like a kite that is waiting for the wind to pick it up. I couldn't tell if you burned me at the stake whether I was going to say yes or no. Do you think it's just because I'm old and can't fool myself now or get much worked up? Heavens above!! I *wish* I knew. I'm waiting for a sign. I told Sherman last night if he wanted to go on as we were on these terms, we would do, but if he didn't think it was worth waiting for, we'd just quit. We couldn't, of course, very comfortably. We have spent about 3 evenings apart in the last month or six weeks and I know I thought I should bust till the next one came around and so did Sherman. Of course I won't promise to come to you. "Circumstances and conditions" can't do it with me; I've got past the place where I can fool myself; what I do, I shall do in cold blood, but I'll tell you the whole truth. You don't know how I ache every night when I come in. But what if I say no after all? Anyhow it will be just as hard for me as it is for him. We're both in the same boat. And I expect we shall meet Mr. Roberts at the Arapahoe Church some Sunday afternoon and stop off at the ranch on the way back! Prince and Fox tied to the belfry outside the church, with my trousseau hitched on Fox in a gunny sack! (tooth brush and a slicker). It sounds pretty easy doesn't it? And there is a fine prospect of work ahead. Talk about killing two birds.

Did I say "unworthy"? Perhaps I meant that because there was a man. I didn't think you and Lou must necessarily think I was bound to annex myself to him. But perhaps I didn't. Anyway I'm glad you didn't say Injun to me. Maybe I'll say yes tonight. I nearly did the other night, but I had made up my mind to wait for your letter. I expect we would both be happy as clams, don't you? I would like to explain to you how many qualities he has and things he combines that I have always liked the thought of, but I'm afraid it would sound queer, not to say, softy. You needn't be jealous. I tell Sherman every time the subject comes up that you are the only man I ever loved. I feel "human" enough, but not "womanly" yet. Don't you think its these N. E. ancestors of mine who just *won't* let me feel when I want to. I've got to calculate first.

We have fourteen girls in the school and Miss Burnett and I are having a great time with them teaching. The school has been the most awful failure and is of very little, if any, use, now, I think, with such an excellent govt. school here and the same church influence there. But Miss Eva and I are trying to do what we can with the forlorn things.

The Pentecost is lovely. He fell down on Sunday, there was a fearful wind, but Mr. Olson says he will put him on top of the house for me.

It has got cool and perfectly lovely. I wish you were here.

Devotedly,
Your trying to be patient,
Gedy

Do you mind letters all on one subject? If it was settled I don't think I'd bother you. I wish you were here to diagnose my case. Well, you are very sweet and patient.

Your most loving,
Gedy

September 24, 1902
FORT WASHAKIE, WIND RIVER, WYOMING

You darling,

I have only a moment before our children's school bell rings but I am so full of what Sherman calls, bliss (!!) this morning, that I must begin now, even if I can't finish till later. Yr. letter and Lou's basket came day before yesterday. Isn't Lou the sweetest thing, almost as sweet as the candy which we all, and the little Injunies, devoured with joyful accord. And it's very nice to have one more Injuny thing, the basket, in my wickyup. I'm going to write Lou today or tomorrow, the dear thing!

Well, we wrote Father last night, both of us. That is Sherman wrote and I put a note in his letter. His letter was just sweet. I didn't want to write at all till we were married but Sherman bucked. Said we ought to do the square thing anyhow, which of course is true but uncomfortable, maybe so . . . I said the word sitting on the packing box under the window the night of that day I wrote you last. I hadn't the least idea I would when I was writing but all of a sudden it hit me hard and I said it and Sherman almost squeezed the life out of me. Say, Red, I don't feel too old at all now! Remember the Worthingtons! I was just thinking this morning that I never think about that part anymore. Well, if I haven't been perplexed, thank heaven that stage has been passed, anymore. I have been awfully agitated, up one minute and down the next; on and off. But yesterday, or rather the night before that, I decided way inside and oh! my eye, we had a good time last night. We made a discovery last night, someday I'll tell you all about it. Aren't you glad you gave me that little diary? I am.

Poor Mary Preston, she certainly has been long suffering. Think of my getting her into a scrap like this! Last week Sherman took us down to the Sub.[35] He had to go on business and we went alone and spent the night. All Arapahoes down there. My, but the lodges were pretty, and it was so sweet to hear a horse galloping by in the night and know for sure there was an Arapahoe on it! It was also awfully sweet to see Sherman in the morning instead of waiting till dark. He didn't know we were going to stay all night so we had all the more fun. We drove down a couple of broncs that didn't know beans. One was Arapahoe and he balked and the other was Shoshone and he went crazy, after the manner of their respective tribes.

Night before last we rode down to the ranch to take Prince to turn him out down there. I sneaked some picnic supper and was caught by Mrs. Roberts in the act! Mary wouldn't go with us. We rode over on a little island back of the house and sat down on the beach to eat where you could see the sweetest little piece of river with the red bluffs on one side and the bushes all turned red and yellow on the other, and the dearest little piece of sunset river with a tepee at the end and the blue hills back of it. I think I'd almost take Sherman for the ranch! He took me inside afterwards and the house looked so sweet and homey. I always supposed the whole place was falling to pieces but it's too sweet for anything, except a honeymoon!! Coming home that night it was awfully dark. I got jay[36] and suggested a short cut thro' a lane and then reviled Poke for riding slowly and finally had the satisfaction of loping at a high rate of speed straight into a barbed wire fence. I was riding that new bronc of Sherman's, we call him Cherokee as he got him from a goldened haired white man who claims to be part Cherokee, and the thing isn't bridlewise so I couldn't get him off the fence, it had been built across the road, true Injun style, till he had scraped me the length of the wire between three posts. It hurt like Sam Hill. I doubled up and thought I certainly would have to fall off. I went to the Post surgeon yesterday, the family made me, rode the bronc and he (not the bronc!) "fixed it up" for me. It's right on my shin and the doctor said it was cut to the bone. I tell Sherman all the gory particulars to see him double up! Ha! Ha!

We have told Mary at last. She has shown apparently no interest till suddenly, at the Sub, she turned on me and asked me out right. She's sweet and most helpful and discreet. We went down to the R. C.[37] mission and were sitting talking with such a sweet old priest who suddenly turned on Sherman and said, "Mr. Coolidge, do you know how many witnesses are necessary for a wedding in this state?" There was a horrible, horrible pause in which I inwardly thanked heaven my Cousin was an Arapahoe and so could keep his face straight as they gravely discussed the question. There we sat, the witness and the parson before us. It was just killing.

We have thought we would go down to the Arapahoe church with Mr. Roberts someday, just us two, and get a few Indians in for witnesses. But last night it struck us we would do it right here in the little Shoshone chapel. The Injun kids and the Robertses would enjoy it so! Mary is going over to Mr. Moore's today to get some white stuff to make me a dress. I never thought about a wedding dress till today but I don't see why I shouldn't have one and maybe a veil too. But oh! I want you Reddy more than anything else in life. I wish you could be with me for that hour. Sherman can take his leave next week and I think we shall do it then. We are going down to the ranch for a month, going away for little trips so we can both be here for our Sunday work and so I can come up for the teaching of these children occasionally. Then if Mr. Roberts likes the idea we'll just come back here to the wickyup for the winter. We have great plans for next summer. We'll have to build on a lean-to for a kitchen. I think we'll get our dinners at the Mission. Sherman assures me he is a good cook! Ye Gods! I hope so.

Reddy, are you *glad?* This Gedy, is, oh! busting. It's such a sweet Injuny thing. I never could like it so much if it weren't Injun. You know when I was a kid I always said I'd marry one. Think how nice it will be to have him to go around with us when we go on our trips in future. We say so all the time we wish Reddy was here.

I caught him grinning to himself the other night. I asked what was the matter and he said maybe he would tell me someday. But after much judicious pumping I got out of him that he wanted to call me Gedy too. I thought you wouldn't mind. So we do. Say, Red, I'm most foolishly happy. I sometimes am afraid I'm not hot enough about him but I guess I am. Mary says to tell you for her it's an awfully bad case!! Isn't she nervy? All our little Injuns, 13 of them, were baptized last night. Mr. Roberts did some and Sherman the rest. They were angelic, even Delia! I got them white ribbons and they looked so nice on their little black heads. I guess we'll hitch them on again next Wed., or Thursday afternoon! Don't you know they'd be charmed. The only thing that almost spoils all these sweet plans is yr. not being here. I don't see how I can get thro' without you, dearest. We never thought of such a possibility, did we? After all, it's only for ten minutes, but it's for such a long ten minutes, such big minutes. I wish they'd come! We've been engaged for two weeks tonight and they seem like two years, anyhow! I don't see how on earth we can stand another week.

Oh! Mr. Mondell was here last week and they had a big political meeting in the council room at the agency. Everybody from all around went (there was a free dance afterwards!) Injuns and whites, except Gedy. Sherman stayed five minutes and then came up here and we had a fine time till one o'clock when the rest of the party got back. But the point of this is that he saw Mr. Mondell and told him how we tried to find Mrs. M. in Washington last spring.

I've got to stop. You'll be bored to death with all this and my leg hurts like Sam Hill. But oh! Reddy, it was worth it for all the petting I got afterwards. I am awfully happy and I'm so glad he knows you and that it was you who did the business that night at [illegible]. What do you suppose Francis will say? I'll write you "every day or two" only too glad of the chance! If you could come out and spend that month at the ranch with us telegraph us and we would wait for *you*, but otherwise don't think of telegraphing for telegrams have to be telephoned from Lander to the Agency officer and are everybody's business.

If only you could come! Oh! Reddy, do. You make me feel like the babes in the wood. You know you would like to honeymoon with us. You shall have Fox and I'll ride Cherokee and we'll go off into the mountains and hunt bears!

October 22, 1902
COOLIDGE RANCH, WIND RIVER, WYOMING
OUR RANCH (OR RATHER, MY RANCH, SINCE THE "WORLDLY GOODS DEAL" OF TWO WEEKS AGO TODAY).

My precious darlingest,

I know you are forgiving me for this silence. I meant to write you in a day or two, as I said in my last letter, but just after I wrote you we fell into all sorts of trouble. I couldn't write you or anybody till I knew how it was coming out, and, since we have been married we have been housecleaning to the exclusion of every other idea.

What do you think I did last night? Got homesick for you all of a sudden and began to weep into one of our best new napkins I was trying to hem. Sherman was sitting at the end of the table singing hymns out of the hymnal (I should say it was nice to marry a parson) and he began to sing that, Oh, Come Ye to Bethlehem, one that I used to make the sewing school children sing when I was going over to you for the Xmas holidays. I told him to stop or he would make me homesick. Then I tried to rub my eyes as tho' the alkali (plenty of it in the worldly goods) had gotten in them. But it saw thro' me. It really is awfully sweet. It wakes me up kissing me this morning, one big one for him and then another big one for Mugsey. Well darling, I want to tell you all about everything. If I don't finish in time to take this up to the mail today, I'll take what I have and continue in our next. We had everything all ready to be married

Wednesday the first. I had asked Marian Roberts to be bridesmaid and Mary was going to be Sherman's best man (!). Marian sneaked her confirmation veil for me and Mary and I made a dress which looked very respectable. I woke up Monday morning saying "day after tomorrow"—and what is it? "Then all smiles stopped together." That evening Sherman went to Mr. Roberts—we were with the family over in the sitting room at the Mission. Everybody was jollying and congratulating us. He came back looking funny. I took him over to the wickyup. "Is it all right?" "No, Mr. Roberts says he won't marry us." I couldn't believe it, but Sherman could, knowing him of old. We had planned to go to Lander the next day to get a present for Mrs. Roberts by way of a fee. His objection was that we didn't give him time enough, he claimed the two weeks which they treat them to in England, and said he wouldn't marry us without my father's consent. I thought Sherman had just got an Injun fit and pulled out too soon and I felt sure that when I explained my relations to my family to him in the morning he would see our point of view. After breakfast I called him out and started in. Sherman made me promise I wouldn't lose my temper and I didn't, but I talked straight from the shoulder, I can tell you. But nothing persuaded him. All he said was, "I shall telegraph your father." "What if he refuses?" (I thought he would.) "I don't know what you can do but publish the bans." I told him this custom was obsolete here, that he was judging by the law of another country and of twenty years ago. "I shall telegraph your father." Then I conceded a point. Said we would telegraph from Lander. Sherman had wanted to do this all the time, but I know my family and was afraid of consequences. A burnt child, etc. Reddy, if we had been strangers, a runaway couple coming in off the streets, he could not have treated us differently. I felt it was such an insult to Sherman. There was no canonical reason why we could not be married if we chose to do it in our own way for our own good reasons. No one on earth had a right to forbid us. You see, he was just substituting his judgment for ours. You *can't* understand or appreciate all this as you could if you had been here and seen the work as I have, his relation with and to his family. It is the most subtle sort of absolute domineering. But that is neither here nor there. We went to Lander and so did he and telegraphed. We stayed till late waiting for the answer but it did not come. It was cold and very miserable and we felt so helpless and insulted. Coming home that night there was a fearful rainstorm, we were soaked and almost frozen and when we got to the agency (Sherman had to walk for the past two miles feeling the road with his feet, Prince nearly tipped us over once), we decided we couldn't go any further so we stopped at Miss Ramsey's, the field matron, and asked her to keep us for the night. They made up a bed for Sherman in the Council Room (where we heard the ghost dance talk) and took me in with them. Then next morning we went up to the Mission and every last one of them thought we had eloped. They had guessed something was up. Then I had to tell Mary and the others there wouldn't be any wedding that day. That was Wed. The telegram came telling us to wait for Father's letters. They were delayed and we did not get them till Sunday night; mine then, and Sherman's Monday morning. Father wrote very kindly and considerately. We were very glad we had waited. You see, we always half wanted to, Sherman more than half. If Mr. Roberts had said all that he said as a friend, as a priest, as one clergyman to another. But think of his standing up like a pope and refusing to marry us. You don't know how it feels, Reddy, and I hope you never will. We were just about sick. Sherman's vacation began Oct. 1st so he used to come and stay with me daytimes, sometimes we'd have a little lunch in the wickyup with Mary P. trying to be cheerful and sometimes he would go home for his meals. I just dragged around. I just had to lie down in the evenings and Sherman would sit and hold my hand and we'd talk about what we could do. A new plan every evening. Everybody was so good to us. Imagine how we felt. Everybody, of course, was saying that Father had refused to let us marry. I don't think anybody really believed our story, it was so improbable. Mary and everybody said they could understand Mr. Roberts' objecting in the beginning—not refusing but that after Father refused his consent, which he never did, there was nothing left for Mr. Roberts to do but to act according to our decision. Anywhere else we could have gone out around the nearest corner and got somebody else, but it just happened that here we were up against it. Of course, Mr. Roberts did what he did from the most conscientious reasons, we never forgot that, but the combination of a conscience with a narrow mind is a pretty hard one on the other fellow. But everybody was so good to us and so considerate and so plainly on our side. I hated to see anybody. We had been *so* happy. Even Mrs. Roberts who never bothers being civil to anybody and rather doesn't like Sherman, was so sweet and good to us and went out of her way to do us little kindnesses, would beg me to stay over there in the evenings till Sherman came and not to bother with the dishes and all that. I certainly loved Sherman, Reddy. He was so good—so just. He would take Mr. Roberts' side to me and show me his point of view. He has got such a clear sensible mind. It made us awfully near together. But we both felt that we were never going to be married. I don't know why. Sherman went all to pieces one night. Put his poor old head down in my arms and just cried like a baby. But all the time I could see your writing on an envelope addressed to my new name and that made me think maybe we would be married after all. When your letter came the other day—the very first letter I ever got too—I told Sherman how I had felt sure we would be married at last.

You want me to tell you all this, don't you? I haven't told anybody else, and I don't suppose I ever shall, it hurts so to talk about it. Well, Monday, after we had talked over Father's letters to us (Mary had gone off camping with the Wests Saturday. She had put off the trip a week for the wedding.), in which he said he would not attempt to decide for me but that he urged us to wait and think things over, we decided to drive to Lander again and telegraph once more, asking for his consent to marry, saying that we had carefully thought over his letters. We did this and answer came in the morning—"Withdraw my power to decide and leave the responsibility entirely with you." Sherman came over with it in the morning early. (We had got the ring the day before. It's Wyoming gold Reddy, Mr. Burnett, the jeweler in Lander, knew the old man who brought the gold down from his mine.) He showed it to Mr. Roberts, told him we had been to the final court, that the power of decision now rested with me and that my decision was final. Mr. Roberts still said no, that my father had asked for delay and it was my duty to comply with his wishes. He still refused. Sherman told him I was the judge of my duty. Sherman came to me perfectly furious, he said, "If you will get ready I'll come for you at two and we'll drive to Lander and see about the license and then take the Casper stage in the morning." Craig, at Casper, is a friend of his, and I had visions of our friend Percy Palmer (!!) giving me away. We had thought of going to Boise to the Bishop. But on account of the expense and because we aren't either us especially stuck on the Bishop, we didn't. We also thought of going to Dr. Roffer. Sherman was ordained there. But think of the position we were in. Suppose Craig or any of them said, "Why weren't you married at home? Mr. Roberts has known you both for years, and if he won't marry you, there must be some reason." We had our telegram to show. "Surely that relieves the priest of all responsibility. There must be some other reason." We saw about the license at Lander and found we had to get it in Casper for another county. Everybody looked at us on the streets and we knew everybody was talking about us. We had our bags and our wraps for the stage trip and Eva Burnett had helped us get off, curled my hair for me! But all the fun was knocked out of us. It was lovely moonlight and we decided we would drive on to the Sub for the night. I sort of hate to stay that way in Lander and we knew Mr. Becker at the Sub and he would be nice to us and we had had such a sweet time down there the other time. We always call it the Garden of Eden, because, as I told you, Adam and Eve were Arapahoes. So we drove down to Eden and got there about nine. Mrs. Becker couldn't have done enough for us and best of all she didn't ask us any questions. I forgot to tell you that, just as we were leaving the Mission, Mr. Roberts came out and spoke to us and we told him we were going away to be married. If Sherman hadn't been, as he so often told me, first, a priest, and second, an Indian, we would have been married by the justice of the peace in Lander until we could get at a priest, but you see, we had to look out for appearances. We got up at the Sub the next morning expecting the stage about ten. Sherman went up to the store to telephone Craig, came back directly to say that Mr. Roberts had telephoned us very early saying if we could come back with the license he would marry us at once. I guess at last it had dawned on him that we meant what we said. He always told me the Arapahoes were stubborn! So we piled in the cart and went back to Lander, got our license, coaxed poor, tired Prince back to the Mission, got there about five and we married at 5:30 or thereabouts.

I'll finish this tonight. Love me, Darling, for I do love you more than ever. My best love, half of it, if not more. No, you don't have to divide love. It's funny stuff, defies mathematics. If you give it at all, you can give it all, as I do to you, darlingest.

Your Gedy Coolidge

October 26, 1902

COOLIDGE RANCH, WIND RIVER, WYOMING

Dearest girl,

I came right near losing my Injun since I wrote you. We were gaily driving a bronc home from the Agency the other day with Fox tied along beside when this bronc ran us up on a bank and spilled Sherman out—pretty near busted his neck. He has been very much suppressed for the last couple of days. I have to pull him up and down in bed and take his clothes (most of them) on and off; in fact, I'm frequently reminded of old Mr. Burns in dispensary whose shirt I was obliged to remove on my first day, much to my embarrassment, as I hadn't the faintest idea which end the creatures went in at.

When I went up to post your letter we found a big box of hymnlers and some books. I think they both must have come from you, the books I'm sure of. You are a dear and we grasped them all very gleefully. Two of the books I have and I am going to sd them back and "su-opp" as old Lou used to say. The Young Ranchman is very appropriate to the occasion and there is some wild Indian talk in it that appealed to my sense of the fitness of things. While I am on the subject, your telegram was the first Mrs. *Coolidge* thing we got. Oh and the very first congratulations from outside. Wasn't it just sweet it should have come from you? We sat and chuckled over the envelopes over your signature for several days in our off minutes. And then your letter as the first one to come too. The very first letter. We had a killing telegram from Francis Stark this morning and a sweet letter from the Bishop, but that is all we have heard from the outside world. It was the sweetest letter you wrote us, Reddy. We just hung over it. But, oh Reddy, why didn't you say you were glad I had married him? I wanted you to say that awfully. He's such a dear. I don't know just what I love in him—you asked me—he's got awfully sweet eyes, but I think what I love most is all the love he gives me. It's the sweetest thing, Reddy, just as sure and there when you want it and such heaps of it. And my eyes Reddy, you wouldn't know me from my hubby's description of me. And I wish you to understand, very pointedly, that he doesn't want to change his cook at all. You cook, however, and be thankful for a few less captured by Indians during the preparation of meals and washing of dishes. However, you can get used to almost anything, even being surrounded by Arapahoes in an average of once in five minutes. And what do you think, there is a bird on our river that says "Ge-de-de-*dee*" just as plain as print. Sherman called me out the other morning to hear him. And, Red, I can't get used to Mrs. Coolidge; we've only just got so we can hear it without giggling. "Missy Coolidge" the little Shoshones at the Mission call me. And even Sherman got mixed up and called me Miss Wetherbee in public last week. We honestly feel almost as tho' you were here. If I cook too much oatmeal, Reddy, Sherman says, "Why, there's enough for Mugsey, too." And we just think how you would love things and how well my pony would suit you. And how lucky it is we have 3 saddles. We are going to build on 3 rooms and one is to be yours. "You'll have to fix it up," Sherman says, "because you know just what she'd like." We have 5 very fair horses. *Don't* you know where the ranch is? It's about half a mile below the springs, right on the edge of Little Wind and under the reddest red bluffs. We rode up in them the other day and my! it's wild up there. We're on the very edge of the very wilderness. It's way off by itself, this ranch, but it doesn't seem a bit far away. We can see the Arapahoes going by on the road and Iron's camp is just close to us. He drops in occasionally to [illegible] in a stray horse and when people actually come to call on us the thrills we experience are most gratifying! We have two rooms and a lean-to, a big one, in which we stuff everything we can't get in the two. We have got them fixed up awfully homey and sweet. You ought to have seen the ruin we came down to that first night. It isn't much but it's capable of being fixed up and it's home anyway. And such a dear, sweet one. We have fair-sized book cases full of Sherman's books—mostly anti-Roman publications, and our Indian things and my Navajo blankets hung on the walls and your photo and my hubby when he was a little boy and Col. and Mrs. Coolidge; and Sherman woke me up in the night to tell me he was dreaming he heard an orchestra playing "Home, Sweet Home"!! But, Red, it's awfully funny to be married. I can't help feeling like a combination of Kate Sanford and Gussie Herring! Why on earth, do you suppose? Oh! we have had a wedding present, 6 knives and 6 forks from a Mr. Smith—a friend of Sherman's here. We are awfully proud. Had two girls to supper last night and used them for the first time. For goodness sake! Red, don't go get us much of a wedding present. We would love china and you could get them to pack it in small packages and send it by mail, we have very little—freight takes two or 3 mos. And express is awfully expensive. When we get the rest of our house I would love to have things nice but now we are just camping and very pleasant it is, too!

Red, I'll never go so long without writing you again. I want to begin in a day or two and finish the wedding story and then I shall be all got up. By the way, we had dinner at the agent's today and, you ought to have seen the account of my wedding in the Cheyenne paper they showed us!!! We pretty nearly busted. Do read our notice in the Churchman last Thursday's, the 23rd I should think and send us a copy. We thought it was a very masterly production.

I must get supper before we go to the Post. Sherman has the service there tonight. The weather is perfectly heavenly, Red, just as warm and sweet. Do tell the Bishop how sweet we think it was of him to have written us. We are going to write him very soon. We narrowly escaped being married on his birthday. If it hadn't been for the elopement we might have waited; it is Alice's anniversary, too.

Loads of love, my darlingest girl,
Grace Coolidge (You don't mind if I put it all in, do you?)

Grace Runs-on-top, would do, too! I've got an awful collection of names when you come to think of the bunch.
And we'd like you to understand we haven't been bored one second. Say, Reddy, couldn't you match it up with Francis? It's so *much* nicer than being engaged you have them all the time you see. I feel awfully smart to think I got married first! He! He!

November 20, 1902
COOLIDGE RANCH, WIND RIVER, WYOMING

Darling Reddy,

It's 2:15. From about two on it begins to seem like a long time between drinks till my hubby gets home again. Somedays I go up to the Agency and have dinner at the hotel with him but, generally, there is too much to be done down here. He went back to work on the first and it's kind of lonely being a widow all day. Honestly, Reddy, don't blame Mrs. Balch. If anything happened to my Runs-on-Top, I'd marry again in five minutes if I got the chance. There's nothing like it, Reddy, for solid, substantial comfort. He's awfully sweet to me, Reddy, and we have such a fearfully good time "giggling" over foolish jokes. And as for your letter, it nearly killed us. "What does he wear?" I wish they could see him chopping wood in the early dawn in the late Dr. Eliphalet Potter's pink-trimmed pajamas!! And who on earth said that about my babies, Reddy? How disgusting. You bet they'll be Injun if there ever should be any. Just like their mother and father. The worst of it is I'm so much more Injun than Sherman, it's often a little confusing. And weren't the articles on us funny! Sherman reads them aloud as people send them to us, with great unction and we quote from them continually, such as, "If the details could be known, the story of their courtship would read like a chapter from Romance." We love that one while washing the dishes or performing other somewhat unromantic duties, we murmur that joyfully to each other. I guess Prince thinks they were romantic. He looks like something to hang something on instead of a horse ever since the elopement. Sherman's shoulder is still troublesome. He's got rheumatism (Bishop Potter's not the only oyster) or something in it. It bothers him awfully at night. Last night he sat right up straight all night long. We have to get up at six when it's as black as pitch. And I've only had the bandage off my leg about a week—talk about honeymoons! I saw the last scrap of ours, a tiny thread, one morning about dawn when I went out to find chips to make a fire to get something hot for my poor hubby's shoulder. He could hardly move. I was sorry to see it going but it's sweet, to start in on a new moon and to know, as Sherman remarked, that it's the same old moon after all. I expect you had better marry Francis, Reddy. Don't listen to your head. You'll never hear of it after you're once married. It's awfully funny but the very minute you've once done it, your whole attitude changes. All the things you regretted, deplored, before, disappear all of a sudden. I suppose that the thing is they are *yours* afterwards, you just accept them with the same equanimity you do your own defects. I suppose being married is forming a sort of mutual toleration society—at best—and, oh! by Jove, it's better than *not* being married. Did I tell you Gladys Roberts said to me, that evening after we were married, "Well, now you'll never be *not* married anymore." I want to finish the story of the wedding to you. I know you want to hear it and, do you know, in writing all that other stuff, I wanted to tell you a bit and also to record it. Somehow, I think I had the same feeling that you had when you asked me to keep your letters. I do keep every scrap of them and always have. Your little Gedy will have all the reading she wants. I'm so sorry you didn't understand what I wrote you. I didn't much think you would and Sherman told me you couldn't, not knowing Mr. Roberts. You will have to see him in his work and with his family to do that. Perhaps if I had first said he was British, it would have conveyed the whole idea without all the details, better than all that writing. But someday you will see.

Well, as we stopped at the hitching post in front of the house that night, it was about five o'clock. Mr. Roberts came out and Sherman had the hitching strap in his hand. I stood up beside Prince, with a-boy-stood-on-the-burning-deck expression. Mr. Roberts advances. Nobody spoke. Mr. R.: "Good evening. Pleasant evening." (We thought there might be room for the pronouncement.) "Won't you come in the house and have some supper?" "No thank you." "When would you like to be married?" "Right away Mr. Roberts!" "Well, if you'll allow me, I'll just go in the house and tell Mrs. Roberts and the children and the school girls."

So we tied Prince and went over to the Wickyup. We washed our faces and hands. Then the children came over and very much excited and hugging us violently. I had on my old black skirt and a red flannel waist with a button off and a hole in it. Sherman didn't even want me to change my dress and won't hear of the wedding dress. Gracious! I didn't want it either. But I put on that old brown poplin, had my hair tied in a kind of a tooth-brush on my neck and never even touched it and there was a button off Sherman's vest. You see, we had our oldest things on for the stage trip. Mrs. Roberts sent over to ask if we wanted the wedding march. And we said no. Then I went in and sat in the church with the children while Sherman washed his face and hands. When I saw him coming, I went outside and met him and he hung his hat up on the wood pile and kissed me and in we went. The children had got buffalo berries—fixed the place up sweetly—it was a sweet wedding and so quick. Then we went and sat on the steps of the house and the children and the little Shoshones pretty nearly hugged the stuffing out of us. Especially Marian who was to have been bridesmaid, you know, and one little girl named Susie Sillman. Wasn't it too bad Mary wasn't there after all? She came back the next Saturday. Then we had supper, got in the cart with our elopement bags and wraps and a teakettle in one of my hands and a saucepan full of eggs which I had bought two weeks before in Lander! (and kept hidden I may add!!) in the other and a canister of tea between my knees. We had to stop at the hotel to get some things of Sherman's and then I remembered I had left the guild sewing at the wickyup and the guild was to meet the next day so I wrote a note to Marian about it and signed my new name. Sherman nearly had a fit when I showed it to him. I have to do new things with my name all the time. Only today I told it to anybody for the first time. There was a blind boy here from the next camp, Iron's, and he asked me my name. Do you know, I can't get used to it at all? Annie Moore was telling a long tale the other day and she began, "Mrs. Coolidge, etc." and do you know, I didn't realize at all that she was talking to me until she got all through, then—all of a sudden it dawned on me. But to continue. Then we drove down here. It was mild and a lovely moon. I said as we came by the Big School, "Wouldn't it be lovely if the band would only play for us" and in a few minutes, sure enough, we heard it. We stopped to listen to "John Brown's Body"! Wasn't that funny? Then we came here. My! it was the worst looking place you ever saw! But what did we care? We were married and off by ourselves at last and we've been married ever since. Then we had a cigarette with our feet up on the stove. That's about all there is to tell. We had the sweetest kind of a letter from Mrs. Coolidge. They are at the Presidio and are having new quarters built for them and we are to go visit them someday. It will be fun. I would like to hear what my hubby was like when he was little. But talk about your mothers-in-law! When I turn the griddle cakes, Sherman says, "Gedy, Mrs. Coolidge used to do that with a knife." And what Mrs. Coolidge did to the dish towels and how she made rice pudding etc., etc. I hear till I get rather tired of it.

Reddy, next time anybody asked you whether he's a little civilized or not, you might tell them that I said to him the other morning at breakfast, "Great heaven, Sherman, did they think I would marry a blanket Indian?" And Sherman answered sadly, "It looks like it, Gedy. You see, they just judged you by themselves." Or quote to them that favorite' little song of yours about the Bartender. "Oh when I am drunk / Just put me in my bunk! For it's no body's business but my own." Which reminds me that I will send you back those two books and for one of them we would like ever so much to have Dr. Eastman's book "Indian Boyhood" (McClure). He's that Sioux who married Miss Goodale,[38] you know.

I feel awfully about Duce. I didn't know she was here. What a price we have to pay for everything in this world. You for Sherman and Duce for these mountains. Or both for both. I wonder if, or how, it will ever be made up to us.

Reddy, how good of you to send the altar lights and vases. We were both so glad. I do think you are awfully good to do it. Don't for pity's sake get us a wedding present too. This is all same. How nice they will look on the new altar. Sherman has the Arapahoe work now, too. Old Yellow Bear still comes. He introduced Sherman to old Fat Mare the other day. "This is a brother," he said. Oh! Reddy, I just love these Arapahoes. There were three boys here almost all day today. They are just like anybody else, only nicer. (What are the two reasons why Sherman will make me happier than anyone else? Maybe one is that he's mine and the other is that I'm his!! I can't think of anything else. You tell me.) Did Auntie tell you about Alice?—She is having the worst sort of trouble with Jean. Sherman is so good, Reddy. I got Auntie's letter telling me about it the other night. Of course I felt awfully badly and I told Sherman. "Oh, Gedy!" he said, "Now our marriage will be that much more trouble to them and your mother." And two or three days after we were sitting by the stove in the kitchen and I said, "I just think about my sister all the time," and Sherman said so sweetly and seriously, "Gedy, I do, too." He has the dearest nature, Reddy, I was sick that night after the letter came about Alice. We went to the Mission for supper to pack up my things. I read my other letters, but those two of mother's enclosed in Auntie's, I was afraid to read till I got home. I thought they were mean about me. I had a kind of chill. Sherman had to get a fire and hot water bottles. My dress is awfully pretty. It came last week and fits beautifully. It was good of you to bother about it and it makes me like it to feel you had something to do with getting it. Reddy, I don't feel that the family has treated me very well. Quite as well as I expected, but not well. Auntie wrote in the one letter I have had from her, that you and Lou had been in to "console" with her. Darn'em! They can't talk that way about my husband to me, Reddy, not after the kind of song and dance I've had all my life. Father wrote nicely, but I didn't hear a word from either of them for almost a month. Alice wrote a very sweet letter. Helen Cophill and Miss Ball wrote me sweet letters too and oh! we've heard from just bunches of people.

I think I'll always write you Mondays after this. Miss Hopkins is right. I love you better and I'm sure when we are together it will be more as you want, now that I have my Injun for a safety valve. Isn't it nice we both love you separately? That's a constant source of reinforcing to me.

Reddy, can you make a cottage pudding? I'm going to bust one upon Sherman for his supper if it doesn't bust me first. Sherman calls this ranch the buffalo burying ground, there are so many buffalo berries on it. Not that that has anything to do with cottage pudding.

Your very happy,
Gedy

You know that Ge-dee-dee-*dee* bird was up at the Post the other day. Sherman told me!

November 25, 1902
COOLIDGE RANCH, WIND RIVER, WYOMING

Dearest Reddy,

We have five white horses on the ranch and it strikes me you ought to be here, too!

Don't rail at me for not writing. Everybody is doing it—I just have to buck and take it. If I had only been twins one could do the cooking and the other write the letters. But as it is there is only me. There isn't much to tell, to begin with, and then I can't settle down for any time. It has been all-fired cold since the first of Nov., but perfectly grand weather and we haven't had a stove in here till this week so we have had to sit, write and eat and dress in the kitchen which is about 12 x 11. So you see there wasn't much time or space, either, for letters. Then of course we are swamped in letters. I wish they would send wedding presents instead of letters. I could easily take their sentiments for granted and when you have to write you might just as well thank for something! Did you know my poor Sherman had a broken collar bone all that time? We never found it out till he had been going around three weeks, carrying wood and water and harnessing horses, etc. He has had his arm in a sling now for two weeks and as it's his right one, it makes him pretty helpless. But he got a week off for sick leave and we had a good time. But there were a few mornings I had to get up and dress myself and him and get breakfast and go to the corral for the horse and harness up and get Sherman off for the Agency by 7:30. It was enough to bust you. Then Herbert Welsh came, Sherman's cousin, and helped out, and now Mr. Olson is here working on our new room. He began yesterday and we are simply thrilled every time the ax falls! Won't your china look grand in it. I bet you got an awful lot, I'm tickled to death, but kind of remorseful. Just think of having a real true wedding present and from you, you sweety. Reddy, it's awfully good of you! And linen from Lou! You ought to have seen Sherman's face when I told him. (Reddy, you must say "thace," too. You know Arapahoes can't tell the difference very well between f and th and Sherman says when he was a little boy, Mrs. Coolidge used to say, "Sherman what *are* you doing?" and he would answer "Just washing my thace and hands." So we always say thace and hands, too.)

Reddy, this is the loveliest life! Olson and Herbert have their tents pitched close to our corral and I grubstake them all. Herbert's delicious. He stood up one morning in the middle of the kitchen and told us Indian stories till our eyes nearly popped out. We forgot about the fire and it went out. He was stuffing wood in the stove the other day and all of a sudden he looked up at me and said, "I'm glad I'm Injun, I'm *glad* I'm Injun and American, too." He really is half white tho' like me, his father was a white man! He says, "Arapahoes pretty smart people. They do get beaten sometimes, but they're pretty smart people." I said, "Yes, I thought so, I took the first one that asked me." The Indians from the west came below us, Iron's, come here a good deal. There's one blind boy "He-sits-in-the-night" who's awfully nice. We have nice congregations at the Arapahoe church and they come up and shake my hand and congratulate me just so nicely as anybody. My! but they're nice, Reddy. I'm crazy to have you come and see them. We are going to have three rooms put on. A big living room, a bedroom for each of us, and this room for your room, all done over and built with a little garden place toward the South. It will be just big enough I think. It will take us some time on account of the money. But Olson will trust us indefinitely. Of course, I'm going to put that $125 in the bank just as we agreed and we'll all use it for [illegible] someday. Sherman is crazy to go to the Holy Land. Maybe we could all go someday.

Reddy, why are you miserable these days? Is it Francis again? You better marry him. It fills a long-felt want and all that theoretic side is rubbish. Of course, I never was wildly in love with my dear hubby, nor he with me, I guess, we are too old for that sort of thing. But we are both just tickled to death the whole time. I don't know whether it seems "worthwhile" or not. It's awfully good to have somebody belong to you and to belong to somebody. You feel as tho' you could stand off the whole world. Look at Alice, she was crazily in love with Jean and what did it all come to? It settles you so. I just can't bear to think of ever going out to the railroad and leaving all this little house and the Indians and my Foxy— and I won't budge an inch without Sherman. Did I ever tell you? I told Sherman this summer that the night before I left N.Y. I dreamt that he and I were getting out at the Bethlehem station. It was night and snowy and the gas lamps were lighted and we walked up the hill, starting for your house. Sherman was carrying something we were awfully particular about, I don't know what it was, and I was dragging on him, and it all seemed so sweet and natural. Do you remember that I wrote you long ago in June that we went to the Shoshone Sun Dance one night? That was the first night I began to like him this way. But it's awfully sad to lose your steady! One day, when we had been married just a little while I drove up to the hotel with him. Involuntarily I turned around and looked down the road toward the agency, like I used to do, to see if he wasn't coming in sight around those bushes by the slaughter house. Then I remembered I would never see him come that way anymore and I felt so badly about it I couldn't even tell him till that night!

The books and libretti came last night. My me! as Sherman says, but the books look nice. I don't have a minute to read, there are so many letters and so much mending (it's awfully exciting when the first washing comes home!) to do. I really ought to devote all my spare time to the cookbook I borrowed from Mrs. Geddes on Sunday. James Moore came in this morning to ask us to dinner tomorrow. It's a pleasure to go but nothing compared with the pleasure of not having to cook that Thanksgiving turkey Mrs. Nickerson[39] gave us or battling with a pumpkin pie. I'm an awful fool at cooking. Goodness only knows when I wrote in my diary last. But, Reddy, I will cuss and swear right here and now that I will write you every week or bust. I'm just *glad* you are looking anxiously for my letters and waiting not so awfully patiently. That's the way I have felt about yours for so long. It's just right for you to have a little turn. All that kind of up against it feeling goes when you marry. Oh! Reddy, he's the sweetest thing. I asked him, in a goofy moment, whether he loved me better than anybody he ever had and he said "Yes, Gedy, except," then he stopped and I said "Well . . . ?" and he looked so sweet and loving and said, "except little Phil." You know, his little brother who died years and years ago, he just adores him, he found his photo the other day and a letter he wrote Sherman. Such a sweet little thace! As soon as we get up our rooms you had better come out to us. It's enough to just live here.

A very nice superintendent has just come to the Big School, a Virginian, a gentleman and a Xtian[40] and judge from the shine on his shoes and his behavior during the Creed last Sunday. He looked very nice. Perhaps you would like him.

Those pictures of Duce are lovely. I'll read the libretti. But where is Citta Morta?[41] I wanted particularly to read that one. Now you know Sherman won't see any sense at all in [illegible]. But I don't think I'd take a subtle man. I guess he wouldn't take me! I like you to be tho', Reddy. It is so superior! It makes me proud of you. Honest, it does.

Well, it's pretty near time to resort to the cookbook again. I've got to sew some shields in those clothes of mine for tomorrow. I'll wear my new dress for the first time. If you could spare us the Churchman it would be nice. Sherman takes the Standard but I don't care for it. If you happen to get a specially good number of a magazine send it along in a book. I will always return either in *time*. Have you got Heralds of Empire by A. C. Laut? It is well criticized.

I'm obliged to send Sherman's love to you. I didn't do it the last time and was severely rebuked. "Didn't I tell you always to do it and didn't you promise to obey?"

I am going to write Lou soon and please tell the Bishop why Sherman doesn't answer his letter. He hurt his shoulder just a few days after the letter came. My! but it's pretty down here, Reddy. The red bluffs and the river and very handily situated for our Sunday work, too.

I will write next week. Do you remember the "Grace" Sherman was engaged to at Hobart? Well, she wrote and told him she has been a widow seven years and also that she was so glad of his happiness as if it were her own. Now don't you think that's ambiguous. Oh these widows!

Your Gedy

December 8, 1902
COOLIDGE RANCH, WIND RIVER, WYOMING

(Married two mos. today)

Oh, no! no! no! Reddy, you mustn't go off and have a house with Lou. What are Sherman and I building you a room for I should like to know? We tell everybody you are coming to live with us. And we believe you are. *Ask you to my house next summer*. Reddy! What on earth are you talking about? Why, precious lamb, this house is as much yours as either of ours as far as occupying it goes. My goodness me! Darling, I should think you were in the blues. The logs for your room came today. A Shoshone named Wildman brought them and they are white pine and beauties. Olson has got the sitting room up ten logs and it is only going to be 12 feet high anyway. Then he puts on the roof and then the foundation!! It's very mysterious and Chinese,[42] don't you think so, putting the foundations in last?

Oh! Reddy, darling, I can't bear to think of you being like you were in Paris that time. How can you be if there is no trunk lost? Oh! get married. I despise Sherman too, quite frequently, and I never feel hot about him as I do about you. I don't love him any better and I don't think as well, anyway. I always tell him I don't. But what does it matter? He's my own Injun and we all have such worthless faults—a few more or less don't matter. Besides that, when you've once stood up there in church and said all those things and got their ring and their name you don't really despise them a bit. Of course I would be glad if my Fox's legs weren't a little weak from too much walking and if he was a little taller but my! me! I don't love him any the less. And then if you should have anything they haven't you're so glad to be able to piece them out. I tell you honestly, Reddy, I would have given every dear thing I have on this earth to have gotten out of marrying Sherman that week before we were married, ending two months ago today, anything under heaven. I thought all those dreadful things that happened to us were signs for me to break off. And there I was just helpless and all alone in the world to decide my fate and his. All on earth I could think of was running away. I couldn't sleep, I was wild. I give you my vow and honor if he hadn't been through so much of that kind of thing I would have broken it off and flown. I think I felt just as you must have done when you threw Francis' ring away. But the very minute we were married, when we were still driving down here with the tea kettle and the saucepan of eggs all my doubts and nerves vanished and I've just been a happy Arapahoe squaw ever since. And yet, oh! Reddy, we have a trouble. I can't tell you what it is and maybe it will go away, but—don't let's talk about Timothy for a while.

Herbert is so nice, Reddy, he gets all the Injun side of things from him and such stories. He is Sherman's cousin, you know, don't you? He is here now helping Olson build. They are so bright, the Arapahoes, and so nice. You ought to see my Sunday School class at the Big School. I never saw smarter children. There is one Sherman is crazy about—little "Woman-Goes-in." I haven't made the slightest preparation for Xmas. I'm paralyzed at the thought. How would you like a half interest in Foxy? Do you think you could get me a fur cap for Sherman? Anything that he wouldn't look like a perfect freak in. He has a vague idea that his size is 7¾. I expect sealskin would be the best or a longer black fur. He thinks he wants black. And would you get me about 20 calendars or cards like at Potts. Get flower ones. Something for about 25 cents. If you could get a half a dozen different ones the rest could be just alike. There are people here like Mrs. Moore and Mrs. Nickerson that I would like to send a remembrance to. And will you get me a big box of holly? As much as you could send by mail. That will be four pounds. Tell me how much these things cost so I can send the cheque. I hope I am not bothering you much. I think I shall be awfully homesick for you at Xmas. But maybe by then you will have written saying you are coming out in a few weeks. Oh, if you only would.

Get a dog, dearie, it's a great help, but a husband does the business better. I want very much to get a portable organ too. They have a small keyboard and cost about $25.00. Sometime can you see about one for me? (In shipping by freight, send by Casper, it is cheaper than by Rawlins.) (And don't try to prepay to Washakie, only to Casper.) Such an organ would be a great thing for the Jonestown work. We have great hopes for the work. Oh, thank heaven I'm one of them and not an outsider anymore.

I love you so, Reddy. Don't think I'm lost. Oh, I'm *not*, I'm *not*. What are you talking about?

Your devoted Gedy.

Sherman sends his best love and says to tell you he is as happy as a clam at high water.

I will now go and black the kitchen stove.

December 27, 1902

COOLIDGE RANCH, WIND RIVER, WYOMING

Darling Reddy,

It does seem absurd that I put off your letters and write others first but I always feel the others on my mind and so yours I wait for a quiet time to write so I can enjoy them. But we have been awfully rushed lately and we had a rather wretched week last week. But I never meant to go as long as this. I think I can surely do better with the new year for I have gotten up with my congratulation letters at last. Your things came last night, Reddy. Oh! we were tickled with them. Especially the one for Sherman. It looks just like an Arapahoe baby. He hung it up over my desk and its thace *is* sweet. He is going to write you. We had a lovely Xmas. It seemed more like Xmas than those doleful ones at home. But I think I was homesick for you before. I told Sherman it was the first Xmas I had ever been away from home and he said it was the first one he had ever been at home. Rather nice of him? Well, first of all, there was no mail in from the East for 3 days before Xmas so his cap didn't come. So I got him a box of cigars. Romantic! We had a little teeny cedar tree on the breakfast table with the cigars and my saddle bags from Sherman and more cigars for Olson and tobacco and a silk hankie for Herbert. It looked awfully cute. Then we went up to the Agency house back for service at ten. The Sunday before Sherman and I went up into Crooked Creek Canyon and got some sweet little spruces. Olson fixed them on standards and we set six of them up in the chancel with red ribbons tied on them. We lighted the candles and Sherman and Mr. Roberts were both in the chancel, we brought up the Arapahoe organ, the Agency one is so fierce, Mr. Bennett (clerk at Lane's and one of our *three* organists—all fighting) wore his cassock and collar. We had a good many Indians there and for once several white people. It was a really sweet service. The Saturday before Xmas we had our Xmas sale and cleared about $35. Pretty good? It was issue morning and lots of the Indians bought. Then we came home from church and fooled around here for a couple of hours. It was so warm that we didn't have our coats on. Then we rode up to the Moore's for dinner at 3. There were a lot of boxes in the P. O. for us and we tied them on my saddle and brought them home and had another Xmas in the evening at home. Now, wasn't that a satisfactory day? Yesterday I spent the day writing letters. Last night we rode up to a dance at the Post, we had to make each other do it. They have started a social club, all these bum agency people. Very exclusive. Olson and halfbreeds not included!! They have had four meetings and as we haven't been once. We thought we had better mosey up last night, especially as they gave us a complimentary bid. Everybody else is stuck for 5 dollars. Olson went up one night to play for them and took Herbert along to watch the people. All the girls dressed up to kill. You know the style. "But," says Herbert, Olson told us, "they've all got government clothes under those fine dresses!" Not bad for an Arapahoe? I've had a half dozen Indians camping on the ranch this week. They have turned the Big School children loose for 5 days and they were waiting for them. Paul Revere (some relation, of course) was here a couple of days. He told me one day "All the Indians are glad of this marriage of Sherman's. They like you first rate. That's what they need, a nice woman." Then the next day he told me again they needed a nice woman and that the Arapahoes didn't like a quiet woman, they liked one that rustled. "How you rustle?" says Paul. I suppose there was some blarney in it, but it was nice, wasn't it? I feel like writing you nothing but how nice the Arapahoes are, Reddy! Do you mind? The last two Sundays we have been bringing three of my Sunday school children home to dinner (we got a fine big wagon at the Sub and now drive around in high style). The first time we took the children down to Yellow Calf's about 5 miles below here where they were having a council. Sherman thought he would have a service there. But he didn't, after all. There was no opportunity. It was a beautiful great big lodge painted red and all stars and moon. The children and I were scared to go in but we went and they all smiled at us and were so nice. They gave Sherman a great welcome and made him sit up with the chiefs. One of the children was Naomi Fatman and a couple of days later old Blind Fatman came up and called on us. He talked with Sherman about Sherman's father and the old times and was as nice as he could be. We think he came to show that he appreciated our having Naomi here.

Of course what I started to say about last night was that we went to the P. O. before the dance and found your things. (The calendars came the night before.) I thought the cap must be in that box and I was sort of disappointed that your thing for me hadn't come. I stayed in the dressing room and opened the things and read your letter and then I found all those sweet things for me. But honestly, the nicest of all was that you sent something to my Injun. He never got another Xmas present except yours and mine, Reddy. That coyote (It's a fox!) is too sweet for anything and the basket and the handkerchiefs. I do love having several things! Last year I remember they mounted up to five!! Everything you send is always sweet. I'm going to have the last year's prayer desk sent out for a Litany desk. Just lend it to the Agency. I don't know how to thank you for getting all those things for me, holly, calendars, cap—everything. The cap is *just* right. Sherman looks like a Russian and a half in it. Says he never hoped to possess anything so elegant. Got quite incoherent coming home and seemed rather mixed as to whether he was indebted to you or me. It really is *exactly* right. Do you hate me for asking you to do all that shopping? Do you suppose I could return any of the calendars? I find I don't need so many as they are late. Will you tell me? Thank you for the holly. It looks quite nice and berryish. But do let me pay for it. There was a Mrs. Otto in the school here, she went away about a month ago. A year or two ago she lost her baby here. He's buried in the Post cemetery. I thought I would take up some of the holly and some pine and put it on his grave today for her. I told her I would take care of it, she hated so to go and leave him and I thought we would probably live here the rest of our days.

I didn't tell you our little puppy was dead. Friday before Xmas we ran over him right in front of our door. I wonder where all his pretty playfulness goes to? I don't know why I felt so bad about him, but it seemed so *mean* for us to kill him, we were so fond of him and he wouldn't leave me a step. We had him up in the Canyon the day before and he cried and cried tumbling up and down the steep sides and through the snow, but he would go with me. Both wheels went over him. Herbert is going to give me a bull puppy of his as soon as it is old enough to take away from the mother, but that won't help our little one. He looked so thin and old when he was dead.

Tomorrow we have no duties at the Big School and we are going over to Big Wind River where most of the Arapahoes camp in winter to have a little tree for them. We are going to stay in Herbert's house and have the tree at Mule's. We won't have much but peanuts and apples, but Sherman will make them a Christmas talk—I'm crazy to go. Herbert wants us to see the ditch the Arapahoes have been building all the way down the valley, six miles, and he said this morning he would take us to see a comedy "Hand" Sunday night and that he would interpret for us. He's a very sweet boy but kind of like Cousin Elmer!!!! The children were so funny when we were at the council at nine mile crossing. They kept whispering, "Do you like to be in a tepee? Do you?" Naomi said to Sherman that he was her brother (there is some relation) and that I was her sister-in-law! They are as bright and quick as anything you ever saw. I'm crazy to have you come and see them. Our big room will be done in less than two weeks. Maybe we'll have a Xmas tree in it for these Arapahoes, unless they go over for the Jonestown one (Big Wind). I will write you and tell you how it was over there.

We still have our little Xmas tree on the table and it looks pretty. It's awfully windy today, the first time for weeks.

Xmas Mr. Moore showed us a clipping about the trial so we knew it was alright with the Bishop. Irvine is unspeakable. My hatred is the only thing I know that can beat him. I guess Irvine is settled now. He must be. He certainly has got a few slaps that ought to last him.

I must stop and stew up some stuff for dinner. But Olson says he sure gets three meals a day down here!! I'm glad he looks at them that way! Reddy, I think I will keep that $125 for once or twice, we have the wagon and building and debts. But there is the $125 in the Wyo. bank which we can both draw on in case of despair. I hate to keep it, but Bishop Leonard wants that $500 for Lucy's house now and I have got to rustle it in the next year. I sent him $100. I should think you would be plumb busted the way you send things to us. How much was the cap? You've *got* to shop for the house for us. Auntie never offered to pay for the house. I wish she would. All she does is nag.

Dear love from us both, my precious, Reddy.

December 31, 1902

COOLIDGE RANCH, WIND RIVER, WYOMING

Red, I'm an awful goof. I discovered when I was dressing this morning and put one on that they were the kerchiefs you were going to make for me. Did you make them? My! what lots of sewing. It's a great thing to be single. All I do is fetch hubby's drawers and wash for the next fair. I'm just *glad* to have them when you made them. Pretty little white hands! I was just thinking today what *would* I do without you? Every time anything at all happens, the first thing I think is "I'll tell that to Red." And I'm always so sorry about the jokes. For they're so quick they won't be funny anymore next summer. I was telling Sherman the other day that you and I always said each New Year's day that we would be together the next one. He said, "She couldn't get to you now even if you telegraphed and we went out to Casper to meet her." It did make you seem far away. I think I miss you more now than I did at Xmas. I was in such a sufficient time that you aren't in a frame of mind to miss anybody. And we were thinking "How would the service go off?" "What day shall we go to Wind River?" and that kind of thing. But now I am wishing it was nearer Spring so you would come soon. We are finally fixed for horses and there are lots of little trips we can all take together next summer. It's *such* a satisfaction to me that you and my hubby like each other independently of me. Isn't it *really* sweet?

Oh, Red, I'm crazy to have you see Big Wind River. We drove over Monday afternoon, you know. My eye! but it was cold. I nearly perished and the wind just howled. We went to the first camp we saw which was Mule's, a friend, and asked for Herbert's house. Mule came out, got a big armful of wood and started in to make a fire for us. But we were too cold to get out so we drove on up to Herbert's, about a mile. We met Herbert and a boy called Bruce Goes Back, an awfully nice boy with a blind mother and a vanished father whom Mule is raising along with half a dozen other children not his own. Bruce and Herbert came back with us and had dinner. I wish you could have seen Herbert's cabin. Two rooms, right in the big timber (like those big trees at Bull Lake) and close to the river. It was *a whole lot* cleaner than my house and everything, whisk broom, toilet soap, everything there. And such a nice cat slept with us all night. H. and his wife are staying at Mule's. Herbert was crazy to have us see a big ditch, 6 miles long, which the Arapahoes made last summer. Nobody paid them, they just made it for themselves. So after we had had dinner and got warm we drove up there, 4 or 8 miles. Bruce and I sat on the floor of the back of the wagon—kept each other warm. Herbert always insists on coming home a different way from the way he went. He took us home from Wind River another way, too. The next morning he came for us and we drove to Smile's. Uncle had a fine big room where we are going to have the services this winter. There was a big stove in the middle and blankets all around the edges. We fixed the tree, a little one, but we had carried it 25 miles, and hung up our popcorn balls and the toys. I went out and fooled around with the children. There were several school children there for the holidays. There was a tepee and the sweetest little giggling heads would pop out of the door and pop in again. As Allie Sitting Bear remarked, "There are about a thousand children in that tepee!" An old woman with a sweet face, something like Grandma Holt's, came up and when she noticed me she shook my hand a long time and just crooned over me and said things. I said, "Allie, what is she saying?" and Allie said she said she was my mother-in-law. I asked who she was and Allie said Mule's mother. Then I remembered that Sherman had told me that Mule's mother and his were life-long friends and even used to live together sometimes. She kept smiling at me and when Sherman came she told him she had seen his wife and that her heart was glad. I thought when all this was happening how I would tell it to you. Then Mule came out and called them in. There were between 50 and 60. Sherman made them a little Xmas talk first and Herbert interpreted. Then we gave out the things. Mule was such a polite host. Jumped up and gave his chair to an old man who came in late. Brought me a chair very politely. There was a beautiful pair of moccasins on the tree. We found them when we took the other things off. They had Sherman's name on them and were from Mule. Wasn't it nice of him? They just treated us white Reddy. I'm afraid I'll have to say Injun instead after this. Fed our horses grain, hitched them up for us. When Mule was camping here Herbert came up and said they were short of meat and we gave them some of ours, but they didn't wait for us to ask but came and asked us if we were sure we had enough. And not a white man but me (and I'm not very bad) within ten miles anyhow! We came home that afternoon. It was a beautiful road home with mountains on the edges everywhere, Wind River, Owl Creek, and Beaver Hills, all snowy now. I'm going to try to write that Xmas tree up for the Spirit of Missions.[43] I guess it's the first one they ever had over there.

I have had some wedding presents at last, disguised as Xmas presents, or combining both, from my friends. Rather mean trick. They all sent such characteristic things. Edith McMulinth Cent. Dic.;[44] Lou, two tiny, tiny salt cellars; Gussie, a six shooter very elegant and very up to date (after deep thought on her part and several letters!); Cousin Elmer, 1 doz. tablespoons, 1 doz. teaspoons, 1 doz. forks!!! Nellie and Bobbie, carvers with deer horn handles, which went to Sherman's heart (so did Gussie's six shooter); Alice Linick carvers, too, with rather [illegible] handles and my initials wrong (G. W. C.) etc. Mrs. Moore told me today that I would have some freight in this week with his, among which would be your barrel. Hurrah! And the altar, hurrah! some more and the organ and a box of groceries from Father. I went up to that baby's grave today and put branches and your holly on it. It looked very green and pretty. Fox was deeply interested so much so that he forgot to eat while I was busy. He had never seen anything like that before. He does take such an intelligent interest in all our doings. Sometimes he whinnies to me from the field as far as he can see me, and if he is going by the door and I call to him, he always stops and grunts. I don't have to tie him up anywhere.

Reddy, the next time you are waiting for the car in Beth. at that corner go into that little hardware shop and get me an apple corer. There is such a thing, I think. You sort of punch out the core with it and it's a nuisance to have to cut them out.

I always used to wish I was married so I could get things out of that store. They looked so lasting and nice.

Tell Lou that pretty lavender thing (what's it for?!) came last night. We are going to the Sub tomorrow for New Year's dinner with Mrs. Becker down there but when we get back I will write her at once. I spend my days writing letters. Why did you send me that article on the Eastmans? On account of the five? There is a very attractive Southern Arapahoe and his breed and a half wife[45] at the Sub both pretty well educated, Carlisle, who know them. Mrs. Warden told me they were lovely children and so pretty.

Well, darling, Happy New Year and come to us soon. That will make our New Year happier than almost anything. You and my hubby are pretty nearly all I have got and I don't know which of you I love best—it's so hard to compare you and besides, I can't tell where one begins and the other leaves off!

Your devoted,
Gede, and when I say devoted I mean it. What do you think?

Little Ge-dee-dee-*dee* was down there at Wind River, several of him. He just screamed at me Gede! Gede! Gee-dee-dee-*dee!* every time I went out of the house. We used up all the calendars. Hubby wore his cap to Big Wind and is very tickled with it.

January 15, 1903
COOLIDGE RANCH, WIND RIVER, WYOMING

Dearest Red,

You ought to see the bulldog!! He isn't a bulldog at all. Only measures 12 in. from the tip of his tail to what ought to be the tip of his nose. And his body is only seven. Paul says he ought to have two other eyes between those two, they go off this way. We tried to cross the river down by the Council house Sunday, but the ice was too thick so we had to come up about a mile to Shoulder Blade's camp where the water stays open from the hot springs (our river never freezes here). It was at Shoulder Blade's that the pup was. Herbert was going over with us in his wagon for wood and he called to us to stop, rushed into the tepee and came out grinning with two pups which he dumped in my lap telling me to take my choice. What I like about Indians is that they don't wait till things are expedient. I might much better have got those pups on the way home. But it was much nicer to have them to take over with us. The other one looks like our little first puppy, but he is kind of stupid (not so the Bulldog!). Sherman thinks it's because he is so young. Everybody likes the bulldog best, but I don't. Sherman calls him a Gros Ventre,[46] which he is, after eating.

We had a small service at Mule's but a good one. You see we said we would come every month and they were a little mixed on account of our having been there two weeks before. There were several old people there and that is always a good sign. After *the* service Mule said to Sherman that he hadn't much but he was going to give a little feast after the service as they do at Councils so the people would feel good. He said he wanted to do everything he could to help. Wanted us to bring an organ over. You know he is the old fashioned kind that doesn't speak English, not Herbert's kind. Herbert stayed over to get the wood and got home yesterday and told us about it. They want a school over there and they talked about the church. Mule and Yellow Calf and a lot of the influential middle-aged ones. They say they would like to see churches all over the reservation and Mule said the women must bring their children to be baptized. They said they had never understood about religion before and they knew it was like theirs only it told them more. They said Sherman stood between them and the white people. Herbert was very enthusiastic. He is going to have the land for the church I think. It was awfully cold over there. We nearly froze last night. Had to take the pups in bed. We made some calls and saw Sherman's little great niece, a quiet little thing about four. Things are booming.

When we got home we found Olson had gone to Lander for lumber. Herbert was away and Paul's day was over so we trotted out our best china and I set the table just fine and we had everything as nice as could be. The tea tasted so different out of those nice little cups. Everything seemed nicer. I guess we shall always have to use the old enamel ware a good deal tho', for the Indians come in so much and they feel more at home with that kind. Yesterday lunch Little Wolf and Kagavah, a very nice Shoshone, dropped in just as we were at the table, one after the other. Kagavah is the man who caught little Sherman in that fight and brought him to Camp Brown on his horse. He told us how Sherman cried! Sherman showed him Little Phil's picture and Kagavah said he remembered the three little boys. Uncle Little Wolf is a fine sign talker and a splendid old man. It was awfully interesting. Lots of Indians come. Arapahoes are fine. They are not a bit cheeky and they never ask for anything or stay when they are not wanted. We are awfully happy.

I haven't heard from you for a long, long time, it seems to me.

Did you know that Auntie is very ill? I got 3 telegrams and a letter from Father. He didn't tell me what the trouble is. I wrote and said I would go home if necessary. But it would be awful going out in winter and I don't see how Sherman could get along. But I didn't tell Father that. I guess Father is pretty nearly wild with Mother away. He depends on her so. I wish we were nearer to the railroad. I am hoping perhaps you saw them when you went to town and can write me something sensible. It's pretty tough all around.

It's time to battle with dinner so good bye, Reddykins.

We both send lots of love. We have a fine plan to take you down to Whiterocks next summer. You must surely come in May or even April.

Devotedly,
Gede

February 26, 1903
COOLIDGE RANCH, WIND RIVER, WYOMING

Mulls came upon me Sunday like a thousand bricks so that settles that. I'm plumb discouraged. But it's fully sweet to know how glad Hubby would have been. For some reason now I haven't felt so well for a month and I'm horribly cheerful in my foolings. Maybe it will be alright yet. I thought last month I was surely that way and it was an awful strain to wait for mulls. It's hard luck. Are you alright, Reddy? I can't help feeling sort of anxious about you. Tell me the truth for heaven's sake. There have been two or three real sad deaths amongst the Indians this last week. I just hate to hear about dying. If I lost you or Sherman I just don't know what I could do. But I put on a new shirtwaist tonight and tied my pigtails with red ribbons and am feeling *very* frisky indeed. I forgot to thank you for the Indian Boyhood,[47] that's why I'm writing. When I got your letter saying you were sending it, it was just hitting me that I hadn't anything for Hubby's birthday and the poor thing never had but one birthday celebration before in his life. So when the book came I hid it away and he was so charmed with it and is sitting reading it now. I read it Sunday evening and Monday morning and during mulls. Don't you think it's good? Sherman remembers all those same things too. Only he's too much of a white man. I also forgot to say anything appropriate about Francis too. And now that I've come to it, there doesn't seem to be anything to say. I feel as you do too about the surprisingness of life. Only premonitions I have the greatest faith in. You know, how from my tenderest youth I always meant to marry an Indian. That's why—partly—I'm worried about the babies. I've always been afraid, horribly—that I won't have any. And the Arapahoes never have any little left over ones[48] like Lucy's—they are so good to that kind! Anyhow I want my own and Sherman's. The real reason I didn't write you for so long—I might as well tell you, was on account of the half hopes. I really had mulls before I posted that last letter to you, but I thought I might as well send it. I am crazy for you to know everything. Do you know, Reddy, I think a friendship like ours is the best safeguard for married life any human creature could have. I find myself again and again in a thousand things thinking, "Why don't I feel the same way about Sherman?" or "Why doesn't he make me feel so and so?" and then I think back to us and our failures and tests too. I'm horribly fond of you. I never knew just how fond till I got another person to measure by, for I *really* have never cared for anybody else one quarter as much as I have you. I haven't the vaguest idea which of you I am fondest of but I know that both of you together are all I want—of this generation, anyhow!

But you must come to us before July. I never heard of such a thing. The winter has broken up now. It has been spring—so we can sit all day with the outside door open and for nearly two weeks. They all say it will stay spring, with the exception of an occasional storm, till it's summer. But think of you on a private yacht! Would that Holmes were there to see. All same stokes outfit!!! Is Lou with you? I thought from your letter she wasn't to be of the party. But her note the other day sounded different. Your room is up six or seven logs. It is to be a lean-to on this big room. We thought that was the best—also cheapest. Give whoever I know in the party my love if they want it. Use your discretion. Tell me everything you do and where you do. I'll look you up in Biddy! We looked up Mrs. Coolidge's hotel in little Bid!

Good night precious,
Your Gedy

March 28, 1903

COOLIDGE RANCH, WIND RIVER, WYOMING

Darling Reddy,

Why in the world don't you write me? You make me feel so left out in the cold. I think it is over a month since I have heard from you and then you told me you were going to sail the next week. It is as long as it was before only now I haven't the faintest idea where in creation you are. Are you sick again? We have been pretty nearly snowed in for the past two weeks, but I have made, or urged others to make frantic efforts to get up for the mail hoping for your letter which has not come. Perhaps Sherman will bring it tonight. This is almost as unsettling as this baby business. About 3 days ago my hopes suddenly revived when I discovered I was 29 inches around the waist and very Bustiferous. I then looked for other signs and found one which is nearly unfailing, rushed to Mrs. Geddes and was mightily reassured by her, tho' I was mullied last week again. This ought to be toward the end of the 3rd month, the time when you begin to get big in the waist. Well, time will tell, if I'm *not* that way, I don't see why on earth I don't get that way, do you? Poor Buddy and I, we are just pining for babies! Well, if I ever begin, don't be surprised if you have to be god-mother once a year right along. We are going to get you a pony for a birthday present as soon as we can find a good one. I thought I had a mate for Fox the other day but he was no good. I told Sherman the other day I thought it would be nice to give you a pony when we could find a good one, he said, "Reddy shall have the best we've got!" Mule was here last night and he told me he was going to drive all his horses about 150 into the corral this summer and I could come and take my choice. He said that was an Indian custom and he wanted to give me a horse. Wasn't that nice!

The work is booming. I want to write you everything but perhaps you don't want to hear!!

Write me, for Heaven's sake, Reddy.

Your troubled and rather mad,
Gede

August 20, 1904
COOLIDGE RANCH, WIND RIVER, WYOMING

Dearest Red,

I meant to write you several days ago to tell you that you have a very sweet, fat and sassy little niece.[49] But gee whiz! You just try herding two young squallers at the same time in bed yourself and see how much time you have left for anything else. And I was bound to have the boy in short clothes for his 4 mos. old birthday[50] which happened 4 days after his sister came, so I had to hem up three dresses for him before I could do another thing. I am afraid Mrs. Moore has told you about young Gracie's arrival. She said she had just had a letter from you and asked Sherman if he thought I would mind if she wrote you and told about the baby, so I don't know what she finally did do. I've had a great time. She came three weeks ahead of time. Monday we found out that Mrs. Iron (the woman who used to scrub for me) had a fearfully infected hand and we rushed down there. It was awful and up we went to the Post and got stuff to make her sleep and drove down again after supper and got her to promise to go up to the doctor with us in the morning. Well, I went to bed rather tired from holding 16 lb. all day, and began to have a tummy ache. Thought it was wind. Sherman rubbed it diligently. No result. It went on all night. When it was daylight I began to notice that it came and went regularly. Had my suspicions. We had men here working the hay so we sent Maurice White Plume up with the buggy with a note to Miss Robinson, the new field matron, a trained nurse, who had promised to come to me, to ask her if she would come down and tell me if I had better send for Dr. Godfrey. I also thought if I didn't need her she could go up with Mrs. Iron. Well, Maurice came back empty handed. But Mr. Woodsworth, knowing what was up, opened my note and telephoned the doctor as Miss Robinson was in Lander. Well, of course that day Doctor Godfrey had another similar case in Lander, so he telephoned Dr. Dewitt at the Post to come down to me. He's a fine young man, the only decent doctor we have ever had at the Post. Father is Surgeon General of the Army. Down he piled in the morning and by that time I was feeling much better. Pains had been every ten minutes, by that time, they were half an hour or more apart. He told me not to get up and he would be down again in the morning. When afternoon came I just made Sherman go down for Mrs. Iron and take her up. I stayed alone all the afternoon and took care of the boy, who, of course, chose that bright particular day to go without a nap. It was lovely!! Well, back came in about five with Mrs. Jones, the Commissary Sergeant's sister from the Post, who had promised to come to me the following Monday anyway. By that time I was at it hot and heavy. Well, she took the baby. Sherman drove Mrs. Iron home. When he came back I asked him to go up on horseback and ask the doctor to come down and spend the night. I never thought it would come that night. Just before he left Mrs. Moore dropped in. She said she had a feeling all day that she must come and see me. She asked me if I wanted her to stay with me and I was dog enough to say I did. Poor Mrs. Jones, she didn't even know where the flour barrel was!! We have a new cabin built out toward the hay field gate for a bedroom for us. I thought that would be a fine place so I was over there. But they thought it was too inconvenient so the baby was born in your room. She didn't come till half past one, Wednesday August 10. It was the deuce but not as bad as I expected, no worse than some cramps I've had only it lasted so long, and that old straining at the end is enough to scare the life out of you. When she did come she jumped right from me to the foot of the bed and hit the doctor right in the arm. It looked just like a trout jumping. Honestly, I had to laugh. He said I had an unusually long, hard time. I suppose I was too old to be having my first baby. She tore me so I had to have five stitches taken the next day. That's why I'm still in bed. Felt fine about two days after. I never minded staying in bed so little. It's because we're so busy with the children. Young Gracie (Sherman will have that her name) has such a saucy, naughty face, and [illegible] me! when Mrs. Moore was working here the first week she lifted up her head and opened her eyes and looked around. She can creep herself along with her legs and lift her head way up and hold it there. Miss Robinson came the next morning and she herds babies and me and Mrs. Jones does the house work. Wasn't I in big luck to get a good nurse and good doctor? The Indians all say the baby looks like Sherman's mother and call her by her name, Ba-ah-noce.

(Like "a" in bath.) Poor Bud, he's just positively mindless over this child. The awful part I haven't told you yet, which is that I can't nurse her. I battled with her for several days and made her take it and even the boy got so he would too, I thought perhaps he could make it flow better than she could, but she just howled with hunger all the time, so here I am with the cheering prospect of two bottle babies. I'm looking for someone to do my work, I've just got to have someone if it takes my last cent. The babies each have a riding pony. We got those bronco mares from old Caboose Aragon at last and two of them have colts. Your Squaw is a perfect monster, she's nearly as big as her mother now. She came in April. She doesn't care much for Squaw but she never leaves Foxy's fat side. The first thing I said while the doctor was still tying the cord, was, now I can ride horse back. The inconvenience of not being able to is something fearful. Foxy just shakes when he walks he is so fat. Your Squaw has never been used since we got back. I pretty nearly sold her to Mr. King of Laramie, husband of Big Eyes, the other day, who dropped in here on his way home from the Park and wanted to buy a couple of ponies for his children. But I wasn't sure the colt was old enough to wean (Bud wasn't here) and then, to tell you the truth I would like to see Squaw stay in the family, if it is all the same to you she'll be such a fine thing to teach the children to ride on. We have been awfully busy with the church building this summer. We've had awful luck with everything (except the man who is doing the work) even to Prince and [illegible] running away with a load of lumber and slowing things up generally. Most dashing! We've got some nice horses now and a new buggy with a top. The old one busted (too much Brook's Lake, I guess) and we fell out one night near the Springs. We sold the old one. The Dews, Jorgensens and Virginia went to the Park the end of last month. I suppose you are awfully mad because I haven't written you, but I just couldn't do one thing more. Ever since we had the boy I have been nearly dead. Up every two hours through the night and the day for two mos. We never thought he would live even, he was just blue and stupid when we got him. But you ought to see him now, weight 16 lbs. has two teeth and looks as tho' he was seven or eight mos. old. If Miss Coolidge will only do as well, we'll be alright. It just jived me a bit to put her on the bottle. I never have approved of it for children. Poor little kid! It's the dickens of a mess, the whole thing of having them, but it's more than worthwhile. But by Jove, there isn't a spot of you that escapes before the child comes, from melancholia to blisters on your feet. I've been just half alive all summer. I ought to have got someone to help me with the work but the money seemed to be too short. Well, we've got two sweet, fat babies, if I can just manage to bring them up alright. Louis is awfully sweet too, he is a regular old Mamma's boy. He's just spoony with me. It's awfully cute when they begin to notice you. I have carried him in the buggy in a baby case (Mrs. Friday's,[51] all made over clean) and driven the team alone. Isn't that pretty smart? You see, he just couldn't roll off my lap that way. It's a fine scheme. I've got one for his sister too! We have a little single buggy we got from Hanscum's, I mean to put forth with Prince and my two in it as soon as possible. I've hardly heard from anybody all summer as I haven't written anybody. Just a few missy letters. But as soon as I get my lady domestic I am going to put in all my time with babies and letters.

We had an awfully nice letter from the Bishop the other day. (Did I say that a ways back, or just think it?) He said you were at Lou's. I guess I'll send this letter there. Tell Lou and tell her her towels have been very much admired by my various nurses and callers. I have a fine big closet now in the new bedroom and have them all spread out. We use our bedroom for a dining room. I have a nice rag carpet on it I made.

I'll send that Miss Wilson's letter and the Bishop's back to you as soon as I am up and can find them. They are in my desk somewhere but I have to ask for so many things I hate to give anybody the job of finding them.

Give Lou and the Bishop our love and little Gracie's too and I'm sure she sends a saucy kiss to her Aunt Annie. You ought to see her suck her thumb and howl when she loses it! The Robertses all think she looks like me, but I think she is more like Sherman.

Much love to you. Yours lovingly, dear Red,
Gede

November 22, 1904
COOLIDGE RANCH, WIND RIVER, WYOMING

Dearest Reddy,

Yes, my boy died just a month ago yesterday. I don't know why I didn't write you. I am still swamped in unanswered letters for one thing, I suppose. You didn't see the little folding rubber bath tub Lou and Edith sent, of course. I used it for a crib for one or the other of them when baths were over. Louis was in that when he died. He had typhoid. We thought it was just teething for he cut four teeth while he was sick. He was sick just two weeks. Then we thought it was pneumonia. I had a very good doctor for him, the one at the Post. I think we did everything. The last day his temperature was over 108 for a while. But I never dreamed he would die. He was such a great big strong boy, he weighed almost 20 lbs. before he was sick and he was just 6 mos. and one week when he died. From Sunday afternoon till Friday when he died, we were up at the hotel to be near the doctor. We left all of a sudden, just bundled up the two babies and their bottles and went up to the hotel. He died there. We were both with him. Mrs. Moore had the little baby. She kept her several nights for me. He died just after sunset. We took him home that night. You know he had been so sick we couldn't handle him any, poor baby. The doctor said he was the sickest baby he had ever seen—and oh! it seemed so good to get him back in my arms again. Miss Robinson, the field matron, an awfully kind woman and a trained nurse, came down with us, she had come over to stay all night with Louis. We rode with old Prince in the little buggy and Sherman walked. When Miss Robinson drove back for him I dressed my boy. Everything I put on him was something somebody had given him. The next morning Miss Robinson drove up for the little coffin and Sherman went down to the church—it is moved now to just above where we used to go to see that sick baby of Dan Friday's—and dug the grave. I stayed with the baby. When Miss Robinson came I put him in the little coffin myself and carried him down to the church. Sherman read the service, we put him in the grave. It was nice that we didn't have to have anyone do anything for him but ourselves. Do you remember the agent's family? They had a baby just a month older than Louis and she died of typhoid nine days after he did. We don't know where they got it. I can't get used to being without him. Miss Robinson can't understand, she is always talking about it. I can't either but I know I loved him best of the two. It seems natural to me. He was all mine and I had such a hard time with him when I felt so badly last summer, and he loved me. This baby seems like Sherman's and Mrs. Moore's and Miss Robinson's and everybody's. It is the worst thing I ever had. I can't get used to it. It seems as tho' next summer he must come back again, or sometime. Think of a little baby going through all that great experience, all that suffering—and then death. Do you think he is a baby now? or what? I will send you one of his pictures. I think you will want one. He was laughing right to me. All I want is to get him back—and I can't.

I think we shall go at the hospital soon. We will put up a log building and put it in charge of the Post doctor. We thought Welty was surely going, but again we are disappointed and we are tired fooling. We have very little money for it but it is so tremendously needed. I feel that I want to spend all my time now that would have been spent on Louis on the Indians. It is all I can do for him.

This baby is still very little. She hasn't outgrown any of her first things yet. We had so much trouble feeding her and we have been up every night, and sometimes nearly all night with her ever since she was born. We have had her on malted milk since Louis was sick and she has begun to pick up splendidly. Yes, we named her Grace Anne. At least it is in memory of our friendship, if no more. Everybody says she is very pretty, so I suppose she is, and she is as smart as anything and laughs and talks. I suppose she thinks she is talking with me—by the hour. Sherman is just silly over her. The night is never too dark or too cold or too sleepy for him to get up with her. You know how fond he is of Phil. She looks exactly like that photo of Phil. I have always tied them both up Injun, or rather, Arapahoe. It seems so much more sensible than putting coats on them. Sometimes I would have them all ready to go out, tied up and their hoods on, and I would lay them on the sofa and there they would lie and eye each other like two fat sparrows on a roof. I can't look at her now without wanting my boy. It seems as tho' somehow he must come back. But if I get another baby as I did him it can't be him, and if I have another it can't be. You think of everything and there is no way. Except to go to him. That is the only way I can ever have them both again. The thing now is to make the best come out of it. I feel all the time that the responsibility rests with me now to see that his death and his life too for that matter of that, were not in vain. That is all I can think of. I hope for you that Blondy[52] is enough of a believer, to be able to help you when your time for trouble comes. I was thinking of that the other night. Seems to me it would be too much to have a husband who couldn't help you by being sure of himself. But that is all life. It comes as it comes.

Yours lovingly
Gede

Love to Lou and the Bishop from us both.

January 9, 1905
COOLIDGE RANCH, WIND RIVER, WYOMING

Dearest Red,

I have been waiting for a time when I should not be so rushed before writing you, but as it doesn't look as tho' that time was likely to come I will just write you a short letter now and longer when I can. It certainly was good of you to put so much in the china barrel and to bother with it all. Sherman certainly appreciated the glass pitcher, you remember his leaning that way, and the lovely thing in that line that you and he bought together, has, I (of course) regret to state, long since left us. We thought the candlesticks were lovely, everything in fact. And didn't you send the glasses? They are just like yr. Bethlehem mission ones. Sherman recognized them at once and they make us think of last Xmas and the magic plate lifter. I hope you will forgive the horned little things I send you all. I hadn't any heart for Xmas, in fact forgot all about it till it was on us, and we were so rushed getting the things for the two trees ready and fixing up the Jonestown church for the first service in it, and getting ready for my dinner. I got rash and asked seventeen people.

Fortunately there was a hard snowstorm and the Jorgensens with their two didn't come, or I shouldn't have had dishes enough to go round. Grace got ever so many things and I think yr. wrapper is sweet. Have always wanted one for her. I haven't put her in short clothes yet, tho' she is 5 mos. old tomorrow. But she is too little and too cold. We call her Toots, pronounced like boots (not feet). Right in the middle of all the Xmas excitement her food went back on her, malted milk that has agreed with her so finely for over two mos. and we have been nearly wild trying to find something she can take. I have tried milk fresh and canned in every modification and nothing suits her. I now feed her on rice water and Mellin's Food preceded by an ounce of beef tea! I expect I will be giving her roasted peanuts next. Lou has had a checkered medical career. Do ask her if she knows what you can feed a baby on who can't digest milk? She is fat and well, red cheeks and giggles, but we are up every night with her still, sometimes for hours. After the malted milk went back on her we were just nearly worn out. One night we went to bed at ten and got up at twelve and from then stayed up till morning. Sometimes one or the other of us would go to bed for a few minutes but that was all. She has had an awful cough for about three weeks and we are afraid it is whooping cough. Poor little Toots, she seems to have had more trouble than anything else. We had quite a wonderful time at Xmas, we thought. There were 13 baptisms at Big Wind. We thought perhaps there would be two or three more at Little Wind, but there were 47 there. There was just one man, Dan Friday, you remember him, the rest were the little school and camp children and babies. The fathers and mothers did it all themselves. It is the first time in the history of the mission that there has been anything like a big demonstration from the camp people. Yellow Calf stood up and just herded the children up and Michael and Josiah and I went practically through the census list to get the right names attached to them. The church was so crowded we had to take out the seats and let as many as could sit on the floor and lots couldn't come inside. Sherman took the children in batches of five up to the altar and then had them stand in the chancel afterwards. They all looked so little and solemn and sweet. Finally the chancel got too crowded and they had to be herded down again. I have sixty-eight godchildren!!! The older girls made the promises for their little nieces and nephews and sisters and brothers. They wanted to. The Carlisle children are doing finely. I do hope the Bishop will go out to see them sometime. Lots of them remember him. I asked Josiah in the church at the Christmas tree if he didn't want their little girl, Catherine, baptized, and he said, "No, we are going to wait till the Bishop comes to have her baptized." Aren't the Arapahoes getting civilized, tho'!!? I pretty nearly giggled. But I guess it is because Josiah means to be confirmed when the Bishop comes next time. But it did sound funny.

Mr. Moore told us the other day that the papers said that fiend Irvine was beginning on yr. father again, and then father sent me a paper about it. We felt very badly about it. But I guess he can't fail to have short work made of him. It doesn't seem as tho' anybody could be so vindictive.

Frank Sayre sent us $25.00 at Xmas time for the Indians, from Montana, wasn't that pretty sweet of him? And such a nice letter with it. He has lots of earnestness, hasn't he for a boy like that? This came pretty near being a long letter after all. Thank you from us all. We just loved everything.

Yours devotedly,
Gede

April 9, 1905
COOLIDGE RANCH, WIND RIVER, WYOMING

Dear Annie,

Just a line to tell you that little Grace is dead too. She was quite sick with pneumonia for about ten days and then for another ten days with the after effects and her little stomach and bowels that have always given her so much trouble. We thought she had really started to get better when she died quite suddenly. It was last Wed. Apr. 5th. She would be 8 mos. old tomorrow. I was fortunate in having a really good doctor and nurse for her and she wasn't anything like as sick as Louis. We don't know what to do without a baby. I am glad to say that in another 6 mos. I ought to have another. That makes something to look forward to.

Sherman got your picture and will write you someday. He feels awfully bad about the baby. They were so fond of each other.

I owe you lots of letters but will try to write them sometime. We were going up to Hanscum's tomorrow for a few days but it is snowing hard tonight and I am afraid we can't go.

Love to the Bishop and Lou from us both.

Yr. Gede

November 2, 1905
COOLIDGE RANCH, WIND RIVER, WYOMING

Dearest Red,

What will you say when I tell you that my little son is dead too?[53] He was the fattest, healthiest, goodest baby you ever saw and no one can believe he is dead. The doctor says that valve that should close in a new born baby's heart didn't close properly in his case. He wasn't very well Saturday night, that is, he wouldn't nurse much, but we didn't think it was much. Sherman went to church as usual and the baby died about an hour before he came home. I was all alone with him. I thought he died a half an hour before he did, but I put him in a hot bath and revived him. He died in my arms. Before he did I Christened him. I was so afraid he would be different from the others. Do you think that was just as good as if Sherman had? It is funny we can't raise children, isn't it? You ought to see those three little graves in a row, Grace in the middle and the boys on the outside.

This picture Mrs. Kneale[54] took of him when he was 6 days old. He was 12 days when he died, Oct. 29. Lots of people came to see him that day. Mrs. Snyder (one of the breeds) with her baby. Gwen Roberts is holding them both. Philip is the one asleep. You can't get much of an idea of him but you can see he is fat and cute. He had his sister's wrapper on and it was too big for him.

I enclose a money order for the $18.00. We sold our Pinto yesterday, that is the first money we had had.

Yrs. Lovingly,
Grace

LATER MISSIVES, 1911–32

November 15, 1911
ENID, OKLAHOMA

Dearest dear,

I have been doing something horribly audacious, horribly! And now I'm coming to you—not as you might hope in order to confess and reform—but to ask to be helped to further audacity. I have been writing a—well, a collection of—in short, some Indian sketches, stories I can hardly call them. Just little snapshots, you know. They are all true—matter of fact, that is—therefore fine in subject, but how I've treated that subject is of course beyond me to judge of. I've done 25 (two of them are not yet written but I'll have them done this week). They ought to be enough for a book, about 40,000 words, I calculate—and all, except 4 wh. I did last spring, written in the past 4 weeks. If you could only write and [illegible], or at least let the [illegible] there'd be some fun in it. (I have a heap of them now high upon the hearth.) But somehow that doesn't seem to be quite playing the game. (I've here reached the point of audacity.) Do you think after you have looked them over and *he* has looked them over that yr. father would be willing to take them in to the Harper people for me and see if by any misplacement of Fate they would be willing to touch them with a ten foot pole? You won't mind reading them, I know, and if after doing so you do not think they are of sufficient merit to ask your father to sponsor you can just tell me and send them a weary round on my own account. But of course if the Bishop would take them in for me the Harper outfit would probably regard them with a more favoring eye. (Hear my solemn litany?) Well, what do you think of all that? Shall I in the course of a few weeks send them on to you—or not? The time has (or seems to me to have) come, the Walrus said. I feel like a squeezed lemon, tho' I've *adored* doing them. It's funny I'm writing again after all those stuffed up years in Wyoming. It's not worth it, I'm convinced but I tell you solemnly *I can't help it*. The things are in you and they stir to get out and what's more they have to come out just as absolutely as the babies do. I know, cause I've felt them both. I thought (to return to earth) that 25 were enough of these tales. I feared more would be monotonous. But

I have about a dozen other titles jotted down. In case anyone thought there ought to be more of them. I tell you this, I don't know at all whether they are a little bit good or just plainly rank! I have one friend here (Mrs. Steen of whom I wrote you) who has written quite a bit for magazines—short stories mostly—she has been awfully good about reading them all, no one else has seen them en masse, and *says* she thinks well of them. But of course one person's opinion is not much. Well, I've *loved* doing them and they can at least be buried with me. Dust to dust. I feel rather spent and utterly naked when anyone has to see the things. Oh! oh! oh!

Darling dear, will you please go into some bookstore and get me Dreiser's Jennie Gerhardt? It is supposed to be very powerful. I hate American novels generally. (Except Owen Wister. Yes, honestly!) But I want to read Jennie Gerhardt. I will repay if you will please mail it to me. And one more thing: (I am afraid you won't care to hear from me again!) I want to get Sallie[55] a big—very big she wants—nonsmashable doll for Xmas. It must have brushable hair. Is there such a combination obtainable? And where? And for how much?

I hate to think of Xmas in this dismal, footless, friendless, near-[illegible] as I lately heard Enid called.

Much, much love and don't keep me hanging in the air forever before you answer this. And don't tell anybody about them because I suppose no publisher will look at them and then I shall be ashameder than ever. Oh! heavens. And all the time I *feel* the broom to be mightier than the pen, though even in my own home, unwielded.

Anyhow I *loved* doing them. Principalities and powers (or even publishers) can't take that away.

Devotedly and distractedly,
Yr. poor Gede

September 15, 1912
FARIBAULT, MINNESOTA

All off! It's a girl. Born the 5th at 6 p.m. sharp. Not much trouble, only a couple of rather vigorous hours after a morning of uncertain qualms.

But I'm feeling a little seedy now as I've had a mess with the milk. It came till it nearly drowned us all and burst me, resulting in a few days of temperature etc. I had the sweetest of doctors and the nicest and kindest of nurses and the baby is a cherub for all she is only getting half rations. Sleeps 5–6 hours at a stretch and at *night!!!* She's a really pretty little thing with a little black fur cap on her heady. Well, all we can do is to echo Sallie's prayer put up the evening little sister was born: "Please give us another, a boy; and, thank you for this one." She is the fattest best looking baby I have had. No wonder I never felt her move. She never wiggles a finger now if just rolling her eyes will do. I must tell you how neatly I did the yob (as my Norwegian girl says). In the first place "girls" are scarce around here. I have been hunting one for some time. This one, a good one too, came to me the evening before the baby did. Then the morning of that day, Wednesday, I sent the family up to St. Paul for two days to the State Fair. When they returned the baby was about 3 hours old!!! Sallie was here but a neighbor took her off in the afternoon. Sallie of course was perfectly charmed seeing the baby before anybody else did. She would like it named Rosebud!!! I don't somehow think that would sound just right when it gets to 50 below around here. No definite name as yet. I'm tired of these Xtian children; I'm going to keep this one a heathen for a while. Sallie has started school. The girls went off last Thursday, poor Virgie terribly torn at having to leave the baby.[56] Effie I think was much more pleased with the new maid than she was with the baby.

And who do you think phoned us from St. Paul Friday morning? The Reverend departmental Secretary Hunting on his way from Berkeley, Cal. to a Missions House Pow Wow in N.Y.!!! The last time I saw him I was in bed with Sallie!! He stayed 24 hours and we had a good time, laughed ourselves perfectly weak. Wasn't it a blessing he hadn't come a week before?

Well, this seems to be all on one subject. I was awfully glad to get yr. letter yesterday. We have had exactly the same kind of a summer here. The heat the day the baby was born and for several days before and after was simply unspeakable. Now we are having the furnace.

Much love to you all and we shall be so pleased to have the blanket. Almost all the baby's presents have been kimonos and jackets!!

Devotedly,
Grace

Sallie's first remark on seeing the baby was: "I wish she was Indian like I am." Now what in the world do you suppose she meant by that?

March 1, 1913
FARIBAULT, MINNESOTA

Dearest Annie,

Just a few lines to tell you that you nearly lost us all three weeks ago tomorrow. R.R. crossing, express train, hit the back wheels of the buggy. I would have had Sherman send you a newspaper account only that it was too lurid. Rosebud, who was picked up on the ground with the back seat (on which she and I had been sitting!) wedged on top of her. They could hardly get her out. But she was absolutely unscratched. None of us were really badly hurt, tho' Sallie and I were pretty well out of business for a few days, and I guess no words could do justice to our appearance. We seem to have landed on our faces. My eyes were swollen shut for a week or more and now I have to stay in the dark or gloom. This is the first letter. And for some reason I am still more or less in bed, tho' I fear that is from weakness of character, not get-up enough to get up. Sherman is stiff and sore. Sallie all right now. They thought she wouldn't live thro' the first night. But it turned out not half as bad as it seemed. She was at the little hospital here a week and I nearly two. Sallie looks like a soubrette now, with bruises all around her eyes. My goodness, this is the kindest place. One friend took the baby and kept her bodily 3 days for me. We were so fortunate in getting the nice nurse we had when she was born so Sherman came home then after 2 days and he and the nurse took care of Rosebud at home. It seems to me the worst of it all is that my milk is gone. The baby adores the bottle tho' and doesn't seem to remember she ever had a mother. Not the least upset. I never saw the train coming, nor knew the least thing about it. S. was driving, we in the back. Wasn't that funny!? The hospital was [illegible] but the doctor is a dear, which is always soothing. I've got a good maid, a wonderful thing to accomplish in Faribault. And I haven't washed a dish for 3 weeks. No great loss without some small gain! I also made very interesting psychological observations while at the hospital and quite enjoyed myself after the first two or three days of terror about Sallie. But think of death having come so close to us once more. No time to sit back on yr. hind legs in this world and feel secure. I looked down into the blankets, driving down that hill on to the crossing, to see if my Rosebud was asleep and then never saw her again for a week! I tell you, you want to tread lightly in this world and keep moving.

We fear this happened because we were all cutting church! The hospital is run by German Lutheran "sisters" (deaconesses). I fear I shocked mine. She insisted on reading out loud to me one day and what do you think she selected? The Xtian Herald!!!![57] Anyhow, I steered her on from article to article till we struck one on [illegible] a bunch of Black Hand[58] Kidnappers in N.Y. I made her read that. It was quite juicy after all.

Where are you moved to? Forgive me for talking so much about ourselves but adventures are rare. My respected nose got broken!!!!

Yrs. Ever,
G.

March 28, 1914
FARIBAULT, MINNESOTA

Dearest Annie,

If I don't hurry up yr. birthday letter won't even be written in the month of March!!! I won't explain or apologize for being late for you know just about the things that I should say and just about how much of them would be true. But I must say I do find letters doubly hard to write from here. In the first place, Faribault is like the land of the Lotus Eaters, nothing ever happens here except that people die and get born, which isn't very interesting to write about—read about, is what I mean. And in the second place, Rosebud the ubiquitous and no maid make a bad combination for time and peace.

Did you know our house tried to burn down this winter? And that, *on the anniversary of last year's excitement!!* Find the hoodoo. (I wish you would, I'm going to bed with my "medicine" next year.) A Faribault-built defective flue did the business. The baby woke a little after 12 (midnight) coughing and strangling. We jumped up and got our various heads out of the window for air. Sherman plunged down stairs into a sea of smoke. We could hear but not find the fire. Well, Sherman took the children across to the house of the woman who cleans for me and stays with the baby, etc. It was 20 below and deep snow. Everybody except us was sleeping with the windows tight shut. He couldn't wake her! But there was a light downstairs in the house next door. The young girl of the family was sitting up with her beau. So he broke in upon Love's Young Dream and dumped the children. In the meantime I was welcoming the fire co. Also gathering up a few of the most important adjuncts of civilization; such as the baby's bottle and a ms[59] upon which I had been toiling all the previous day which carelessly happened to be Sunday. They chopped two big holes, one upstairs in the study and one in the dining room, downstairs. We were insured and really got three rooms papered for nothing, but oh! the mess. Nearly 3 weeks cleaning up after a two hour fire! And you don't know what it is to keep Rosebud off newly varnished floors. Also Sherman went East two days after the fire and remained till the worst was over. He was mainly in Washington on Indian Society business and didn't get up to N.Y. On his way home he stopped over Sunday at Carlisle with the children. They had been confirmed the month before and he was there to give them their first Communion, at Mr. McMillan's church. A coincidence. They have been having a great shake-up at Carlisle. The Supt. (Friedman) has been fired for stealing, etc., principally from the athletic funds! The govt. employees are a credit to any country, really, aren't they? The children say that the immediate result is that the food is a little better and that they have two mattresses on the beds instead of one!

Have you read The Fugitive, The Dark Flower, Press Cuttings, etc.? None of them up to the full powers of their authors, do you think? In fact, far from it. I wonder why authors must publish when they must know that they are not doing their best. I suppose for the sake of the incoming checks. I belong to two rather nice little reading clubs here. We read the plays, principally—on account of length—that come out. A few days ago somebody—not me—said, "Let's read some Browning." Somebody else produced The Blot etc. and threw it at me. And we began. And such is the power of real literature, that there was not a person in that club, even the lightest and most unliterary, who did not cry with one voice, "This is the best we have ever read. This is the real stuff!" As for me who had to read it out loud at sight, my hands were positively cold and shaking with the effort. Miss Bennett certainly left us all a legacy of joy in the doors of certain poets which she opened to us. But I'll bet if she had lived on thro' this next twenty years she wouldn't waste one week on Tennyson. I saw him classed, the other day, with the minor poets, emotionally at any rate. Well, many happy returns to you and young Talbot. Is it 39 you are?

Well, that's not so bad as 40 as you will find out in the course of a year. And is my godson Pip really 4? No, he can't be. Francis is 7, Dora nearly 6. Yes, he is. Do you ever intend to have another? I am rapidly giving up hope, myself.

I have sent for yr. father's new book.[60]

Love to you all from all of us.

Yrs. ever,
G. C.

Rosy's favorite toy is that little doll Dora sent Sallie. It is nearly chewed up now.

February 9, 1932
BROADMOOR, COLORADO SPRINGS, COLORADO

Dearest girl,

I never meant to wait such ages before writing but I have had such stacks of letters to write and hard ones. But I am beginning to see daylight and now I don't know what to do with myself. This place suddenly doesn't seem to be a home anymore; just a house. Sherman was always here the steady one and I the one that always wanted to be up and off. The girls are here but their being here always seems to have such a temporary quality to it. It doesn't add to the home feeling.

Of course you are the understanding one: my first thought was what a wonderful thing for him to slip away like that almost with stillness. Sallie says that he knew that he was dying and she is quite sure he didn't mind. I don't see why he shd have. Sherman was always very calm and sure in his feelings; the thing that I fear dread is not in any sense death, but horrors. I used always to be afraid when he came in late for dinner, for instance, that he had fallen in the street or been struck by a machine. You know how he always drifted along! People here used to tell me how they wd honk at him—usually in vain. He has been rather miserable for the last couple of years, bad dizzy spells and odd panting breathing. Especially the dizziness tortured him. And he was also worried about losing his memory for names, etc., tho' I must say that was not very bad. I think he is just plain lucky to have escaped the trials of old age and ill health and I am so thankful that he did not outlive me. For some reason I always had it in my mind that I shd die first. You know how dependent he always was. Rosie said, "Papa was witty and funny and had a good clear mind and a personality that everybody remembers with pleasure. Maybe if he had lived on longer all that might have changed." I was so glad she marked that out for herself.

The phone rang early Sunday morning. She woke up and heard it and came down and took the message. Then came in my room and woke me up. I never dreamed of that message coming so by phone. I thought any such message wd have been sent over. But I suppose it was because it came at night when the town office was closed. About ten days before the day he died he had been in Sallie's little Monte Sano Hospital and L.A. (he had gone there after Xmas with her because we felt such confidence in those doctors there who had done so much for Sallie) for observation. They were giving him a cryptoscopic examination, a horrid severe and unpleasant thing as you likely know, when he suddenly had a very bad heart failure. Sallie wired me, in fact for several days we wired back and forth. He improved immediately, but altho' they knew his condition was serious it did not seem to be necessary for me to come on at once. And I hated to go.

Especially about leaving Rosie alone here. Even now I can't really regret not going. He was charmed with the doctor. Sallie's great friend Josephine was interning in the hospital and was with him a lot and Sallie was there. I had a wire from Sallie that Sat., after that he was continuing to improve. Late that evening they called her to the hospital and before 3 he died, quite easily, unconscious an hour before he died.

I have had terribly nice letters about him from old friends, all kinds of friends, from my old gardener, yesterday, up. The services were really quite inspiring. They were held the day after the Convocation (in Pueblo) at Bp. Johnson's suggestion and nearly all the clergy of Colo. came. They were the pall bearers. Sherman wd have loved all that part of it, wdn't he! He always felt the clergy were his blood relations. Of course I thought every way about how I cd take him up home to Wyo. but it just wasn't practical. There is no cemetery on the reservation, and in Jany and a bitter cold Jany, at that, it just couldn't be. The place here is hilly and piney and attractive. So we let it do. It doesn't matter much anyhow. It was an awfully cold day. A lot of our friends came down from Denver and they nearly froze going back.

I have a strange feeling as tho' I had been delivered over hand and foot to the next generation.

I only hope you will come in Apr. I may possibly go on to Calif. and Honolulu earlier. I feel so sort of stupid and restless and we are having a disgusting cold winter. But then I may not. I wd love to make that trip with you. Bring yr. Francis and we can take Rosie with us. They wd enjoy it. But I don't at all have to take her. My grim old Swedish cook can hold her down all right here.

Yes, you are right in saying that I did make Sherman's life richer and happier. The last 12 or 15 years he very much came to himself. And how he loved Rosie!!

Well, thank you dear girl for yr. wire and yr. letter (also for those books that came this very day). I loved getting them both.

My best love to you. Isn't it funny to think that you were the one who first brought us together? At Rongis that night. Do you remember? I can't write one other word.

Gede

Poems

THE OFFERING OF THE GODDESS

Coolidge-Heinicke Collection (1911)

But a heathen maid am I, poor and lorn,
Divine, men called me, and knelt before
My shrine. They poured oblations, wine and corn,
Ambrosia of the north; nay, more,
Blood, on my altar's stones. The blood of beasts.
Ah! yes, and blood of men. They wafted prayer
To me; from sacrificial beasts
Rich viands laid they on my altar there,
The smoke of incense fires stained the far blue.

Dear Christ, I was alone and very blind!
In lands remote from Thee I lived, nor knew
Of Thy sweet life, Thy sacrifice, designed
Of God, our Father before the birth of time.

But now, since Thou hast touched my closed eyes,
I burn to lay some treasured thing of mine,
There, at Thy Cross' foot. Wouldst Thou despise
a maiden's penitential offering?

Yet what to give have I, who from Thee took
Prayers and devotion, justly Thine? The Spring
May give Thee lilies; men, through bitter tears may look
Their homage. I, though plucked and depleted,
I, who took, now yield, of my infamous fame,
Their Symbol—I, Thine innocent merry, defeated—
Lord, at the Cross I lay—my heathen name.

ON FINISHING A BOOK

Coolidge-Heinicke Collection (1911)

I step about from room to room,
And here, and there,
Nor find I ever what I seek
Anywhere.

The last leaf's turned, ended the tale,
The least, the most
Of you, eager, I read, and now—
You're lost.

I loved you so, for you my tears,
My anguish gave,
And yet you hide from me as in
A grave.

Of him who fathered you I'd ask.
If he were by.
But ah! I think he's lost you too,
As I.

Where shall I find again, as yours,
So high a strain?
E'er so shall tremble, weep, or love
Again?

And so I slip about the house
Seeking and lone,
I know, alas! for ever more
You're gone.

NOTES

SHERMAN AND GRACE COOLIDGE

1. Marion Gustin, "Arapaho Is Distinguished Churchman," Sherman Coolidge Files, Warren Hunting Smith Library, Geneva NY (hereafter WHSL). The Eastern Shoshone Reservation, established in the 1860s, was later renamed Wind River Reservation in the 1930s. See "The Arapaho Arrive: Two Nations on One Reservation," WyoHistory.org, June 23, 2018, https://www.wyohistory.org/encyclopedia/arapaho-arrive-two-nations-one-reservation#_ftnref1.
2. Grace Coolidge to Anne Talbot, October 22, 1902, Coolidge-Heinicke Collection, Colorado Springs Pioneers Museum (hereafter CHC); "Indian Husband Approved," *New York Times*, CHC; and "Society Girl's Heart and Hand Captured by an Indian," *Denver Post*, October 24, 1902, Sherman Coolidge Biographical File, American Heritage Center, University of Wyoming–Laramie (hereafter AHC).
3. G. Coolidge to Talbot, November 20, 1902, CHC.
4. "Society Girl's Heart," AHC.
5. Sherman Coolidge, "A Sketch from Real Life," CHC.
6. Ellis, *Pioneers*, 13–14.
7. Sherman Coolidge, "The Death of Brave Heart (Big Heart)," CHC.
8. Wagner, *Powder River Odyssey*, 28.
9. Coolidge, "A Sketch from Real Life," CHC.
10. Fowler, *Arapahoe Politics, 1851–1978*, 42–44.
11. Coolidge, "Death of Brave Heart," CHC.
12. Coolidge, "Indian of To-Day," 88.
13. For a thorough examination of the nature of violence on the Great Plains, see Blackhawk, *Violence over the Land*.
14. Coolidge, "A Sketch from Real Life," CHC; and Fowler, *Arapahoe Politics*, 47–48.
15. See "Early Life of Rev. T. Sherman Coolidge," CHC; Coolidge, "Sketch from Real Life," CHC; G. Coolidge to Talbot, January 15, 1903, CHC; Fowler, *Arapahoe Politics*, 47–48; Markley and Crofts, *Walk Softly*, 143–44; and Stamm, *People of the Wind River*, 56–57, 220. The quote is found in Markley and Crofts, *Walk Softly*.
16. Charles Frederick Larrabee to Coolidge, May 31, 1887, CHC.

17. Coolidge, "Sketch from Real Life," CHC; and Reid, "Westerners," 47.
18. Larrabee to Coolidge, May 31, 1887, CHC.
19. Sophie Coolidge to Grace Hebard, December 29, 1930, Grace Raymond Hebard Papers, American Heritage Center, University of Wyoming–Laramie (hereafter GHP).
20. "Canon Coolidge Pays His Debt of Love: Colorado Minister Visits White Foster Mother in Washington," *Washington Post*, June 26, 1931, CHC.
21. S. Coolidge to Henry Whipple, February 4, 1877, Henry Benjamin Whipple Papers, Gale Family Library, Minnesota Historical Society, St. Paul (hereafter HWP).
22. Van Orsdale, "Rev. Sherman Coolidge, D.D.," 86.
23. Coolidge to Whipple, February 4, 1877, HWP; and Coolidge, "American Indians," 253.
24. Van Orsdale, "Rev. Sherman Coolidge, D.D.," 86.
25. Fowler, *Arapahoe Politics*, 49–53.
26. Carlson, *Plains Indians*, 142, 150–62; Hedren, *Powder River*, 36; and Ostler, *Plains Sioux*, 60, 77, 144.
27. Ellis, *Pioneers*, 15.
28. Sherman Coolidge, "Sherman Coolidge Autobiographical Notes," CHC; and Gustin, "Arapaho Is Distinguished Churchman," WHSL.
29. Sarah Allen to Coolidge, February 11, 1877, CHC.
30. Van Orsdale, "Rev. Sherman Coolidge, D.D.," 85–86.
31. Fowler, *Arapahoe Politics*, 63–65; and Stamm, *People of the Wind River*, 128–29.
32. The Bureau of Indian Affairs (BIA), originally the Office of Indian Affairs, was created in 1824 as a branch of the U.S. Department of the Interior. It was officially renamed the Bureau of Indian Affairs in 1947. See C. L. Henson, "From War to Self Determination: A History of the Bureau of Indian Affairs," *American Studies Today Online*, accessed April 27, 2020, http://www.americansc.org.uk/Online/indians.htm.
33. Markley and Crofts, *Walk Softly*, 145–46, 151–52.
34. Coolidge, "Indian of To-Day," 93; and Spalding, "Second Annual Report," 617–18.
35. Affidavit of A. D. Lane, May 3, 1887, Records of the Bureau of Indian Affairs, National Archives and Records Administration, Washington DC (hereafter RBIA); Coolidge to Whipple, May 8, 1887, HWP; and Thomas M. Jones to Whipple, May 15, 1887, HWP.
36. Allen, *And the Wilderness Shall Blossom*, 272n386.
37. Fowler, *Arapahoe Politics*, 91, 99, 106.
38. Fowler, *The Arapaho*, 79; and Fowler, *Arapahoe Politics*, 106–7.
39. "Church Periodical Club," 441; "Diocese News," April 1885, 494–95, 586; "Diocese News," May 1885, 658; "Chicago," 727; and "Pennsylvania," 444.
40. "Newark," 169.
41. G. Coolidge to Anne Talbot, July 4, 1896, CHC.
42. "The Coolidge Family," Finding Aid, CHC; Ellis, *Pioneers*, 18; G. Coolidge to Talbot, January 1, 1897, CHC; G. Coolidge to Talbot, February 28, 1897, CHC; and "Society Girl's Heart," AHC.
43. G. Coolidge to Talbot, ca. late 1890s, via Philip Heinicke, email to author, December 19, 2020.

44. Ellis, *Pioneers*, 18–20, 24; "Coolidge Family," Finding Aid, CHC; and "The Ogontz School 1850–1950," Penn State University Libraries, accessed September 3, 2020, https://libraries.psu.edu/about/collections/ogontz-school-1850-1950.
45. G. Coolidge to Talbot, August 20, 1902, CHC.
46. G. Coolidge to Talbot, February 9, 1932, CHC.
47. Coolidge to G. Coolidge, November 1897, CHC; and G. Coolidge to Talbot, November 4, 1897, CHC.
48. G. Coolidge to Talbot, November 12, 1899, CHC.
49. G. Coolidge to Talbot, February 26, 1903, CHC.
50. G. Coolidge to Talbot, June 21, 1901, CHC.
51. G. Coolidge to Talbot, March 4, 1902, CHC.
52. G. Coolidge to Talbot, March 17, 1902, CHC.
53. G. Coolidge to Talbot, June 25, 1902, CHC; and G. Coolidge to Talbot, September 10, 1902, CHC.
54. G. Coolidge to Talbot, August 20, 1902, CHC.
55. G. Coolidge to Talbot, October 22, 1902, CHC.
56. Gardner Wetherbee to G. Coolidge, October 6, 1902, CHC.
57. G. Coolidge to Talbot, October 22, 1902, CHC.
58. G. Coolidge to Talbot, November 20, 1902, CHC.
59. G. Coolidge to Talbot, November 20, 1902, CHC.
60. G. Coolidge to Talbot, November 25, 1902, CHC.
61. "Coolidge Family," Finding Aid, CHC.
62. G. Coolidge to Talbot, March 13, 1903, CHC; G. Coolidge to Talbot, October 25, 1905, CHC; and "Society Belle Turns Squaw," GHP. The article was later reprinted as "Very Silly Woman or Exaggerated Story," 21.
63. G. Coolidge to Talbot, February 26, 1903, CHC; and Fowler, *Arapahoe Politics*, 107, 324n59.
64. "Coolidge Family," Finding Aid, CHC.
65. "Indian Troubles in Boise," 248.
66. Nathaniel Seymour Thomas to Coolidge, June 13, 1910, CHC.
67. G. Coolidge to Talbot, April 16, 1913, CHC.
68. Wetherbee to G. Coolidge, January 12, 1910, CHC.
69. Coolidge to G. Coolidge, September 5, 1910; Coolidge to G. Coolidge, October 5, 1910; and Coolidge to G. Coolidge, November 10, 1910—all in CHC.
70. Coolidge to G. Coolidge, October 15, 1910; Coolidge to G. Coolidge, November 30, 1910; G. Coolidge to Talbot, ca. spring 1911; and draft letter from Coolidge to Francis Key Brooke, ca. April 1911—all in CHC.
71. G. Coolidge to Talbot, January 25, 1912, CHC.
72. Coolidge to G. Coolidge, February 13, 1912, CHC.
73. "Coolidge Family," Finding Aid, CHC.
74. G. Coolidge to Talbot, March 28, 1914, CHC; and G. Coolidge to Talbot, April 16, 1913, CHC.

75. "Conference Evening at Haskell Indian School," 300.
76. Hertzberg, *Search for an American Indian Identity*, 36–37. Also see Deloria, "Four Thousand Invitations," 25–43. Deloria states that the SAI "worked actively to preserve elements of Native cultures and societies from destruction."
77. *Report of the Executive Council*, 157–58.
78. Coolidge, "Opening Address," 227–28.
79. Coolidge, "American Indians," 251.
80. Montezuma, "Let My People Go," 33–34.
81. Hertzberg, *Search for an American Indian Identity*, 135.
82. "Important Topics Considered," 218–19; and Coolidge, "Opening Address," 227–28.
83. "Gardner Wetherbee," Find a Grave, accessed August 22, 2020, https://www.findagrave.com/memorial/130563888/gardner-wetherbee.
84. G. Coolidge to Coolidge, April 26, 1916, CHC.
85. G. Coolidge to Talbot, August 11, 1915, CHC.
86. See Grace Coolidge, "Two Indian Stories," *Outlook*, March 23, 1912, 651–55. *Collier's* ran such writings as a handsomely illustrated series titled "Tepee Neighbor Sketches." Also see Grace Coolidge, "The Victory," 16–17.
87. G. Coolidge to Talbot, December 14, 1912, CHC.
88. Parker, "Editorial Comment," 24; Arthur C. Parker to Grace Coolidge, October 12, 1917, Society of American Indians Papers, Cornell University Library, Ithaca (hereafter PSAI); and Myfanway Thomas Goodnough, "Sherman Coolidge," *Rock Springs (WY) Miner*, February 22, 1935, AHC.
89. G. Coolidge to Talbot, April 29, 1918, CHC.
90. Gustin, "Arapaho Is Distinguished Churchman," WHSL.
91. "Election of Officers," 125; and Hertzberg, *Search for an American Indian Identity*, 175–76, 193–94.
92. Hertzberg, *Search for an American Indian Identity*, 202–3; and Parker, "Ruth Margaret Muskrat," 320.
93. Harry B. Hunt, "This Little World: Washington," *Daily News* (San Francisco), September 18, 1923, 16.
94. Heinicke email to author, December 16, 2020.
95. Robert I. Woodward, "Notes about the Reverend Sherman Coolidge," Sherman Coolidge File, Cathedral of St. John in the Wilderness Archives, Denver (hereafter SJWA); and Goodnough, "Sherman Coolidge," AHC.
96. "Coolidge Decries Injustice in Barring Native Indians from American Citizenship," *Colorado Springs Gazette*, June 13, 1927, 10; G. Coolidge to Talbot, July 15, 1931, CHC; and G. Coolidge to Talbot, July 24, 1931, CHC.
97. "Coolidge Family," Finding Aid, CHC.
98. G. Coolidge to Talbot, February 9, 1932, CHC.
99. "Coolidge Family," Finding Aid, CHC. Also see Woodward, "Notes about the Reverend Sherman Coolidge," SJWA; and Goodnough, "Sherman Coolidge," AHC.
100. G. Coolidge to Talbot, February 9, 1932, CHC.

101. Irving P. Johnson, eulogy for Sherman Coolidge, CHC.
102. G. Coolidge to Talbot, April 25, 1937, CHC; and Goodnough, "Sherman Coolidge," AHC.
103. "Coolidge Family," Finding Aid, CHC.
104. "Grace Darling Wetherbee Coolidge," Find a Grave, accessed June 20, 2020, https://www.findagrave.com/memorial/34466606/grace-darling-coolidge.
105. Ellis, *Pioneers*, 29.
106. Reid, "Westerners," 47.
107. "Canon Coolidge Is Claimed by Death," *Wyoming State Tribune*, January 25, 1932, AHC; and Goodnough, "Sherman Coolidge," AHC.

NOTES ON SHERMAN COOLIDGE

1. G. Coolidge to Coolidge, November 13, 1917, CHC.
2. Arthur C. Parker to Coolidge, December 1, 1912, PSAI; and Coolidge to G. Coolidge, February 13, 1912, CHC.
3. See, for instance, Eastman, *Indian Boyhood*; and Standing Bear, *Land of the Spotted Eagle*, which was originally published in 1933.
4. The only reprints of Coolidge's "The Function of the Society of American Indians" (1914) appears in Peyer, *American Indian Nonfiction*, 345–49; and Peyer, *What the Elders Wrote*, 159–62.
5. Eastman, *Indian Boyhood*, 286–88.
6. Standing Bear, *Land of the Spotted Eagle*, 16.
7. Spalding, "First Annual Report," 587.
8. Coolidge to S. Coolidge, March 25, 1877, HWP.
9. Coolidge, "Report from Sherman Coolidge," August 1885, 425.
10. Coolidge, "Indian of To-Day," 88–89.
11. See Coolidge to Hebard, May 31, 1926, AHC; Hebard, to Coolidge July 25, 1926, AHC; and Coolidge to Hebard, July 30, 1927, GHP.
12. Sherman Coolidge, "Crow and Eagle," CHC.
13. Sherman Coolidge, "The Colt," CHC; and Sherman Coolidge, "A Little Gambler," CHC.
14. Sherman Coolidge, "A Horse Race," CHC.
15. Coolidge, "Death of Big Heart," CHC.
16. See Coolidge, "Indian of To-Day," 87–88.
17. Coolidge, "Sketch from Real Life," CHC, does discuss these events very briefly and appears to be written by Coolidge in the third person.
18. Coolidge to Whipple, May 8, 1887, HWP.
19. Hobbs, "The Centennial of the *Spirit of Missions*," 300.
20. Ethelbert Talbot to Coolidge, July 21, 1890, CHC.
21. Coolidge, "Report from Sherman Coolidge," 424–25.
22. Coolidge, "Report from Sherman Coolidge," December 1898, 598; and Coolidge, "Report from Sherman Coolidge," January 1899, 14.

23. Fowler, *The Arapaho*, 61–77, 80–85.
24. G. Coolidge, "Christmas Tree," 280–83.
25. Coolidge, "Education of Indians," 594–95.
26. Coolidge, "Indian Speeches," in Barrows, *Proceedings*, 98.
27. Fowler, *Arapahoe Politics*, 97.
28. Coolidge, "Indian of To-Day," 87–94.
29. Coolidge, "Sherman Coolidge Autobiographical Notes," CHC.
30. G. Coolidge to Talbot, August 25, 1902, CHC.
31. Coolidge, "Indians in Wyoming," in Department of the Interior, *Report on Indians Taxed*, 10:628–29.
32. G. Coolidge, "Wanted: To Save the Babies," 19; and U.S. Senate Committee on Indian Affairs, *Hearings*, 93–95.
33. *Report of the Executive Council*, 127.
34. Coolidge, "Indians in Wyoming," in Department of the Interior, *Report on Indians Taxed*, 10:628–29.
35. See Coolidge, "Function of the Society of American Indians," 185; and Parker to Philip Gordon, March 23, 1917, PSAI.
36. *Report of the Executive Council*, 91–92.
37. Coolidge, "The Indian American," 21.
38. Coolidge, "Indian of To-Day," 87–88.
39. Coolidge, "Function of the Society," 186.
40. Coolidge, "Indian American," 20–24.
41. Parker to Coolidge, May 1, 1913, PSAI.
42. Coolidge, "American Indians," 251–55.
43. Coolidge, "The American Indian of Today," 33–35.
44. See untitled article, in the *Trail* 6, no. 5 (October 1913): 6–9. The *Trail* was a monthly published for the Society of Sons of Colorado.
45. Coolidge, "Function of the Society of American Indians," 186–90.
46. "Conference Evening at Haskell Indian School," 300.
47. Sherman Coolidge, "American Indian Day," PSAI.
48. Speroff, *Carlos Montezuma, MD*, 358.
49. Montezuma, "Let My People Go," 33–34.
50. Parker to Coolidge, June 7, 1916, PSAI.
51. Lewandowski, *Ojibwe, Activist, Priest*, 47.
52. Parker to Gordon, November 19, 1915, PSAI.
53. G. Coolidge to Talbot, December 1, 1915, CHC.
54. "Important Topics Considered," 218–19.
55. Fowler, *Arapahoe Politics*, 96, 105.
56. U.S. Senate Committee on Indian Affairs, *Hearings*, 93–95.
57. Hertzberg, *Search for an American Indian Identity*, 117, 153.
58. Coolidge, "Opening Address," 227–28.
59. "Open Debate on the Loyalty," 252–56.

60. "Newspaper Comment," 266–67.
61. "Tribal War Averted at Indian Meeting," 1916, PSAI.
62. "Escaped Massacre to Be Taken by White Folk and Educated for Ministry—Story of an Indian Boy," 1916, PSAI.
63. "Cedar Rapids Platform," 223–24.
64. Speroff, *Carlos Montezuma, MD*, 361.
65. Boyer et al., *Enduring Vision*, 663–67.
66. Speroff, *Carlos Montezuma, MD*, 413–14.
67. Hertzberg, *Search for an American Indian Identity*, 170.
68. Gertrude Bonnin to Parker, August 6, 1917, PSAI.
69. "Five Civilized Tribes," 143; and "What Indians Are Thinking," 143–44.
70. Speroff, *Carlos Montezuma, MD*, 363, 420–25.
71. Reid, "Westerners," 47.
72. Speroff, *Carlos Montezuma, MD*, 415.
73. Sherman Coolidge, "Ye Cannot Serve God and Mammon," ca. 1920, CHC.
74. Coolidge, "Indian of To-Day," 93.
75. Hoxie, *This Indian Country*, 274.
76. "Coolidge Decries Injustice," 10.
77. G. Coolidge to Talbot, February 9, 1932, CHC.

NOTES ON GRACE COOLIDGE

1. G. Coolidge to Talbot, April 30, 1897, CHC; and Joshua Kineber to G. Coolidge, April 21, 1899, CHC. Kinebar was the associate secretary of the *Spirit of Missions*. In his letter to Grace, he addresses her as "My dear Sir." Kinebar also indicates that he might publish her submission, though it never appeared in the periodical.
2. See Coolidge, "Two Indian Stories," 651–55; and Coolidge, "The Victory," 16–17.
3. See Cornell, introduction to *Teepee Neighbors*, by G. Coolidge, xxii–xxv.
4. Coolidge, *Teepee Neighbors*, 9; and G. Coolidge to Talbot, December 14, 1912, CHC.
5. G. Coolidge to Talbot, November 15, 1911, CHC.
6. G. Coolidge, "Arapahoe Christmas Tree," 113–15.
7. G. Coolidge, "Christmas Tree," 280.
8. G. Coolidge to Talbot, December 31, 1902, CHC.
9. Coolidge, "Arapahoe Christmas Tree," 113–15.
10. Coolidge, "Christmas Tree," 280–83.
11. Fowler, *The Arapaho*, 61–77.
12. George Garfield (on behalf of the Arapaho council) to William H. Ketcham, January 12, 1902, Bureau of the Catholic Indian Missions Records, Raynor Memorial Libraries, Marquette University Archives, Milwaukee (hereafter BCIMR); and Fowler, *Arapahoe Politics*, 106–7.
13. Fowler, *The Arapaho*, 80–85.
14. G. Coolidge to Talbot, April 16, 1913, CHC.
15. Goodnough, "Sherman Coolidge," AHC.

16. Coolidge, "Wanted: To Save the Babies," 17.
17. G. Coolidge to Talbot, ca. May 1911, CHC.
18. Coolidge, "Wanted: To Save the Babies," 17–22.
19. G. Coolidge, "White Plague," 171–74.
20. G. Coolidge, "Carpenter Who Had No One," 101–2.
21. G. Coolidge, "Justice on a Reservation," 30–35.
22. G. Coolidge to Talbot, April 30, 1897, CHC.
23. Heinicke email to author, December 16, 2020.
24. G. Coolidge to Talbot, July 4, 1896, CHC.
25. G. Coolidge to Talbot, April 2, 1897, CHC.
26. G. Coolidge to Talbot, June 24, 1897, CHC.
27. G. Coolidge to Talbot, September 10, 1897, CHC.
28. G. Coolidge to Talbot, April 16, 1899, CHC.
29. G. Coolidge to Talbot, March 30, 1899, CHC.
30. G. Coolidge to Talbot, ca. January 1899, CHC.
31. See Ehrenhalt and Laskey, *Precious and Adored*.
32. G. Coolidge to Talbot, January 16, 1899, CHC.
33. G. Coolidge to Talbot, April 16, 1899, CHC.
34. G. Coolidge to Talbot, May 9, 1899, CHC.
35. G. Coolidge to Talbot, June 10, 1901, CHC.
36. G. Coolidge to Talbot, June 21, 1901, CHC.
37. G. Coolidge to Talbot, November 24, 1901, CHC.
38. G. Coolidge to Talbot, September 10, 1902, CHC.
39. G. Coolidge to Talbot, June 25, 1902, CHC.
40. G. Coolidge to Talbot, July 21, 1902, CHC.
41. G. Coolidge to Talbot, August 5, 1902, CHC.
42. See Lewandowski, "Marie Baldwin," 35–52.
43. See G. Coolidge to Talbot, June 20, 1903; G. Coolidge to Talbot, March 13, 1924; G. Coolidge to Talbot, August 4, 1919—all in CHC.
44. G. Coolidge to Talbot, August 20, 1902, CHC.
45. G. Coolidge to Talbot, August 25, 1902, CHC.
46. G. Coolidge to Talbot, September 10, 1902, CHC.
47. G. Coolidge to Talbot, August 25, 1902, CHC.
48. G. Coolidge to Talbot, September 1, 1902, CHC.
49. G. Coolidge to Talbot, September 10, 1902, CHC.
50. G. Coolidge to Talbot, October 22, 1902, CHC.
51. In the early 1890s, for instance, Coolidge carried on courtships with two women—Rebecca Buttroff and Nettie Smith. See Coolidge to Rebecca Buttroff, October 17, 1891; Buttroff to Coolidge, November 22, 1891; and Buttroff to Coolidge, ca. December 1891—all in CHC. See also Coolidge to Nettie Smith, June 1, 1891, CHC; and Coolidge to Smith, July 3, 1891, CHC.
52. John Spalding to Whipple, May 10, 1887, HWP.

53. G. Coolidge to Talbot, November 20, 1902; and G. Coolidge to Coolidge, September 17, 1911, CHC.
54. E. Talbot to Coolidge, October 18, 1902, CHC.
55. Coolidge to G. Coolidge, November 20, 1902, CHC.
56. Uncle Nye to G. Coolidge, November 12, 1902, CHC; and Aunt Sarah to G. Coolidge, January 29, 1907, CHC.
57. Coolidge to G. Coolidge, October 5, 1910, CHC.
58. G. Coolidge to Talbot, December 27, 1902, CHC.
59. G. Coolidge to Talbot, August 20, 1903, CHC; and "Coolidge Family," Finding Aid, CHC. According to the Finding Aid, Louis was born April 14, 1904, and died on October 21, 1904.
60. G. Coolidge to Talbot, November 22, 1904, CHC; and "Coolidge Family," Finding Aid, CHC. According to the Finding Aid, Grace Ann was born prematurely on August 10, 1904, and died April 5, 1905, at eight months. Grace's transcribed correspondence suggests these dates are correct, but they nonetheless seem a biological impossibility. It is therefore likely that the transcription is incorrect, with the culprit being Grace's often-illegible handwriting.
61. G. Coolidge to Talbot, April 9, 1905, CHC; and "Coolidge Family," Finding Aid, CHC.
62. G. Coolidge to Talbot, November 22, 1904, CHC; and "Coolidge Family," Finding Aid, CHC.
63. G. Coolidge to Talbot, November 2, 1905, CHC.
64. G. Coolidge to Talbot, November 22, 1904, CHC.
65. Thomas, "Some Children of Wyoming," 120.
66. Coolidge, *Teepee Neighbors*, 16; and G. Coolidge to Talbot, February 26, 1903, CHC.
67. Application for Enrollment in a Non-reservation, Effie Coolidge, Student File, Carlisle Indian School Digital Resource Center, Archives & Special Collections, Waidner-Spahr Library, Dickinson College PA (hereafter, ECSF); and G. Coolidge to Talbot, December 26, 1906, CHC.
68. Application for Enrollment in a Non-reservation School, Virginia Coolidge, Student File, Carlisle Indian School Digital Resource Center, Archives & Special Collections, Waidner-Spahr Library, Dickinson College PA (hereafter VCSF); and G. Coolidge to Talbot, May 2, 1907, CHC.
69. G. Coolidge to Talbot, March 25, 1925, CHC.
70. G. Coolidge to Talbot, November 15, 1911, CHC.
71. Cornell, introduction to *Teepee Neighbors* by Coolidge, xxiv–xxv. The full quote from Mencken reads: "The great quality of pity is in it. . . . It is a book that leaves something behind it. It is simple, and it is moving."
72. G. Coolidge to Talbot, November 15, 1911, CHC.
73. G. Coolidge to Talbot, September 15, 1912, CHC.
74. G. Coolidge to Talbot, March 1, 1913, CHC.
75. G. Coolidge to Talbot, March 28, 1914, CHC.

76. G. Coolidge to Talbot, October 23, 1928, CHC; and "Coolidge Family," Finding Aid, CHC.
77. G. Coolidge to Talbot, October 23, 1928, CHC.
78. Heinicke email to author, December 16, 2020.
79. G. Coolidge to Talbot, July 15, 1931, CHC; and G. Coolidge to Talbot, July 24, 1931, CHC.
80. G. Coolidge to Talbot, October 1, 1931, CHC.
81. G. Coolidge to Talbot, January 1, 1933, CHC.
82. G. Coolidge to Talbot, February 9, 1932, CHC.
83. G. Coolidge to Talbot, May 1911, CHC.

DISPATCHES FROM A MISSIONARY

1. Sharp Nose (ca. 1840s?–1901) was the uncle of Sherman Coolidge and an influential Arapaho chief who was there to greet his nephew when he returned to the Wind River Reservation in 1884. Tragically, Sharp Nose's son died at the Carlisle Industrial Indian School in Carlisle, Pennsylvania, in 1883. The news came while Sharp Nose was guiding President Chester A. Arthur on a trip through Yellowstone. See Fowler, *The Arapaho*, 63–78; Fowler, *Arapahoe Politics*, 106; and Stamm, *People of the Wind River*, 222.
2. John Franklin Spalding (1828–1902) was the Episcopal bishop of Colorado from 1873 until his death. Spalding was responsible for the territories of Wyoming, New Mexico, and Arizona as well. He authored several books, including *A Devotional Manual* and *The Church and Its Apostolic Ministry*. His son Franklin Spencer Spalding became the bishop of Utah. See "Obituary of John Franklin Spalding," *Living Church*, March 15, 1902, 711.
3. At that time, the bishop was Ethelbert Talbot.
4. Fremont Arthur was a friend of Sherman Coolidge's and an Episcopal lay missionary who had his own camp where he sought converts. Arthur unfortunately died of tuberculosis as a young man at nearly thirty years old. See Coolidge to G. Coolidge, January 19, 1899, CHC; and Markley and Crofts, *Walk Softly*, 85.

EARLY ARTICLES AND STATEMENTS

1. A. M. Johnson was the Wind River Industrial School's superintendent who was exiled from the reservation after participating with Coolidge in the conspiracy against the Jesuits. See affidavit of A. D. Lane, May 3, 1887, RBIA.
2. Black Coal (ca. 1840–93) was a blood relative of Sherman Coolidge's and an influential chief among the Arapahos for decades, having been instrumental in arranging the Northern Arapahos' relocation to Wind River in the 1870s. Black Coal later helped establish agricultural cooperatives at Wind River after Washington denied his quest to win a reservation for the Northern Arapahos. See Fowler, *Arapahoe Politics*, 63–65; and Stamm, *People of the Wind River*, 128–29.

3. George L. Randall (1810–73), the bishop of Colorado Territory, began missionary work at Wind River in 1871 and founded a day school for the Shoshones. In 1873 a Shoshone Episcopal mission was established under President Ulysses S. Grant's peace policy near then Camp Brown. When Randall returned to Wind River that year, Arapaho warriors attacked him and his small, mixed congregation. Randall and his flock were spared when the raiders wrongly assumed the group was armed and retreated. The stress caused by the incident and the Wyoming weather were blamed for the bishop's subsequent death by pneumonia. See "Bishop Randall," *New York Times*, September 29, 1873; and James Bowen Funsten, "The Indian as a Worker," *Outlook*, December 1905, 877–78.
4. J. I. Patten was the acting agent at the Shoshone and Bannock Agency in the mid-1870s. See his report in the U.S. Office of Indian Affairs, *Annual Report*, 148–55.
5. Rev. Joseph Witherspoon Cook (1836–1902) was the Episcopal missionary to the Cheyennes in the late 1860s and the religious instructor to the young Philip Joseph Deloria (1853–1931), or Tipi Sapa (Black Lodge), the Episcopal priest and leader of the Yankton Nakotas. See Trask, "Episcopal Missionaries," 87–101; and Stamm, "Boom-Town Evangelism," 132–53. Cook's enduring work, *Diary and Letters of the Reverend Joseph W. Cook, Missionary to Cheyenne*, was published serially in the *Wyoming Churchman* from 1917 to 1918.
6. Little Wolf was the Arapaho chief who was instrumental in making peace with the Shoshones in 1870. From 1889 he was part of the Arapaho business council, which made several trips to Washington DC, to advocate for greater tribal control over the resources at Wind River. See Fowler, *The Arapaho*, 66; and Fowler, *Arapahoe Politics*, 48, 323n50. Coolidge discussed his blood relation to Little Wolf in an interview conducted in 1918. See Reid, "Westerners," 47.
7. This is a reference to Ely Samuel Parker (1828–95), a Seneca U.S. Army officer and diplomat who fought in the Civil War while serving as a secretary to Gen. Ulysses S. Grant. Known for writing the final draft of the Confederate terms of surrender at Appomattox, Parker later became the first Native commissioner of Indian affairs when Grant won the presidency in 1868. Arthur C. Parker, his great nephew, penned his biography, *Life of General Ely S. Parker*. See also Porter, *To Be Indian*, 41–44.

SHERMAN AND THE SOCIETY

1. William Prescott (1726–95), an American colonel of the Revolutionary War period, was famous for his exploits in the Battle of Bunker Hill (1775). Prescott is known for his many quotes, among them his purported order to his soldiers: "Do not fire until you see the whites of their eyes." See "William Prescott," Military Hall of Honor, accessed January 10, 2021, https://militaryhallofhonor.com/honoree-record.php?id=2976.
2. Coolidge gave this speech at the Anti-Saloon League Convention in Columbus, Ohio, in November 1913.

3. Carlos Montezuma (ca. 1866–1923) was born a Yavapai (a tribe associated with the Apaches) in present-day Arizona. Originally named Wassaja, or "Beckoning," Montezuma was kidnapped from his parents by Pima warriors and sold to Carlos Gentile, an Italian photographer, in 1871. Gentile later placed Montezuma in the home of a Baptist minister in Urbana, Illinois. There, Montezuma went on to become one of the first Native men to earn a Western medical degree. After working for the Indian Health Service and the Carlisle Indian Industrial School, he established his own practice in Chicago. Montezuma was instrumental in the founding of the Society of American Indians, but he often criticized the organization for tolerating the BIA's wardship. He felt the bureau should be abolished entirely and was confident that once Indians had their freedom and rights, they would flourish in white society. See Hertzberg, *Search for an American Indian Identity*, 43–45; and Lewandowski, *Ojibwe, Activist, Priest*, 34–35, 47.
4. Charles Alexander Ohiyesa (Winner) Eastman (1858–1939) was an internationally known Santee Dakota physician and writer, one-term SAI president (1917), and husband of the poet and writer Elaine Goodale Eastman (1863–1953). Together, Eastman and his wife authored numerous books on his Dakota childhood and the ways and beliefs of his people. Eastman was also an instrumental figure in the Young Men's Christian Association (YMCA) and in the founding of the Boy Scouts. See Speroff, *Carlos Montezuma, MD*, 337–38.
5. Red Jacket (1715–1830), the chief of the Seneca Wolf tribe, fought for Britain during the American Revolution. In 1792 he changed his allegiance, concluded a peace treaty with Washington, and later fought against the British in the War of 1812. See Wilson and Fiske, eds., "Red Jacket," 205.
6. Perhaps it is a reference to A. M. Johnson, the Baptist minister and onetime superintendent at the Wind River school with whom Sherman Coolidge attempted to conspire against the St. Stephens Catholic mission.
7. Sophie Coolidge very likely chose the date February 22 because it was George Washington's birthday.
8. Cato Sells (1859–1948), the commissioner of the Bureau of Indian Affairs from 1913 to 1921, was known for his virulent opposition to the notion that American Indians descended from Mongolians. See Whisenhunt, "Cato Sells," 40–48; and "Our Indians Not Yellow: Cato Sells Banishes Books That Teach Them They Are Mongolians," *New York Times*, December 28, 1914.
9. The Carter Code Bill, proposed by the Chickasaw Oklahoma representative Charles D. Carter (1868–1929), sought to define the legal status of Native peoples, while the Stephens Bill, named after Texas representative and chairman of the Committee on Indian Affairs John Hall Stephens (1847–1924), sought to open a court of claims that would allow Indian nations to seek compensation for treaty violations. See "Platform of the Second Annual Conference," 71–74; Hertzberg, *Search for an American Indian Identity*, 117; and Speroff, *Carlos Montezuma, MD*, 289.

10. Charles E. Dagenett (1872/3–1941), a graduate of the Carlisle Indian Industrial School and Dickinson College, joined the Indian Service in 1904. In 1907 he became the bureau's highest-ranking Native employee as the supervisor of employment. See Speroff, *Carlos Montezuma, MD*, 337.
11. Luther Burbank (1849–1926) was an American botanist, horticulturalist, and pioneering scientist who developed hundreds of strains of plants, including the russet Burbank potato, which now predominates in modern food processing. See Smith, *Garden of Invention*.
12. Henry Roe Cloud (1884–1950), in 1910, became the first Indian to graduate from Yale University. Roe Cloud joined the society at just age twenty-five and went on to found the American Indian Institute, a preparatory school for Indian boys in Wichita, Kansas. In 1933 he was appointed the superintendent at the Haskell Indian School in Lawrence, Kansas. See Speroff, *Carlos Montezuma, MD*, 336.
13. Philip Bergin Gordon, or Tibishkogijik (Looking into the Sky, 1885–1948), of French-Ojibwe ancestry, in 1913 became the first Indigenous Catholic priest to be ordained in the United States. Gordon had been impressed by Montezuma's condemnations of the BIA at the 1915 SAI confidence in Lawrence, Kansas, and had joined the doctor in his fight for the bureau's abolition. See Lewandowski, *Ojibwe, Activist, Priest*, 3–4, 47–48.
14. Marie Louise Bottineau Baldwin (1863–1952) was the daughter of Jean Baptiste Bottineau, a lawyer involved with the land claims of his Turtle Mountain Band of Ojibwes. Baldwin herself earned a degree from the Washington College of Law in 1914 and enjoyed a long career in the Bureau of Indian Affairs. See Cahill, "Marie Louise Bottineau Baldwin," 65, 69–70, 73.
15. Gertrude Simmons Bonnin (1876–1938), a Yankton Dakota writer and activist, was best known by her pen name, Zitkala-Ša (Red Bird, in Lakota). Bonnin, educated in Quaker institutions from age eight, worked at the Carlisle Indian Industrial School in the late 1890s. Her semi-autobiography for the *Atlantic Monthly* in early 1900 is today a seminal text of Indian boarding school literature. She returned to Yankton in the early 1900s and married an Indian Service clerk, Raymond Telephause Bonnin, with whom she relocated to the Uintah and Ouray Reservation in Utah. At Uintah, she began a community center movement much praised by the society. Bonnin later moved to the Washington DC area, where she founded the National Council of American Indians in 1926. See Lewandowski, *Red Bird, Red Power*, 11–13.

A SERMON AND A PROTEST

1. He is possibly referring to Eastern Shoshone chief Washakie.
2. Irving Peake Johnson (1866–1947), the bishop of Colorado from 1918 to 1938, later delivered Sherman Coolidge's eulogy. See "Rt. Rev. I. Johnson, Long a Bishop, Dies; Retired Leader of Episcopal Diocese of Colorado Edited Witness, Church Paper," *New York Times*, March 2, 1947, 60; and Johnson, Eulogy for Sherman Coolidge, CHC.

ARTICLES

1. She is referring to Robert Browning's poem "Amphibian."
2. Herbert Welsh, Sherman Coolidge's half-white cousin, was once involved in an unsuccessful conspiracy to keep Herman G. Nickerson as the Wind River agent after the Arapahos had forcefully rejected his policies regarding allotment. Nickerson paid Welsh two dollars to lobby for him in the Arapaho camps, though the scheme garnered no support. See George Garfield (on behalf of the Arapaho council) to William H. Ketcham, January 12, 1902, BCIMR. Herbert Welsh is mentioned as being Coolidge's half-white cousin in G. Coolidge to Talbot, November 25, 1902, CHC.

WRITINGS

1. The term "issue wagon" refers to the government wagon that delivered monthly rations to the Indian reservations.

LETTERS

1. Gracie's dog.
2. A nickname for Pacci the dog.
3. Nellie Hart, whose father, Rev. Dean Hart, ministered at St. John's Episcopal Church in Denver. See Ellis, *Pioneers*, 18.
4. Eleonora Giulia Amalia Duse (1858–1924), an Italian actress who was preeminent in her day. See Sheehy, *Eleonora Duse*.
5. A reference to Lucretia Hale's *The Peterkin Papers*, a collection of short stories about the fictional Peterkin family published in 1880.
6. A quote from "Two in the Campagna" by Robert Browning.
7. Grace's sister.
8. Grace was then carrying on a "platonic" correspondence with a mysterious Greek soldier who was fighting in the Greco-Turkish War of 1897. See G. Coolidge to Talbot, April 30, 1897, CHC.
9. A reference to Byron's 1810 poem, "Maid of Athens, ere We Part."
10. A popular camera at the time.
11. Ethelbert Talbot had recently been elected the bishop of central Pennsylvania, and the family had relocated to Bethlehem.
12. Richard Wagner's 1869 opera, *Das Rheingold*.
13. Lilli Lehmann (1848–1929), a German operatic soprano associated with Wagnerian repertory. See Macy, *Grove Book of Opera Singers*, 274.
14. Francis Donaldson, Anne Talbot's future husband.
15. Olga Nethersole (1867–1951), an English actress who rose to international fame on the stage at the turn of the century. See "Olga Nethersole Dies at Age of 80," *New York Times*, January 11, 1951, 25.
16. Dr. George and Grace Hunting. George later took the position of superintendent of St. Mark's Hospital in Salt Lake City, Utah. See G. Coolidge to Coolidge, December 25, 1906, CHC.

17. Abiel Leonard (1848–1903), the second bishop of the Episcopal Diocese of Utah from 1888 to 1903. Leonard died of typhoid fever in St. Mark's Hospital, Salt Lake City. See "Bishop Leonard Gone from Life," *Salt Lake Daily Herald*, December 3, 1903.
18. Lucy Carter, a missionary appointed to Utah in 1899. See "Abstract of Proceedings," 8.
19. Meaning bareback.
20. James Bowen Funsten (1856–1918), the bishop of Wyoming and Idaho from 1898 until his death. See Hawley, *History of Idaho*, 381–82.
21. Short for missionary.
22. Grace's nickname for Sherman.
23. Mrs. Julia Hereford (Sings First), Sherman Coolidge's half-sister, had been either adopted or sold to John Felter of Evanston, Wyoming, after the Shoshones captured her in 1870. She later married John R. Hereford, born June 18, 1874, in Sweetwater, Wyoming. Hereford died on October 3, 1941, at the age of sixty-seven. He is buried in Washakie Cemetery alongside Julia, who lived to the age of eighty-two, dying on September 9, 1946. See "John H. Hereford," Find a Grave, accessed June 20, 2020, https://www.findagrave.com/memorial/146659736/john-r-hereford; and "Julia Felter Hereford," Find a Grave, accessed June 20, 2020, https://www.findagrave.com/memorial/146659844/julia-hereford. Also see Coolidge, "Sketch from Real Life," CHC.
24. Buckskin, John Roberts's horse. See Markley and Crofts, *Walk Softly*, 113–14.
25. Likely a term for menstruation.
26. Meaning evening.
27. Meaning *ter in die*, or "three times a day" in Latin.
28. Marian, a misspelling of Marion, refers to Marion Roberts, one of John and Laura Roberts's daughters.
29. Grace and Sherman's nickname for Anne Talbot.
30. A popular baby food at the time.
31. A reference to Ethelbert Talbot's ongoing conflict with one of his fellow Pennsylvania clergymen, Rev. Dr. Ingram N. W. Irvine. According to news reports, Talbot had attempted to unfrock Irvine, charging him with "improper language and conduct toward females." Irvine claimed he had been wrongfully accused and that Talbot had initiated a conspiracy against him. A church board of inquiry ultimately exonerated Talbot of any misconduct. See "People Talked About," 99.
32. Another horse.
33. Likely a whirligig toy, which is perhaps referred to as the Pentecost in the following letter dated September 10, 1902.
34. Meaning New England.
35. Short for the Arapaho subagency.
36. Slang for "silly person," also the derivation of "jaywalking." See entries for "jay" and "jaywalking" in Stevenson, *Oxford Dictionary of English*, 937.
37. Meaning Roman Catholic.
38. Elaine Goodale Eastman (1866–1953), a child poet and the former superintendent of Indian schools in the Dakotas. See Sargent, *Life of Elaine Goodale Eastman*.

39. Wife of Herman G. Nickerson, the agent at Wind River from around 1899 to 1902. See Fowler, *Arapahoe Politics*, 106–7; and Nickerson, "Report Concerning Indians in Wyoming," 414–15.
40. Meaning Christian.
41. Referring to *La Città Morta* (*The Dead City*), an 1898 play in five acts by the Italian writer Gabriele D'Annunzio.
42. A politically incorrect way of saying "backward."
43. Grace was successful in having her account published in the *Spirit of Missions*. It is found earlier in this volume under the title "An Arapahoe Christmas Tree."
44. Meaning the *Century Dictionary*.
45. Meaning the wife was half white.
46. Gros Ventre is French for "fat stomach." It is also a reference to a band of Arapahos, the Gros Ventres, which split from the northern and southern bands in the eighteenth century and became a member of the Blackfeet Confederacy. See Pritzker, *Native American Encyclopedia*, 319.
47. *Indian Boyhood*, Charles Eastman's 1902 autobiographical book, which originally ran in a six-part series for *St. Nicolas: An Illustrated Magazine for Young Folks* from December 1893 to May 1894. See Carlson, "'Indian for a While,'" 604.
48. Meaning orphaned Indian children.
49. Grace Ann Coolidge, born prematurely on August 10, 1904, and died April 5, 1905, at eight months. "Coolidge Family," Finding Aid, CHC.
50. Grace had become pregnant not long after she gave birth to Louis Coolidge on April 14, 1903. Louis died on October 21, 1904. See "Coolidge Family," Finding Aid, CHC. The reference to "4 months" is likely a transcription error caused by Grace's handwriting. It is more likely that a period of at least six months had passed.
51. Wife of Northern Arapaho chief Friday, a fluent English speaker. See Fowler, *Arapahoe Politics*, 43.
52. Likely a nickname for Francis Donaldson.
53. Philip Coolidge, who was named after Sherman's younger brother. Philip was born on October 17, 1905, and died twelve days later on October 29 due to a congenital heart defect. See "Coolidge Family," Finding Aid, CHC.
54. Likely Edith Kneale, the wife of agent Albert H. Kneale (1880–1943), who held the position of agent on several reservations in the West during his long career. Caxton Printers in Caldwell, Idaho, published his memoir, *Indian Agent*, posthumously in 1950.
55. Grace's first surviving daughter, born in 1907.
56. Virginia and Effie were students at the Carlisle Indian Industrial School during this period.
57. Meaning the *Christian Herald*.
58. An apparent reference to the Mafia.
59. Short for "manuscript."
60. Talbot's *Bishop among His Flock*.

BIBLIOGRAPHY

ARCHIVAL SOURCES

AHC. Coolidge, Sherman. Biographical File. American Heritage Center, University of Wyoming, Laramie.

BCIMR. Bureau of the Catholic Indian Missions Records. Raynor Memorial Libraries, Marquette University Archives, Milwaukee.

CHC. Coolidge-Heinicke Collection. Colorado Springs Pioneers Museum, Colorado Springs.

ECSF. Coolidge, Effie. Student File. Carlisle Indian School Digital Resource Center, Archives & Special Collections, Waidner-Spahr Library, Dickinson College PA.

GHP. Hebard, Grace Raymond. Papers. American Heritage Center, University of Wyoming, Laramie.

HWP. Whipple, Henry Benjamin. Papers. Gale Family Library, Minnesota Historical Society, St. Paul.

PSAI. Society of American Indians. Papers. Cornell University Library, Ithaca NY.

RBIA. Records of the Bureau of Indian Affairs. National Archives and Records Administration, Washington DC.

SJWA. Coolidge, Sherman. File. Cathedral of St. John in the Wilderness Archives, Denver.

VCSF. Coolidge, Virginia. Student File. Carlisle Indian School Digital Resource Center, Archives & Special Collections, Waidner-Spahr Library, Dickinson College PA.

WHSL. Coolidge, Sherman. File. Warren Hunting Smith Library, Hobart and William Smith Colleges, Geneva NY.

PUBLISHED SOURCES

"Abstract of Proceedings of the Board of Managers." *Spirit of Missions* 64, no. 1 (January 1899): 7–10.

Allen, Anne. *And the Wilderness Shall Blossom: Henry Benjamin Whipple, Churchman, Educator, and Advocate for the Indians*. Afton MN: Afton Historical Society Press, 2008.

Barrows, Samuel J., ed. *Proceedings of the Seventh Annual Meeting of the Lake Mohonk Conference of the Friends of the Indian*. New York: Lake Mohonk, 1889.

Blackhawk, Ned. *Violence over the Land: Indians and Empires in the Early American West*. Cambridge: Harvard University Press, 2008.

Boyer, Paul, Clifford E. Clark Jr., Joseph F. Kett, Neal Salisbury, Harvard Sitkoff, and Nancy Woloch. *The Enduring Vision: A History of the American People.* Vol 2, *From 1865*. Boston: Houghton Mifflin, 2000.

Cahill, Cathleen D. "Marie Louise Bottineau Baldwin: Indigenizing the Federal Indian Service." *Studies in American Indian Literatures* 25, no. 2 (Summer 2013): 63–86; and *American Indian Quarterly* 37, no. 3 (Summer 2013): 65–86.

Carlson, David J. "'Indian for a While': Charles Eastman's *Indian Boyhood* and the Discourse of Allotment." *American Indian Quarterly* 25, no. 4 (Autumn 2001): 604–25.

Carlson, Paul H. *The Plains Indians.* College Station: Texas A&M University Press, 1998.

"The Cedar Rapids Platform." *American Indian Magazine* 4, no. 3 (July–September 1916): 223–24.

"Chicago." *Churchman* 71, no. 5 (May 1895): 727.

"Church Periodical Club." *Church Standard* 74, no. 1 (January 1898): 441.

"Conference Evening at Haskell Indian School: An Extract from the Haskell *Indian Leader.*" *Quarterly Journal of the Society of American Indians* 3, no. 4 (October–December 1915): 292–302.

Coolidge, Grace. "An Arapahoe Christmas Tree." *Spirit of Missions* 68, no. 1 (January 1903): 113–15.

———. "The Carpenter Who Had No One to Set Him Straight." *American Indian Magazine* 5, no. 2 (April–June 1917): 101–2.

———. "A Christmas Tree that Bore Souls." *Spirit of Missions* 70, no. 4 (April 1905): 280–83.

———. "Justice on a Reservation: A Story of an Actual Happening." *American Indian Magazine* 6, no. 1 (Spring 1918): 30–35.

———. *Paddy-Paws: Four Adventures of the Prairie Dog with a Red Coat.* Chicago: Rand McNally, 1914.

———. *Teepee Neighbors.* Boston: Four Seas Press, 1917.

———. "The Victory." *Collier's* 50, no. 25 (September 1913): 16–17.

———. "Wanted: To Save the Babies, or Capricornus and a Coroner." *American Indian Magazine* 5, no. 1 (January–March 1917): 17–22.

———. "The White Plague." *American Indian Magazine* 5, no. 3 (July–September 1917): 171–74.

Coolidge, Sherman. "The American Indian of Today." *Quarterly Journal of the Society of American Indians* 2, no. 4 (January–March 1914): 33–35.

———. "American Indians for the Honor of Their Race." *Red Man* 6, no. 7 (March 1914): 251–55.

———. "Education of Indians." *Churchman* 55, no. 5 (May 1887): 594–95.

———. "The Function of the Society of American Indians." *Quarterly Journal of the Society of American Indians* 2, no. 3 (July–September 1914): 186–90.

———. "The Indian American: His Duty to His Race and to His Country, the United States of America." *Quarterly Journal of the Society of American Indians* 1, no. 1 (January–April 1913): 20–24.

———. "The Indian of To-Day." *Colorado Magazine* 1, no. 2 (May 1893): 87–94.

———. "Indians in Wyoming." In *Report on Indians Taxed and Indians Not Taxed in the United States (except Alaska) at the Eleventh Census: 1890*, edited by the Department of the Interior, 628–29. Washington DC: Government Printing Office, 1894.

———. "Opening Address of the President at the Sixth Annual Conference of the Society of American Indians." *American Indian Magazine* 4, no. 3 (July–September 1916): 227–28.

———. "Report from Sherman Coolidge." *Spirit of Missions* 50, no. 8 (August 1885): 424–25.

———. "Report from Sherman Coolidge." *Spirit of Missions* 51, no. 8 (August 1886): 57.

———. "Report from Sherman Coolidge." *Spirit of Missions* 61, no. 3 (March 1896): 118.

———. "Report from Sherman Coolidge." *Spirit of Missions* 62, no. 7 (July 1897): 550.

———. "Report from Sherman Coolidge." *Spirit of Missions* 63, no. 12 (December 1898): 598.

———. "Report from Sherman Coolidge." *Spirit of Missions* 64, no. 1 (January 1899): 14.

———. "Report from Sherman Coolidge." *Spirit of Missions* 64, no. 5 (May 1899): 229.

———. "Use Your Citizenship Worthily of the Gospel of Christ." *Journal of History* 7, no. 1 (January 1914): 298–301.

Cornell, George L. Introduction to *Teepee Neighbors*, by Grace Coolidge, xv–xxvi. Norman: University of Oklahoma Press, 1984.

Deloria, Philip J. "Four Thousand Invitations." *Studies in American Indian Literatures* 25, no. 2 (Summer 2013): 23–43; and *American Indian Quarterly* 37, no. 3 (Summer 2013): 25–43.

"Diocese News." *Churchman* 71, no. 4 (April 1885): 494–95.

"Diocese News." *Churchman* 71, no. 5 (May 1885): 658.

Eastman, Charles. *Indian Boyhood*. New York: McClure, Philips, 1902.

Ehrenhalt, Lizzie, and Tilly Laskey, eds. *Precious and Adored: The Love Letters of Rose Cleveland and Evangeline Simpson Whipple, 1890–1918*. St. Paul: Minnesota Historical Society Press, 2019.

"Election of Officers." *American Indian Magazine* 6, no. 3 (July–September 1918): 125.

Ellis, Amanda M. *Pioneers*. Colorado Springs: Dentan Printing, 1955.

"Five Civilized Tribes Doing Their Bit." *American Indian Magazine* 5, no. 3 (July–September 1917): 143.

Fowler, Loretta. *The Arapaho*. New York: Chelsea House, 1989.

———. *Arapahoe Politics, 1851–1978: Symbols in Crises of Authority*. Lincoln: University of Nebraska Press, 1982.

Hawley, James H. *History of Idaho: The Gem of the Mountains*. 4 vols. Chicago: S. J. Clarke Publishing, 1920.

Hedren, Paul L. *Powder River: Disastrous Opening of the Great Sioux War*. Norman: University of Oklahoma Press, 2016.

Hertzberg, Hazel W. *The Search for an American Indian Identity: Modern Pan-Indian Movements*. Syracuse: Syracuse University Press, 1971.

Hobbs, G. Warfield. "The Centennial of the *Spirit of Missions*." *Historical Magazine of the Protestant Episcopal Church* 4, no. 4 (December 1935): 300–309.

Hoxie, Frederick. *This Indian Country: American Indian Activists and the Place They Made*. New York: Penguin, 2012.

"Important Topics Considered." *American Indian Magazine* 4, no. 3 (July–September 1916): 217–19.

"Indian Troubles in Boise." *Churchman* 95, no. 2 (February 1907): 248.

Kneale, Albert H. *Indian Agent*. Caldwell ID: Caxton Printers, 1950.

Lewandowski, Tadeusz. "Marie Baldwin, Racism, and the Society of American Indians." *American Indian Culture and Research Journal* 44, no. 1 (Spring 2020): 35–52.

———. *Ojibwe, Activist, Priest: The Life of Father Philip Bergin Gordon, Tibishkogijik*. Madison: University of Wisconsin Press, 2019.

———. *Red Bird, Red Power: The Life and Legacy of Zitkala-Ša*. Norman: University of Oklahoma Press, 2016.

Macy, Laura, ed. *The Grove Book of Opera Singers*. Oxford: Oxford University Press, 2008.

Markley, Elinor R., and Beatrice Crofts. *Walk Softly, This Is God's Country: Sixty-Six Years on the Wind River Indian Reservation, Compiled from the Letters and Journals of the Rev. John Roberts, 1883–1949*. Lander WY: Mortimore Publishers, 1997.

Montezuma, Carlos. "Let My People Go." *American Indian Magazine* 4, no. 1 (January–March 1916): 32–33.

"Newark." *Church Standard* 74, no. 12 (December 1897): 169.

"Newspaper Comment." *American Indian Magazine* 4, no. 3 (July–September 1916): 266–67.

Nickerson, Herman G. "Report Concerning Indians in Wyoming." In *Annual Reports of the Department of the Interior for the Fiscal Year Ended June 30, 1900*, 414–15. Washington DC: Government Printing Office, 1900.

Olson, James C. *Red Cloud and the Sioux Problem*. Lincoln: University of Nebraska Press, 1965.

"Open Debate on the Loyalty of Indian Employees in the Indian Service." *American Indian Magazine* 4, no. 3 (July–September 1916): 252–56.

Ostler, Jeffrey. *The Plains Sioux and U.S. Colonialism from Lewis and Clark to Wounded Knee*. Cambridge: Cambridge University Press, 2004.

Parker, Arthur C. "Editorial Comment." *American Indian Magazine* 6, no. 1 (Spring 1918): 15–24.

———. *The Life of General Ely S. Parker: Last Grand Sachem of the Iroquois and General Grant's Military Secretary*. Buffalo: Buffalo Historical Society, 1909.

Parker, Robert Dale, ed. "Ruth Margaret Muskrat, Cherokee, 1897–1982." *Changing Is Not Vanishing: A Collection of American Indian Poetry to 1930*, 320–29. Philadelphia: University of Pennsylvania Press, 2011.

"Pennsylvania." *Churchman* 77, no. 3 (March 1898): 444.

"People Talked About." *Leslie's Weekly* 95, no. 2443 (July 3, 1902): 99. https://www.google.com/books/edition/Frank_Leslie_s_Illustrated_Newspaper/JG8gxzCzIN4C?hl=en&gbpv=1&dq=bishop+ethelbert+talbot+on+trial+1902&pg=PA99&printsec=frontcover.

Peyer, Bernd C., ed. *American Indian Nonfiction: An Anthology of Writings, 1760s–1930s*. Norman: University of Oklahoma Press, 2007.

———, ed. *What the Elders Wrote: An Anthology of Early Prose by North American Indians.* Berlin: Dietrich Reimer, 1982.

"Platform of the Second Annual Conference of the Society of American Indians." *Quarterly Journal of the Society of American Indians* 1, no. 1 (January–April 1913): 71–74.

Porter, Joy. *To Be Indian: The Life of Iroquois-Seneca Arthur Caswell Parker*. Norman: University of Oklahoma Press, 2001.

Pritzker, Barry M. *A Native American Encyclopedia: History, Culture, People*. Oxford: Oxford University Press, 2000.

Reid, Mabel. "Westerners." *Sunset: The Pacific Monthly* 41, no. 5 (November 1918): 47.

Report of the Executive Council on the Proceedings of the Annual Conference of the Society of American Indians. Washington DC, 1912.

Sargent, Theodore D. *The Life of Elaine Goodale Eastman*. Lincoln: University of Nebraska Press, 2005.

Sheehy, Helen. *Eleonora Duse: A Biography*. New York: Knopf, 2003.

Smith, Jane S. *The Garden of Invention: Luther Burbank and the Business of Breeding Plants*. New York: Penguin, 2010.

Spalding, John. "First Annual Report of the Missionary Jurisdiction of Wyoming Territory." *Spirit of Missions* 49, no. 11 (November–December 1884): 587.

———. "Second Annual Report of the Jurisdiction of Wyoming." *Spirit of Missions* 50, no. 11 (November–December 1885): 617–18.

Speroff, Leon. *Carlos Montezuma, MD, a Yavapai American Hero: The Life and Times of an American Indian, 1866–1923*. Portland OR: Arnica Publishing, 2005.

Stamm, Henry E. "Boom Town Evangelism: The Reverend Joseph W. Cook and St. Mark's Church, Cheyenne, Wyoming, 1867–1870." *Anglican and Episcopal History* 66, no. 2 (1997): 132–53.

———. *People of the Wind River: The Eastern Shoshones, 1825–1900*. Norman: University of Oklahoma Press, 1999.

Standing Bear, Luther. *Land of the Spotted Eagle*. Boston: Houghton Mifflin, 1933. New edition. Lincoln: University of Nebraska Press, 1978.

Stevenson, Angus. *Oxford Dictionary of English*. Oxford: Oxford University Press, 2010; online version, 2015.

Talbot, Ethelbert. *A Bishop among His Flock*. New York: Harper & Brothers, 1914.

Thomas, Nathaniel S. "Some Children of Wyoming." *Spirit of Missions* 75, no. 2 (February 1910): 120.

Trask, David S. "Episcopal Missionaries on the Santee and Yankton Reservations Cross-Cultural Collaboration and President Grant's Peace Policy." *Great Plains Quarterly* 33, no. 2 (2013): 87–101.

U.S. Office of Indian Affairs. *Annual Report of the Commissioner, Bureau of Indian Affairs to the Secretary of the Interior for the Year 1878*. Washington DC: Government Printing Office, 1878.

U.S. Senate Committee on Indian Affairs. *Hearings before the Committee on Indian Affairs, United States Senate, Sixty-Fourth Congress, First Session, on H. R. 10385, an Act Making*

Appropriations for the Current and Contingent Expenses of the Bureau of Indian Affairs, for Fulfilling Treaty Stipulations with Various Indian Tribes, and for Other Purposes, for the Fiscal Year Ending June 30, 1917. Washington DC: Government Printing Office, 1917.

Van Orsdale, J. T. "Rev. Sherman Coolidge, D.D." *Colorado Magazine* 1, no. 2 (May 1893): 85–86.

"Very Silly Woman or Exaggerated Story." *Albuquerque Indian* 1, no. 8 (January 1906): 21.

Wagner, David E., ed. *Powder River Odyssey: Nelson Cole's Western Campaign of 1865: The Journals of Lyman G. Bennett and Other Eyewitness Accounts*. Norman: Arthur H. Clark, 2009.

"What Indians Are Thinking about the War." *American Indian Magazine* 5, no. 3 (July–September 1917): 143–44.

Whisenhunt, William B. "Cato Sells: A Texan as Commissioner of Indian Affairs." *East Texas Historical Journal* 32, no. 2 (October 1994): 40–48.

Wilson, James G., and John Fiske, eds. "Red Jacket." *Appletons' Cyclopedia of American Biography*. Vol. 6. New York: D. Appleton, 1900.

INDEX

Page numbers in italics indicate illustrations.

www.ingramcontent.com/pod-product-compliance
Lightning Source LLC
Chambersburg PA
CBHW060808310726
48980CB00002B/277

* 9 7 8 1 4 9 6 2 3 4 0 5 6 *